POLLS, POLLSTERS, AND PUBLIC OPINION

A vast literature exists on theories of public opinion – how to measure, analyze, predict, and influence it; however, there is no synthesis of best practices for interpreting public opinion: The existing knowledge is disparate and spread across many disciplines. *Polls, Pollsters, and Public Opinion* presents a systematic analytical approach for understanding, predicting, and engaging public opinion. It tells the story through the eyes of the pollster and draws an analytical road map for examining public opinion, both conceptually and practically. Providing a theoretical and conceptual foundation, as well as debunking popular myths, this book delves into the science of polling, offering tools analysts can use to assess the quality of polls. It also introduces methods that can be used to predict elections and other sociopolitical outcomes while understanding the nuances of messaging, engaging, and moving public opinion.

Clifford Young is President at Ipsos Public Affairs in the United States and an adjunct professor at Johns Hopkins SAIS. He is an expert on consumer and public opinion trends, corporate reputation, elections, and scenario construction. He also, oversees Ipsos' media partnerships, including ABC News, Axios, NPR, C-SPAN, Thomson Reuters, *USA Today*, and the *Washington Post*.

Kathryn Ziemer is a clinical psychologist and clinical director at Old Town Psychology. She founded Old Town Psychology in 2018 and has built it into an award-winning mental health clinic that combines research and clinical work. She is an expert on attitude formation, emotion development, cognitive biases, and behavior change. She previously worked as a research scientist at Ipsos Public Affairs.

METHODOLOGICAL TOOLS IN THE SOCIAL SCIENCES

Series Editors

Paul M. Kellstedt, *Associate Professor of Political Science,*
Texas A&M University
Guy D. Whitten, *Professor of Political Science and Director of the European*
Union Center at Texas A&M University

The Methodological Tools in the Social Sciences series is comprised of accessible, stand-alone treatments of methodological topics encountered by social science researchers. The focus is on practical instruction for applying methods, for getting the methods right. The authors are leading researchers able to provide extensive examples of applications of the methods covered in each book. The books in the series strike a balance between the theory underlying and the implementation of the methods. They are accessible and discursive, and make technical code and data available to aid in replication and extension of the results, as well as enabling scholars to apply these methods to their own substantive problems. They also provide accessible advice on how to present results obtained from using the relevant methods.

Other Books in the Series

Polls, Pollsters, and Public Opinion

A Guide for Decision-Makers

CLIFFORD YOUNG

Ipsos Public Affairs

KATHRYN ZIEMER

Old Town Psychology

CAMBRIDGE
UNIVERSITY PRESS

Shaftesbury Road, Cambridge CB2 8EA, United Kingdom

One Liberty Plaza, 20th Floor, New York, NY 10006, USA

477 Williamstown Road, Port Melbourne, VIC 3207, Australia

314–321, 3rd Floor, Plot 3, Splendor Forum, Jasola District Centre,
New Delhi – 110025, India

103 Penang Road, #05–06/07, Visioncrest Commercial, Singapore 238467

Cambridge University Press is part of Cambridge University Press & Assessment,
a department of the University of Cambridge.

We share the University's mission to contribute to society through the pursuit of
education, learning and research at the highest international levels of excellence.

www.cambridge.org
Information on this title: www.cambridge.org/9781108479554

DOI: 10.1017/9781108855310

First published 2024

A catalogue record for this publication is available from the British Library

Library of Congress Cataloging-in-Publication Data
Names: Young, Clifford (Clifford Alexander), author. | Ziemer, Kathryn, 1984– author.
Title: Polls, pollsters, and public opinion : a guide for decision-
makers / Clifford Young, Kathryn Ziemer.
Description: Cambridge, United Kingdom ; New York, NY : Cambridge
University Press, 2024. | Series: Methodological tools in the social
sciences | Includes bibliographical references and index.
Identifiers: LCCN 2023050911 | ISBN 9781108479554
(hardback) | ISBN 9781108855310 (ebook)
Subjects: LCSH: Public opinion | Public opinion – Political aspects. |
Public opinion polls. | Political science – Decision making.
Classification: LCC HM1236 .Y68 2024 | DDC 303.3/8–dc23/eng/20231204
LC record available at https://lccn.loc.gov/2023050911

ISBN 978-1-108-47955-4 Hardback
ISBN 978-1-108-79000-0 Paperback

Contents

Figures

Graphs

Quadrants

Tables

Acknowledgments

We first must thank Ipsos and its CEO Ben Page for supporting this book; it would have not been possible without them. You can't talk of Ipsos without mentioning Didier Truchot – the indefatigable visionary and founder of the company. He has truly built a machine that captures the pulse of the world. Our project has included twenty-five years of discovering what it means to be a pollster, a decade of delving into people's psychology, fourteen years of graduate-level students serving as guinea pigs, and much multidisciplinary collaboration. We also thank our professional mentors – all giants in the field in their own right: Tom Smith, Orjan Olsen, Darrell Bricker, Robert Worcester, Clara Hill, Mary Ann Hoffman, and John Vidmar – from them we drew immensely. There is a whole slew of people who helped with early versions and pieces of this project. They are too numerous to note individually, so a big collective thank you. A personal shout-out to Catherine Morris, a gifted data journalist and Ipsos alum, who edited the manuscript and made it much better. And, finally, a warm remembrance of James Davis, whose first-year logic of causal order course is the origin story of this book.

The Three-Hatted Pollster

Public opinion is a driving force in democracy – governments must be responsive to the needs of their citizens. It determines who will govern and which policies will be more likely to succeed. Yet, given constant societal flux, pinning public opinion down with precision requires a nuanced understanding of context. Political and economic actors so often underestimate or misunderstand public opinion.

This book is for the user of public opinion data presented through the lens of the principal purveyor of such data, the pollster. By users, we mean decision-makers, or those who counsel decision-makers, many of whom see public opinion as an ephemeral and easily manipulable phenomenon.[1] Nevertheless, contrary to these perceptions, practice and scientific evidence show that public opinion is a stable, measurable, and, ultimately, predictable phenomenon.[2] Furthermore, when it is ignored, desired outcomes on the policy and political fronts are less likely to be achieved.[3]

Under certain conditions, public opinion can indeed be seemingly unpredictable.[4] The key from an analytical perspective is to know the conditions under which public opinion is more susceptible to volatility. Analysts must be able to identify the characteristics of these unique circumstances.

The pollster's work does not stop there; this is only the beginning. Substantial empirical evidence underscores that, in some cases, public opinion is only a secondary or tertiary factor in determining an outcome. Again, analysts need to be able to identify when this may be the case and respond accordingly. This book will examine public opinion conceptually

---

[1] Butler & Dynes (2015) "How Politicians Discount the Opinions of Constituents with Whom They Disagree," in *American Journal of Political Science*. Volume 60, Issue 4, pp. 975–989.

[2] Page & Shapiro (1992) *The Rational Public: Fifty Years of Trends in American Policy Preferences*. University of Chicago Press.

[3] Newport, Shapiro et al. (2013) *Polling and Democracy: Report of the AAPOR Task Force on Public Opinion and Leadership*. AAPOR Task Force.

[4] Bishop (2004) *The Illusion of Public Opinion and Artifact in American Public Opinion Polls*. Rowman & Littlefield Publishers.

and in practice, while laying out an analytical road map for pollsters on how best to analyze and engage public opinion.

A vast literature exists on theories of public opinion; on how to measure it and how to analyze it.[5] Still others exist on predicting public opinion and on how to influence it.[6] So, what does this book contribute?

MISSING ELEMENTS IN THE PROFESSIONAL LITERATURE ON PUBLIC OPINION ANALYSIS

Telling this story through the eyes of the pollster is easier said than done. Why? Well, simply, there is no synthetic treatment of best practices in interpreting public opinion. As we see it, the existing knowledge base on public opinion is disparate – spread across many disciplines, including political science, survey methods, political psychology, statistics, social psychology, cognitive psychology, behavioral economics, data science, and sociology. These literatures do not necessarily talk to each other.

Such a global understanding of the activity of the pollster is especially important now. Take the recent polling misses; they should give everyone pause. After the polls blithely promised a victory for Hillary Clinton over Donald Trump in the 2016 US presidential elections, their accuracy has justifiably come under question. The US 2016 election is by no means the exception. Take Argentina in 2019, or the United States in 2020, or Brazil in 2022, and so on. How can we put such performances into a broader context?

The reality is that the raw tool at the pollster's disposal – the survey – was refined for an era when people had fewer communication options. Now, almost everyone has a digital footprint, and landlines are going the way of the dinosaurs. Access to people has never been so varied yet so difficult. Naturally, the industry is aware of these issues and adapting its methodologies. Context matters to make sense of this.

Despite the very real challenges the polling industry faces, we can say, with confidence, that polls still offer real, meaningful, and actionable

---

[5] Some examples include Stimson (1999) *Public Opinion in America: Moods, Cycles and Swings.* Routledge; Page & Shapiro (1992) *The Rational Public: Fifty Years of Trends in American Policy Preferences.* University of Chicago Press; Bishop (2004) *The Illusion of Public Opinion and Artifact in American Public Opinion Polls.* Rowman & Littlefield Publishers; Groves et al. (2009) *Survey Methodology* (2nd edn.). Wiley; Davis (1985) *The Logic of Causal Order.* SAGE Publications; and Bradburn & Sudman (1990) *Polls and Surveys: Understanding What They Tell Us.* Jossey-Bass.

[6] Some examples include Tetlock & Gardner (2016) *Superforecasting: The Art and Science of Prediction.* Crown and Manheim (2010) *Strategy in Information and Influence Campaigns: How Policy Advocates, Social Movements, Insurgent Groups, Corporations, Governments and Others Get What They Want.* Routledge.

insights. The key is understanding how to interpret the results given our reality. Remember that polling results represent public opinion at a given moment in time. It is, by definition, always retroactive. Yet, when interpreted correctly, public opinion can give us a glimpse of the future, helping us make better decisions today.

The pollster also must contend with a world that is ever more polarized. The public is increasingly tribal in nature, and suspicion of the "other" is high. The fractured nature of public opinion makes it very difficult for practitioners to gain an overarching understanding of it as an analytical variable or decision input. Once again, context matters.

A polling professional today needs to understand a broad range of disciplines as noted previously. Complicating this, even if properly motivated, any given professional cannot necessarily be expected to integrate this vast literature without the requisite time, motivation, and resources. As such, there is not a single book that melds these different fields into one synthetic practically oriented approach. That's what this book aims to achieve.

A POLLSTER'S TALE[7]

As a freshly minted PhD from the University of Chicago, I thought of myself as hot stuff. Trained in the science of polling, I could do no wrong. Or so I thought, until theory met practice.

My first poll and paying client was for a group supporting a candidate for the presidency of *Jockey Clube Brasileiro* – a social club and horse racing track located in the city of Rio de Janeiro. I know it sounds crazy – a poll for an election in a social club. But these people had lots of money and were passionate!

Like any well-trained quantitative social scientist, I fretted about my sample design; it needed to be representative of the member base of the club. *Check!* I worried about the questionnaire design, no biased questions. *Check!* I also thought about my analytical plan for data analysis; I wanted to tell a clear simple story. *Check!*

All good; all great. The poll went well; the data looked great. On the day of the client presentation (really a chat by phone), I was pumped. Pumped, that is, until the client asked me, "So, will I win? What do I need to do to win?"

I sat there dumbfounded, without a ready answer. In fact, at that moment, I realized I lacked the knowledge base needed to provide the proper context and meaning for the client. Sure, I was well trained in the science of polling but had no framework, nor the requisite gray hairs, to shed light on what it all meant.

---

[7] This story and other individual tales in this book are based on the experience of Clifford Young.

Questions raced through my mind, "Will he win? What are his chances? And what can he do to change them?" I had no idea where to start.

To add insult to injury, the client came back to me the next day. He had gotten his hands on the other side's poll. Yes, they had one as well! And it was at odds with our own.

The client, of course, asked a very reasonable question, "What's up? Are they right or are we right?" He was asking me to assess the polls. Again, I sat there speechless, not only because I spoke halting Portuguese at the time, but because I had no reasonable response but my own logic – a bad place to be as a scientist and expert. I had no empirically based **rules of thumb** to anchor my analysis. No context.

I would only learn later in my career that, indeed, such analytical heuristics do exist. That there are multiple ways to assess the relative odds of a given candidate. But this knowledge, for me, would be years in the making. Users of public opinion data naturally face the same challenges as newly minted pollsters.

THE KNOWLEDGE GAP

Most professionals working as pollsters have had similar trials by fire. Their training gave them the skills to tackle certain dimensions of public opinion but left them wholly unable to address others.

For instance, the political scientist may be well versed in theories of public opinion, elections, and election forecasting but less so in the science of polling, messaging, and cognitive psychology/behavioral economics. Meanwhile, students of international studies and conflict have been exposed to approaches to assess political risk but lack a broader toolbox of skills. A cognitive psychologist will have a strong base in information processing, behavioral economics – and hence messaging and engagement – but, again, not necessarily in the other requisite fields.

To truly excel in the field, the practitioner would ideally be versed enough in all disciplines to incorporate them into their day-to-day work. Or, at least, be knowledgeable enough that they will be aware of their own blind spots and weaknesses.

WHAT THE BOOK IS AND IS NOT

We want to be clear from the outset what this book is and what it is not. First and foremost, this book is not a treatment of the use of public opinion in assessing the impact of public policies at a tactical level. In other words, we are not attempting to answer questions around something as specific as whether a healthcare policy bill should include one feature over another. For that, the reader should turn to the vast literature commonly referred to as program evaluation, impact evaluation, or evidence-based policy assessment.

The focus of this book, instead, is to aid the user of public opinion data in developing a systematic analytical approach for understanding, predicting, and engaging public opinion. More fundamentally, we want to help the reader understand how public opinion can be employed as a decision-making input. By decision-making input, we mean a factor, or variable, to assess, predict, or influence an outcome.

First, this book will unpack the different ways that public opinion can be utilized to interpret and predict sociopolitical outcomes. By sociopolitical outcomes, we mean elections, referenda, political or policy agendas, specific legislation, crises, scandals, and other existential threats to government and societal stability. In this case, public opinion can be thought of as a single decision input when assessing sociopolitical outcomes. For instance, government approval ratings are critical predictors of electoral outcomes. However, using government approval ratings alone to predict an electoral outcome is definitively *not* the most robust method. It is only when combined with other inputs, such as whether the incumbent is running, that our ability to accurately pick the winner is significantly improved. We will learn that multiple input forecasts are preferable to single input ones.

Second, our book makes a simplifying assumption that decision-makers – both political and economic – are heavy users of public opinion data. Both theory and practice support this assumption. Political theory, in the form of the median voter model,[8] suggests that parties and politicians are vote maximizers. As such, politicians will generally approximate their policy offer to the preferences of the average voter.[9] Policy disputes are typically won by those who meet public opinion where it is. We see this in practice all the time, although there are notable exceptions to this rule.

Third, this is not a book on polling or survey methodology; however, methods and methodological robustness will be a theme throughout, especially as it relates to our ability to use public opinion as an assessment tool. We will delve into this in greater detail in Part II of this book. Analysts must

---

[8] Also known as "Hotelling's Law," median voter theory posits that politicians adopt stances that incline toward the perspective of the median voter.

[9] Downs (1957) "An Economic Theory of Political Action in a Democracy," in *Journal of Political Economy*. Volume 65, Issue 2, pp. 135–150.

be able to determine if the measurement of public opinion is flawed, even if they are not experts in the science of polling.[10]

For more than eighty years, since Gallup correctly predicted that Roosevelt would beat Landon in 1936, the scientific survey sample, and its workhorse, the poll, has been the primary mechanism for understanding public opinion. Prior to surveys, decision-makers used a variety of methods to assess public opinion, including elections, crowd sizes, local newspaper editorial board opinions, riots, protests, and mass marches. Later developments in questionnaires and survey methods further reinforced the poll as the preeminent tool for gauging the mood of the people.[11] Over the years, the poll has largely become synonymous with public opinion.[12]

But our data world is significantly changing, and, as a result, so have our approaches to assessing public opinion. Looking forward, alternative methods to the poll will only grow in volume and application. Even today, analysts are increasingly employing nonpolling data sources to assess public opinion. Alternative data sources include analyzing social media, satellites, drones, ground sensors, APIs (application programming interfaces), aggregate cell phone data, and prediction marks. Think of the protests in 2022 that roiled Iran in the wake of the death of Jina Amini at the hands of the country's "morality police." Observers were able to track the spread of the protests through videos posted online = just one example of many.

Fourth, the book is about the use of public opinion across all domains – both political and nonpolitical. Most of the examples, however, are of elections. The reason for this is twofold. First, elections can be easily validated – we know the "true value" when the election returns come in. And second, most of these data are publicly available. In contrast, we have managed thousands of nonelectoral engagements, but they are proprietary in nature. We attempt to sprinkle in such examples when possible.

To date, the concept of the pollster has referred to an individual or organization that measures, analyzes, and interprets public opinion. But does this designation still apply in a world where the poll is no longer the sole vehicle to gauge public opinion? We argue, "yes." While technological advances have expanded the means and methods of tracking public sentiment, the importance of public opinion as a decision input has never

---

[10] See Lazersfeld (1968) "Forward," in *The Logic of Survey Research* edited by Morris Rosenberg. Basic Books, Inc.

[11] Bradburn & Sudman (1988) *Polls and Surveys: Understanding What They Tell Us.* Jossy-Bass.

[12] Converse (1987) "Changing Conceptions of Public Opinion in the Political Process," in *Public Opinion Quarterly.* Volume 51, Issue 2, pp. 512–524.

Table 1.1 *The three-hatted pollster*

	Part II	Part III	Part IV
	The Data Scientist (to Assess)	The Fortune Teller (to Predict)	The Spin Doctor (to Convince)
Primary Client Type	Media and all other clients	Private sector and financial sector	Politicians, governments, and private sector
Analytical Focus	Maximizing accuracy	Forecasting outcomes	Developing the most convincing message
Typical Questions	Is my public opinion data biased?	Who will win the next presidential election?	What is the winning message?

been more important. No matter the method to measure public opinion, an expert – the pollster – must give meaning to it. We believe that the traditional concept of the pollster is as meaningful today as it always has been. In this book, we focus on public opinion as a decision input, not the poll, even though we present polling data to illustrate our case.

ORGANIZATION OF THE BOOK

The pollster has three primary identities that we will explore in detail in this book. As a framing device, we will refer to the pollster as the "three-hatted pollster," reflecting the pollster's distinct identities as a **data scientist, fortune teller**, and **spin doctor** (Table 1.1). These relate to the pollster's primary functions: to assess the polls and related inputs, to predict public opinion outcomes, and to utilize these inputs to shape compelling messages that will resonate with chosen audiences. The pollster wears multiple hats, but before we unpack the various dimensions of the three-hatted pollster, we will explore the concept of public opinion, how our understanding of it has evolved over the centuries, and whether public opinion is a reliable, stable input or something more elusive and volatile.

Part I: What Is Public Opinion?

Part I includes **two chapters** of review and discussion of the relevant scientific and academic literature on public opinion, opinion formation, its effect on outcomes, and popular myths about it.

In Chapter 2, we examine public opinion as a concept. What is it? How has it been defined over the years? How has it been conceptualized by philosophers and social scientists? We also discuss how decision-makers employ public opinion as a decision input and examine the **concept of convergence**. Specifically, to what extent, and under what conditions, are decision-makers aligned with public opinion?

This, of course, is a central underlying analytic theme of our approach – that decision-makers use public opinion as an input because there is a real link between public opinion and sociopolitical outcomes. Put differently, if aligned with public opinion, decision-makers (candidates, politicians, policymakers) are more likely to win elections, push their policies and agendas forward, and win the messaging battle; but, if not, they won't achieve success.

In Chapter 3, we explore the formation of attitudes. For the practitioner, understanding how humans process information and come to their opinions is critical in influencing public opinion. This was a crucial piece of the puzzle that was poorly understood until recently. First, we look at **the multi-attribute model** – a commonly used model by social psychologists and economists. In particular, we detail how attitudes can predict public opinion. We call this the static process or model. Second, we examine how information is cognitively assessed and how emotions shape public opinion. This we call the dynamic model.

In Chapter 4, we ask the simple question: Is public opinion stable or not? Many decision-makers have seen it as an ephemeral, whimsical thing; some social scientists do as well.

We come down squarely on the **aggregate stability** side of this debate: that public opinion is a stable, predictable phenomenon under most conditions. We argue that, for public opinion to be a decision input, it must be stable and predictable. However, we also detail under what conditions public opinion is more likely to change or be volatile. Ultimately, any analyst of public opinion must be able to identify when a movement in public opinion is real and when it is merely noise.

THE THREE-HATTED POLLSTER

In Parts II–IV, we show practically how to employ public opinion as a **decision input**. As noted earlier, we use the concept of the "the three-hatted pollster" to organize the primary ways in which pollsters use public opinion: (1) to assess; (2) to predict; and (3) to convince.

Part II: The Data Scientist

In Part II, *The Data Scientist*, we include three chapters (Chapters 5–7) on how to measure public opinion through a systematic discussion of the science of polling and data scientific assessment tools. The intent here is *not* to train the next generation of pollsters or data scientists *but* to equip the analyst with tools to assess the quality of their data sources.

In Chapter 5, we discuss the types of errors in polls. Specifically, we define concepts such as bias, error, the law of large numbers, and the margin of error. We employ a simplified version of *total survey error* – a commonly used bias assessment framework.[13]

Our framework includes sampling and non-sampling error as the two dimensions that make up the concept. Sampling error is measured by the margin of error (MOE). Non-sampling error includes coverage bias, non-response bias, measurement error, and estimation error. Special attention will be given to *coverage bias* and *estimation error*. We find that they account for most of the polling misses. Specifically, we examine the challenges of estimating who is a likely voter – a special case of estimation error.

In Chapter 6, we apply our total survey error framework to the problem of a single poll. In this case, we assess an election tracking poll during the 2016 US presidential election. In July of that year, results from the Ipsos/Reuters election tracker were at odds with the market. Why was this the case? To answer this, we take the analyst step-by-step through the assessment process.

In Chapter 7, we use our framework to assess an aggregate of polls. We look at why the polls got the 2015 Greek referendum wrong. Was the problem down to sampling error or non-sampling error? A likely voter problem or coverage bias? Here, we determine through a process of elimination the most likely culprit. We also discuss concepts like spread, aggregation, and average absolute error (AAS).

Part III: The Fortune Teller

In Part III, *The Fortune Teller*, we include three chapters on using public opinion as an input to predict sociopolitical outcomes. The focus will be on rules of thumb and benchmarks, *not* on sophisticated statistical methods.

In Chapter 8, we detail the varying types of cognitive bias associated with prediction and discuss how to minimize them. We draw upon the

---

[13] Here, total survey error (and similar derivations) can be depicted as a triangle, with the two legs being the sampling and nonsampling errors and the hypotenuse being the total survey error.

cognitive psychology and behavioral economics literature, steeped in *prediction misattribution.*

We examine the weakness of expert prediction using the 2016 US presidential election as an example. Here, we discuss three broad classes of cognitive bias: (1) single input learning styles; (2) confirmation bias; and (3) binary thinking. We also look at herding and availability bias. Finally, we discuss methods to reduce such biases, including **triangulation**.

In Chapter 9, we take a special look at election prediction. This comprises a full review, from the simplest heuristics to more sophisticated aggregated election and poll-based forecasting models. Again, the treatment here is *not* concerned with statistical techniques *but* simple analytical frameworks, easily accessible to all. This chapter will also discuss combinatorial forecasting methods that mix, or triangulate, multiple sources. Again, the 2016 US presidential election will be our case study.

In Chapter 10, we look at a broad class of public opinion outcomes, such as approval ratings, referenda, impeachments, mass social protest, regime stability in nondemocratic societies, and big-picture scenario construction. Specifically, our focus will be on approval ratings and context-based approaches. Approval ratings both predict outcomes, like elections, and are a critical guide to engaging public opinion. Given their importance, the analyst needs to understand what impacts them. To do so, we provide a road map for the pollster. In terms of context analysis, pollsters are also required to paint the big picture for decision-makers. This can be done in multiple ways. We detail examples using main problem questions as well as multi-item indexes that capture underlying values and beliefs.

Part IV: The Spin Doctor

Part IV includes **two chapters** on how to message, engage, and move public opinion. Again, it will be a discussion of conceptual models and their application in practice.

In Chapter 11, we present conceptual frameworks to help the pollster engage public opinion. Here, we detail two frameworks: (1) the structural perspective and (2) the packaging perspective. In the structural perspective we discuss concepts like segmentation, message themes, messenger credibility, priority linkage, proof points, framing, and messenger–message fit. We also show how the multi-attribute model and its rankings and ratings can be redeployed to aid with messaging. In the packaging perspective, we show how emotions give special meaning to public opinion through words. The focus will be on concepts such as cuing, priming, hot cognition, packaging, and sticky messages.

In Chapter 12, we take the framework presented in Chapter 11 and apply it to a concrete case study. Here, we use both the structural and packaging perspectives to assess the 2022 Brazilian presidential election. Critically, we show the optimal communications strategy for both the Lula and Bolsonaro campaigns and then determine who did better and why – all this based on public opinion.

CONCLUDING THOUGHTS

In Chapter 13, we review the primary points made throughout the book – the key takeaways. We also discuss some odds and ends not discussed in the preceding chapters. These include the pollster in society and reexamining the concept of public opinion as a decision input. We spend some time assessing non-survey inputs as a gauge of public opinion. Here, we think pollsters should have a framework for looking forward. Our data world is changing, but basic scientific concepts like bias, error, validation, and reliability are not.

PART I

THE FUNDAMENTALS OF
PUBLIC OPINION

Public Opinion is the thermometer a monarch should constantly consult.
—Napoleon Bonaparte

Accurately assessing public opinion is not as simple as running a poll and taking the results at face value. While the survey is indeed essential for establishing a base from which interpretation will follow, that is just the beginning. Context matters.

In this section, we will discuss the different ways in which public opinion has been defined and operationalized over the centuries. Why is this important for the pollster? We will answer this question in this section of the book.

In Chapter 2, we will focus on critical concepts that undergird our conceptualization of public opinion. Some include the link between the public and those who govern, public opinion's stability, opinion as an attitude, and convergence. Pollsters need to understand these to do their job properly. Why is public opinion important? Is it stable? What is the role of emotions in opinion formation? All these are questions that the pollsters must frequently answer.

In Chapter 3, we examine how attitudes are formed. Here, we see attitude formation is a function of prior beliefs and information. We understand this process through two complementary lenses: the static process and the dynamic process. The static model thinks of attitudes as a combination of ratings and rankings. We term this the **multi-attribute model** – a commonly used approach in psychology and economics. The dynamic model concentrates on how humans process information. Things like words, symbols, and memory networks take on practical significance. Ultimately, both models have many applications for the practitioner.

In Chapter 4, we try to answer the basic question – is public opinion stable or not? We examine "the Yeas" and "the Nays" – two opposing perspectives on public opinion. All this provides critical context for the pollster.

2

What Is Public Opinion?

At a very basic level, the public is a force that political leaders – autocratic and democratic – have long had to reckon with. Think, for instance, of spontaneous expressions of dissatisfaction and strife, such as bread riots during times of famine. Ensuring that the people are generally contented, or at least, pacified enough that they will not rise up against their rulers, has been a vital concern for those in power from time immemorial. But the incorporation of the will of the people into the body politic is a relatively modern innovation, at least relative to the full sweep of human history.

The oldest examples of public opinion's incursion into governance lie in the participatory democracy of Athens and the representative republic of ancient Rome. In Athens, male citizens, or the "demos"; and the "civitas," or citizen, who formed the voting "populus" of the Roman Republic, influenced those who governed. In Athens, this occurred in the form of open debate and direct voting. In Rome, elections determined who would be eligible for public office via the Senate.[1] Suffrage back then was limited to free men. It would be another few millennia before it would be broadly extended to women and people of more limited means.

PUBLIC OPINION AS A PHILOSOPHICAL CONCEPT

It was not until 1600s Europe that public opinion as we know it today began to develop conceptually and practically. This came about as cracks appeared in the façade of the absolute power of monarchs, giving rise to new ideas and experiments in government. The backdrop to this was the emergence

---

[1] Hillard (2019) "Ventus Popularis?: 'Popular Opinion' in the 70s and Its Senatorial Reception." In C. Rosillo-López (Ed.), *Communicating Public Opinion in the Roman Republic* (pp. 211–240) (Historia Einzelschriften; Vol. 256). Franz Steiner Verlag.

of new social and economic groups that challenged the traditional authority of the monarchical systems in Europe. Ultimately, this gave rise to the European Enlightenment. In this context, Enlightenment philosophers, such as John Locke, Jeremy Bentham, Adam Smith, and Charles Montesquieu, articulated natural rights and advocated for limited government. *They saw public sentiment as an important mechanism for ensuring virtuous self-regulation*.

Jean-Jacques Rousseau – a French-Swiss philosopher of the eighteenth century – most clearly articulated the concept of public opinion in his defining 1792 book, *The Social Contract*. He referred to it as **the general will**, which he believed reflected the sentiments of all citizens in alignment with the common good. This he distinguished from **the will of all**, the motley collection of more self-centered wills and interests of individuals and groups. In a well-ordered society, there is no distinction between the general will and the will of all, as individuals will be motivated by the need to align with the common interest. Such an altruistic society exists solely in theory, as Rousseau himself admitted.

Still, Rousseau saw the general will as the legitimizing force of governance. In contrast, the prevailing wisdom of the day saw the sovereign, or monarch, as being granted their right to govern by God, not the people. Rousseau wrote during a time of great upheaval in France. Long wars and economic downturns had seriously undermined the legitimacy of the monarchy and would ultimately lead to the bloody dissolution of the *ancien régime*.

Most importantly for the pollster, Rousseau articulated *the inextricable link between the public and those who govern* – it is impossible to think of one without the other. This is key for understanding public opinion as a decision input: that it influences, or impacts, those who govern and, consequently, outcomes such as elections and public policy.

MOBOCRACY AND AMERICAN SKEPTICISM

Enlightenment philosophy was fully unleashed for the first time in the American democratic experiment, soon to be followed by the revolution in France. In America, it took some time for the democracy we know today to take root. Initially, America's founding fathers were skeptical of full, direct democracy, believing that there should be limits on the extent to which the people participate in governance. Their greatest fear was "mobocracy," in which an unchecked populace would inevitably fall prey to the allure of demagogues.

Setting aside the idea of a unicameral Congress because it was thought too susceptible to the vicissitudes of the mob, the founding fathers sought a compromise. Enfranchised citizens would be permitted to vote for representatives to the lower house of Congress, the House of Representatives. But members of the Senate, the upper house, would be elected by state legislatures, a practice that remained in place until 1912. Senators would serve for six years, instead of the two years granted to members of the House of Representatives – although some framers of the Constitution would have preferred that senators serve for life.

The design of the Senate was viewed even back then by some as hewing to close to an aristocratic model for comfort. But the founding fathers believed that the senate's design was necessary to circumvent the possibility of their fledgling republic's descending into mob rule. *The Federalist Papers: No. 62* and *63*, attributed to James Madison or Alexander Hamilton, outlined the argument for a legislative body that would serve as a necessary counterbalance to the whims of the people.

Writing in *Federalist 63*, the authors foresaw instances in which the public, "Stimulated by some irregular passion, or some illicit advantage, or misled by the artful misrepresentations of interested men, may call for measures which they themselves will afterwards be the most-ready to lament and condemn." The Senate would serve as a check "in these critical moments."

Public opinion is still viewed by some as inherently ephemeral and whimsical, prone to manipulation. The founding fathers' concerns reverberate still today. Why is this important?

In our view, the practitioner needs to understand that public opinion can seemingly be volatile, unstable, and unpredictable under certain conditions – the key, is to identify those conditions. We will elaborate on this in detail later in Chapter 4.

THE POLL AS PUBLIC OPINION: "ONE PERSON, ONE COUNT" VERSUS WEIGHTED AVERAGES

With the advent of the modern polling industry in the 1930s, the poll itself became synonymous with public opinion – a "one person, one vote" conceptualization, often called "majoritarian aggregation," or "simple aggregation."[2] Here, public opinion became associated with the averaging of individuals in a population, with each person weighted equally.

---

[2] Converse (1987) "Changing Conceptions of Public Opinion in the Political Process," in *The Public Opinion Quarterly* Vol. 51, Part 2: Supplement: 50th Anniversary Issue (1987), pp. S12–S24 (13 pages). Published by: Oxford University Press.

Practically speaking, this is exactly how we take an average in our standard poll today.

We often associate this perspective with George Gallup and his successful prediction of Roosevelt over Landon in the 1936 US presidential election. This served as an important legitimizing proof point for the science of polling and led to the subsequent rise of the polling industry.

The polling industry has gone through substantial change since the 1930s. It first met big science during WWII with the classic example of *The American Soldier* by George Stouffer and colleagues – the first big survey, big data project of its kind. Still later in the 1950s and 1960s, polling experienced a revolution in its methods and statistical sampling. Intellectual giants such as Kish, Campbell, Converse, and Lazarsfeld transformed polling into a truly scientific endeavor. Much of what we will discuss in this book finds its origins in this period.

EFFECTIVE PUBLIC OPINION

There were many critics of the "one person, one vote" notion of public opinion. Blumer argued that not all individuals have equal power or influence and, therefore, should not be "weighted" equally.[3] This "effective public opinion," or "weighted aggregation," perspective underscores the disproportionate impact that certain groups have on sociopolitical outcomes.

Take, for instance, Table 2.1 with data from the 2016 US elections. Clearly, the opinion of likely voters is not the same as that of registered voters. It is even more distant from that of the general public. This is important because, ultimately, the people who vote determine election outcomes. As Obama said, "elections have consequences." In this case, effective public opinion, or effective publics, would reflect the viewpoint of those who vote – not the general population. This has real implications for our ability to understand which way the winds are blowing leading up to an election. As Table 2.1 shows, the 2016 likely voter pool was more conservative than the general public. This alone suggests that the resulting 2016 election would reflect a more conservative bent than that seen among the broader population.

To make the most of public opinion polling data, we need to understand which population is most relevant. When seeking to determine who is most

---

[3] Blumer (1948) "Public Opinion and Public Opinion Polling," in *American Sociological Review* Vol. 13, pp. 542–554.

Table 2.1 *Outcomes by different effective publics*

2016 Preelection polling	All	Registered voters	Likely voters (70%)	Likely voters (55%)
Ballot (Clinton's lead vs. Trump)	+6	+6	+6	+4
Partisan identity (Difference Democrats vs. Republicans)	+6	+6	+5	+3
Ideology (Difference liberals vs. conservatives)	–14	–13	–17	–19
Nativism (Difference agree vs. disagree)[a]	+50	+53	+55	+56

[a] The nativism question reads: "When jobs are scarce, employers should prioritize hiring people of this country over immigrants. Do you Strongly Agree, Agree, Neither Agree/Nor Disagree, Disagree, Strongly Disagree."
Source: Ipsos-Reuters Election Poll 2016

likely to win an upcoming election, it is the pollster's job to determine who will vote and who will not. Again, this is precisely because elections are determined by **effective public opinions**.

Meanwhile, when a polling outfit works with companies and organizations to shed light on their public reputation, what the general population thinks is often uninteresting. Instead, corporate decision-makers see groups with a direct business impact – such as regulators, the press, the financial sector, NGOs, and other interest groups – as much more relevant. The application of effective public opinion in practice is highly contingent on the specific problem at hand, varying from client to client and context to context.

ATTITUDE AS PUBLIC OPINION

Modern polling relies on two scientific pillars.[4] The first is the sample survey – the probabilistic selection of a random sample of individuals from a population of interest.[5] The second is attitude measurement. Much of the foundational work on attitude measurement was done by social

---

[4] Lazersfeld (1968) "Forward," in *The Logic of Survey Research*, edited by Morris Rosenberg. Basic Books, Inc., New York.
[5] See Kish (1965) *Survey Sampling.* John Wiley & Sons; Cochran (1977) *Sampling Techniques.* John Wiley & Sons.

Table 2.2 *Components of attitude measurement*

	Description	Example
Direction	2 Categories (Positive and Negative)	Approve or Disapprove of the Job Trump Is Doing
Intensity	4,6,8, Categories	Strongly Approve or Moderately Approve
Neutrality	Neutral or No Opinion Category	Neither Approve Nor Disapprove

psychologists in the 1920s.[6] The attitude became the predominant instrument by which to measure public opinion.

An attitude is defined as a positive or negative predisposition toward an object. An object can be a person, organization, country, bill, policy, or any other thing that can be evaluated positively or negatively using a scale. Attitudes also possess three key elements: (1) direction, (2) intensity, and (3) neutrality.

Let's define our terms (Table 2.2). First, direction refers to whether the person's affect, or attitude, is positive or negative. So, one might approve or disapprove of Trump's handling of his job; or have a positive or negative evaluation of a company; or support or oppose a given bill. These are all examples of direction. Second, intensity refers to whether a person has a stronger or weaker attitude toward the given object. So, again a person might strongly approve or just approve of the job Trump is doing. Or, someone might strongly oppose a bill or only do so moderately. Third, some might not have an opinion on a given issue or be ambivalent about it. For instance, respondents might say they neither approve nor disapprove of Trump's handling of his job.

This simple notion of an attitude is used extensively in polling. The most ubiquitous question in public opinion might be that of presidential job approval – we find it in the United States and around the world. This makes sense given the critical link between the public and those who govern. Other examples as noted in Table 2.3 include favorability toward people, politicians, organizations, groups, symbols, and countries. Still others might involve whether people support or oppose a bill, policy, or law. Ultimately, there are myriad ways to construct attitudinal scales, the

---

[6] Thurstone (1927) "A Law of Comparative Judgment," in *Psychological Review* Vol. 34, Issue 4, pp. 273–286.

Table 2.3 *Examples of question wording and attitude measurement*

Scale	Objects	Example
Approve vs. Disapprove	Presidents, governors, mayors, governments, and other executives	Q. Do you approve or disapprove of President Donald Trump's job?
Favorable vs. Unfavorable	People, politicians, organizations, groups, symbols, and countries	Q. Do you have a favorable or unfavorable opinion of Joe Biden?
Support vs. Oppose	Bills, policies, issues, laws	Q. Do you support or oppose the repeal of the 1975 Public Affairs Act?

full extent of which lies beyond the scope of this book. However, public opinion analysts at a minimum should understand the measurement logic behind attitudinal questions.

CONVERGENCE: THE LINK BETWEEN DECISION-MAKERS AND THE CITIZEN

Public opinion does not exist in a vacuum. But in order for it to be a meaningful decision input, it must have a real-world impact on government policy and other sociopolitical outcomes. Even the earliest conceptualizations of public opinion linked it squarely with those who govern. At a theoretical level, philosophers, like Rousseau, understood that public opinion was the root of legitimacy for those who govern. Practically, leaders must align themselves with what the people want in order to stay in power.

Downs articulated the decision-maker citizen link with his **median voter model.**[7] He argued that politicians and parties seek to garner the most votes by molding their policy agenda to the perceived preferences of the median, or average, voter. We can see this convergence play out in elections all the time. In the United States, candidates focus their rhetoric and solutions to the partisans during the primaries and then typically pivot to the moderate middle in the general elections.[8]

---

[7] Downs (1957) "An Economic Theory of Political Action in a Democracy," in *Journal of Political Economy* Vol. 65, Issue 2, pp. 135–150.

[8] Here, it is worth noting that not all contexts are so simple as to be defined by the median voter. These are known as nonmedian voter scenarios. In multicandidate elections, other factors become more salient in the voting calculus, such as ideological proximity to the

Table 2.4 *Likelihood that a given outcome will
align with public opinion*

	Percent convergence
Electoral convergence	80–85%
Domestic policy convergence	70%+
Foreign policy convergence	50%

Source: Estimated from 2011 AAPOR Task Force; Page and
Shapiro (1983); Young and El Dash (2015)

To get highly specific, think of the shifting rhetoric of Don Bolduc, the Republican New Hampshire senatorial candidate in the 2022 US midterms. Before the primaries, he staunchly denied the legitimacy of the 2020 election. After winning, he suddenly changed his tune.[9] We see similar – albeit perhaps less extreme – behavior in other countries that have two rounds of elections, such as Brazil or France.

An extensive scientific literature also shows strong convergence between what the public wants and the enactment of policies. This body of evidence demonstrates that such alignment happens globally and at every level of government – national, state, and local.

The degree of convergence varies by type of outcome. It can be as high as 80–85% for elections as seen in Table 2.4, and around 70% for domestic policy issues such as healthcare, tax policy, education, and civil rights. When it comes to foreign policy the level of alignment can be as low as 50%. This is generally because the public is less proximate to foreign policy, making it more susceptible to input from special interest groups.[10]

Our own empirical experience as pollsters demonstrates the concept of convergence. Two elections serve as proof points. Take the 2019 Argentine presidential election, in which Alberto Fernández unseated the sitting president, Mauricio Macri. It is unusual for an incumbent president to lose.

The key to unlocking this riddle is in "jobs and the economy." This is what Argentines were worried about and what Macri polled poorly on

party, incumbency, and clarity of responsibility for policy impacts. For more information see Williams and Whitten (2015) "Don't Stand So Close to Me: Spatial Contagion Effects and Party Competition," in *American Journal of Political Science*, Vol. 59, Issue 2, pp. 309–325.

[9] The Editorial Board, "This Republican's Pivot Should Fool No One," *The Boston Globe*, September 17, 2022.

[10] Page and Shapiro (1983) "Effects of Public Opinion on Policy," in *The American Political Science Review* Vol. 77, Issue 1, pp. 175–190.

relative to Fernández. The economy at the time was contracting −2.5%. Ultimately, Macri was not credible on the top concern of the day. He did **not converge** with what Argentinians wanted at the time.

The 2020 US election is yet another example. The coronavirus reigned supreme as the number one issue. But Trump flouted it and, as a result, was seen as weaker on the pandemic relative to Biden. Trump lost; Biden won.

Public opinion shapes issues beyond elections as well. For instance, there was a time in the not-too-distant past when advancing a bill supporting same-sex marriage would have been unthinkable. Indeed, in 2008, California's sought to ban same sex-sex marriage via Proposition 8. This passed but was ultimately overturned in court. However, soon after that, a number of states enacted same sex marriage legislation. This was capped off by the famous Supreme Court *Obergefell vs. Hodges* decision in 2015, which legalized gay marriage in all fifty states.

How did this legislative sea change occur? Well, a supermajority of Americans supported same-sex marriage at the time (70–80%). The courts and state legislatures were merely converging with the prevailing attitudes of the time.

OPERATIONALIZING PUBLIC OPINION
FOR THE POLLSTER

So, how should we put this all together?

We learned multiple things in this short review (Table 2.5). First, that public opinion has been linked conceptually and historically to governance. Political decision-makers must align or be convergent with the needs of the people if they hope to maintain power. From an analytic perspective, public opinion impacts sociopolitical outcomes – the empirical evidence shows this. If it did not, public opinion would not be a worthy analytic input to understand the world.

Second, public opinion has been articulated in different ways at different points in time. Today, it has become synonymous with the poll. But public opinion can also be thought of as an attitude, the public most relevant to the decision-maker, or the link between those who govern and those who are governed.

Third, public opinion must be able to express itself to be relevant. Decision-makers have to "see it and feel it" in order to react to it. Today, we employ polls to gauge the mood of the public. But there are myriad other ways to gauge public opinion, including the outcome of elections,

Table 2.5 *Selected concepts and descriptions*

Concepts	Description
Convergence	The link between those who govern and those who are governed. Fundamental aspect of public opinion that recognizes its importance in legitimizing those who govern.
One Vote, One Poll	With the rise of modern polling, the poll becomes synonymous with public opinion. Here, each person is treated equally in importance.
Effective Public Opinion	View of public opinion that sees some groups as more important than others. Each person is not treated as equal. Best example is of those who vote versus those who don't.
Attitude	A positive or negative predisposition toward an object. The measurement workhorse of polling.
The Enlightenment	Important period of European history beginning in the seventeenth century that saw the rise of modern philosophy and science and its impact on society. For public opinion, increasing recognition of the public as a virtuous force for governance.
General Will	Concept first articulated by Rousseau. Emphasizes the importance of the public as a legitimizing force for governance.
Ancient Greeks and Romans	The primordial elements of public opinion are found in the Greek city states and the Roman Republic.

riots, strikes, demonstrations, and the sentiment of organized groups who put out publications and position papers.

Finally, we learned that public opinion is a stable and predictable phenomenon. However, it can seem capricious at times. The job of the pollster is to help the decision-maker in separating the wheat from the shaft.

3

Attitude Formation at the Individual Level

Up until this point, we've mostly talked about public opinion at the aggregate level. However, this begs the question. How are attitudes born, or rather formed? When we disaggregate public opinion, we're ultimately talking about attitudes at the individual level. It's in an individual's head that a mix of present state and new information develop into an opinion. It is only natural that understanding this process aids in identifying key levers and influence points for pollsters.

$$AF = PriorBelief + Information$$

In a general sense, attitude formation (AF) is a function of a person's prior beliefs (PB) and new information (I).[1] Information sources are not the focus of this book. But some include traditional news, social media, entertainment, friends and family, experts, and elites. Here, the concept of credibility is critical. We will learn later in this chapter that if information is not credible, it will not be properly ingested.

As pollsters, we operationalize attitude formation using two complementary models that we call **the static process** and **the dynamic process**. These both are based on the extant science and empirical evidence. The static model conceptualizes attitude formation as a moment in time; it thinks of information as a given or as a distant influence. It is also derived from social psychological models that see attitudes as a function of rankings and ratings of different attributes.

The dynamic model recognizes how humans filter and process information from their environment. Here, emotions, words, and symbols are the grist of the attitude formation mill. In the 1980s, cognitive psychology began to shed light on how the brain works. We now know far more today

---

[1] See Zaller (1992) *The Nature of Mass Opinion Cambridge*. University Press.

about information processing than a few decades ago. This significantly helps pollsters in their work. Our dynamic approach incorporates these insights.

As indicated earlier, both the static and dynamic models are important in understanding attitude formation. We'll first cover the static model and how to measure it in a scientifically sound and intuitive way. Then we'll cover the dynamic model and detail ways to operationalize it.

THE STATIC MODEL: DECOMPOSING ATTITUDES INTO RANKINGS AND RATINGS

So how does our static approach see attitude formation? Practically, we often think of attitudinal formation as a weighted average of the rankings and ratings of attributes.[2] This is often called **the multi-attribute model**.[3] Here it is worth noting that the model is only a crude approximation of the attitude formation process.

Figure 3.1 shows this in detail. Here, presidential approval is a function of the combination of policy "rankings" and "ratings" of these policies. Ratings of policy might represent the president's score on each attribute (unemployment, immigration, etc.). Often, these are measured by asking questions like, "How well is the president handling the problem

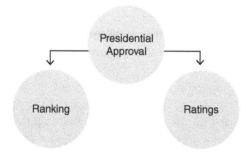

Figure 3.1 Decomposing attitudes into rankings and ratings

[2] Fishbein & Ajzen (1975) *Belief, Attitude, Intention and Behavior: An Introduction to Theory and Research*. Reading, MA: Addison-Wesley; Ajzen (1991) "Theory of Planned Behavior," in *Organizational Behavior and Human Decision Processes* Vol. 50, pp. 179–211; See also Krosnick (1988) "The Role of Attitude Importance in Social Evaluation: A Study Of Policy Preferences, Presidential Candidate Evaluations, and Voting Behavior," in *Journal of Personality and Social Psychology* Vol. 55, Issue 2, pp. 196–210.

[3] Huber (1974) "Multiattribute Utility Model: A Review of Field and Filed-like Studies," in *Management Science* Vol. 20, Issue 10, pp. 1393–1402.

of unemployment?" Policy priorities can be captured by evaluating the importance the public places on each attribute. This is typically done by asking questions like, "How important is tackling the problem of unemployment?" Or, we might ask respondents to rank order a list of public policies or issues.

DEFINITION OF TERMS

Attributes: We consider multiple attributes of an object (or person) when forming an opinion. When evaluating Joe Biden, Americans consider his performance on key issues, such as the economy, public health, and the environment. They also consider personality traits such as his trustworthiness, strength, and decisiveness, as well as demographic characteristics, such as his age, gender, and race.

Ratings: People also rate how well an object performs on a particular attribute. For example, most Americans might consider Joe Biden stronger on the economy and public health, but less so on social justice, immigration, and crime.

Rankings: Not every attribute is created equal – some matter more to us, others less. In early 2021, the economy and jobs as well as public health and disease were more important to Americans than crime, immigration, or the environment.

So, how does this work in practice? Let's take President Joe Biden's approval ratings as an example.

When combining attributes via their ratings and rankings, we can create an equation to capture people's attitudes. The following equation provides a way to calculate the "preference score" of an object. Think of the preference score as a proxy for an approval rating. Using our example of Joe Biden's approval ratings in early 2021, each of his attributes (i) is given a rating (a) of how he scores on that attribute (Table 3.1). Each attribute is also given a priority rank (b) of how important that attribute is to the individual.

$$\sum_{i=1}^{n} a_i b_i$$

Ratings and rankings are multiplied together so that priorities act as a weight on the overall score. The partial scores for each attribute are then added together to create an overall preference score for that object (score in the preference score line). The higher the score, the greater the preference for that object. Put practically, if Biden rates high on public health (65%), he will correspondingly have a high overall preference score (52%).

Table 3.1 *An example of President Biden's rankings and ratings on public priorities*

Attributes	Scenario 1 rating (*a*) (%)	Scenario 2 rating (*a*) (%)	Rankings (*b*) (%)	Scenario 1 preference score (%)	Scenario 2 preference score (%)
Economy and Jobs	52	52	33	17	17
Public Health	65	45	30	19	13
Immigration	41	41	17	7	7
Crime	40	40	13	5	5
Environment	51	51	7	4	4
Preference Score				52	46

Source: Reuters/Ipsos survey of 1,005 American adults, conducted February 17–18, 2021

This played out in reality – at the start of his term, COVID was still a top priority. If the public rated him lower on public health (45% versus 65%), given its importance, Biden's preference score would go down (46% versus 52%). **Here, we can see how attitudes can change over time – fluctuating along with shifts in ratings and rankings.**

ATTITUDES, RANKINGS, AND RATINGS

The decomposition of attitudes into rankings and ratings has several interesting properties. First, the rankings of issues (or attributes) are very stable over time. Indeed, in Graph 3.1, the wave over wave correlation of what people consider to be the main problem in their country is very high (0.89 or higher on average).[4] This is important to note because such priorities can be treated by the pollster as fixed in the short to medium term. Of course, events like terrorist attacks or COVID can radically reconfigure the public's priorities on short notice. But such cataclysmic events are the exception, *not* the rule.

Second, the two components of an attitude can be recomposed in analytically useful ways. See, for instance, the analysis in Quadrant 3.1. At the start of Biden's term in February 2021, we plotted rankings on the issues on the Y-axis against his ratings on the X-axis. When measured against the average of both, this allows us to construct a quadrant that identifies his key pillars and vulnerabilities.

---

[4] See Wlezein & Jennings (2011) "Distinguishing between Most Important Issues and Problems," in *Public Opinion Quarterly*, Vol. 75; Young and Ziemer (2018) "Cognitive Butterfield Part 1: A Framework for Assessing Optimal Engagement Strategies," *IPSOS POV*, May 2018.

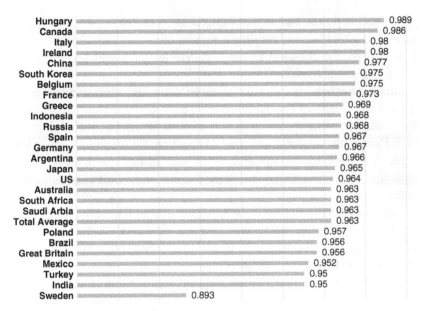

Graph 3.1 Average rank order correlation of main problems wave-to-wave in twenty-three countries
Source: Ipsos Global Advisor 2007–2011

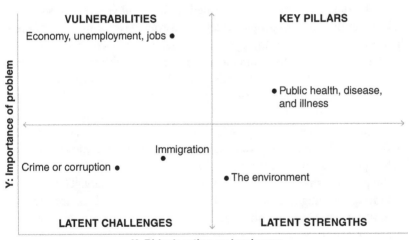

Quadrant 3.1 Four box quadrant analysis, Biden on ranking and ratings
Source: Reuters/Ipsos survey of 1,005 American adults, conducted February 17–18, 2021

In February 2021, Biden was vulnerable on the economy, unemployment, and jobs. Here, he was perceived to be relatively weak on these issues (low ratings). Yet, these same issues – the economy and jobs – were important to the public (high ranking).

On the other hand, his "key pillar" was public health, disease, and illness[5] – it was an issue where he was thought to be particularly strong (high rating). But it was also an issue that was highly important to the public (high ranking). His strength on this metric would help keep his numbers aloft. At the time, we made the argument that Biden was "surfing" the COVID wave. And, that as long as COVID stayed the number one problem, his approval rating would remain high.[6]

This is indeed how it played out for Biden, at least for the first year of his presidency. Eventually, the economy supplanted COVID as the main issue, placing a downward pressure on Biden's approval ratings. We will revisit Biden's standing on the main issue in Chapter 9.

Key here is how the pollster can use the basic building blocks of public opinion to conduct a thorough analysis of it. We will explore this in detail throughout the rest of the book.

DYNAMIC MODEL: EMOTIONS AND WORDS

Understanding how attitudes are formed at the cognitive level helps give the pollster insight into how people perceive and evaluate information. Different than the static approach, the dynamic model explicitly considers *information*. Up until recently, the brain remained largely a black box where little was understood about how humans processed information (Figure 3.2).

However, the cognitive psychological revolution in the 1980s finally unlocked the brain and its mysteries. Cognitive psychological insights began to spread to the other social and behavioral sciences in the 1990s, sparking new subdisciplines like political psychology and behavioral economics. Ultimately, such approaches have made public opinion an actionable decision input.

The primary strength of the static model is its simplicity. The rankings and ratings paradigm is powerful. However, the model does not properly account for what is going on in our heads and consequently how we process information.

---

[5] Given the salience of COVID at the time, "public health, disease, and illness" was likely perceived by most people as equivalent to the coronavirus pandemic.

[6] Young (2021) "President Biden Will Become a Casualty of His Own Success." *The Hill*, April 28, 2021.

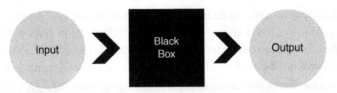

Figure 3.2 The brain as a black box

Information Processing

Cognitive science shows us that humans don't coldly calculate the rankings and ratings of each attitude attribute and then deliberately and deductively form opinions.[7] Remember our multi-attribute model. This would be impossible given the complexity of the world. Think of the innumerous assessments we make every day. We would succumb to cognitive overload and cease to function if required to employ a rational deductive method on everything. Instead, our brains evolved to be resource and energy efficient, developing cognitive mechanisms to make the most optimal decisions while consuming the least resources. These cognitive mechanisms are heuristics, or cognitive shortcuts, that have both pros and cons. On the one hand it makes our brain much more efficient. On the other hand, it can result in cognitive biases, which we'll discuss more in Chapter 8.

Most information processing happens outside of our awareness. This is because we can hold little information in our short-term memory at any one time. As such, our attitudes are a function of a dynamic ongoing process where we take in and filter information from our environment, which in turn influences our perceptions, opinions, and decisions. The result? We often come to our opinions without consciously thinking through them. Moreover, our decision-making is adaptive and influenced by a wide range of factors, including the context, our goals, long-term memory, our knowledge, and our bodily sensations.[8]

One of the key aspects of this process is the ***credibility of the information.*** First, information is assessed. And, if credible, it is then integrated into an overall opinion. If not credible, it is discarded.

[7] Kim & Garrett (2012) "On-line and Memory-based: Revisiting the Relationship between Candidate Evaluation Processing Models," *Political Behavior* Vol. 34, pp. 345–368.

[8] Venkatraman et al. (2020) "Disrupting System 1 Thinking: Better Science for Smarter Marketing," September 2020. www.ipsos.com/sites/default/files/disrupting-system-1-thinking-ipsos-esomar.pdf.

Again, this process is done in an automatic, subconscious manner. Here, it is important to stress that the credibility of information rests in how it is *packaged*. For instance, we intuitively understand that a "Biden infrastructure bill" will not be as compelling to a Republican as a "Trump infrastructure bill." Or that a person in firefighter garb who screams, "Get out!" of a building will be more credible than a clown yelling the same. Some information is more credible than other.

To understand this, let's detail some key points from cognitive psychology about how we process information. We will first examine memory-based information processing and then transition into a discussion of online information processing. Scholars posit that ultimately, both processing systems are pulled into play when individuals are confronted with new information.[9] But here we will investigate what each one means. Think of them as analytical heuristics to help us operationalize the dynamic model in practice.

Our brains are organized around two broad information processing functions: short-term memory and long-term memory. Our short-term memory reflects our conscious, more deductive selves.[10] Here, we systematically analyze and assess information. The problem is that our short-term memory has very limited processing capacity – only something like 7 bits of information, less than a Commodore 64 or even a floppy disk![11]

Long-term memory has an almost infinite capacity to hold and process data. Much of the brain's ability to process information rests here. Cognitive science shows that we are continually processing information and updating our attitudinal predispositions as a result of this. As already mentioned, this happens almost subconsciously as only the most critical information reaches the short-term memory in order to avoid overloading our meager processing power.

Here, emotions are important as they serve as a way for the long-term memory to communicate with the short-term, focusing the brain on the most critical issues and threats at hand. Feelings – such as "thinking something

[9]   Kim & Garrett (2012) "On-line and Memory-based: Revisiting the Relationship between Candidate Evaluation Processing Models," in *Political Behavior* Vol. 34, pp. 345–368.

[10] Kahneman (2011) *Thinking Fast and Slow*. Farrar, Straus, and Giroux; Taber (2003) "Information Processing and Public Opinion," In David O. Sears, Leonie Huddy, and Robert L. Jervis, eds., *Handbook of Political Psychology*; Kinder (2003) "Communications and Politics in the Age of Information" In David O. Sears, Leonie Huddy, and Robert L. Jervis, eds., *Handbook of Political Psychology*. London: Oxford University Press.

[11] Kinder (2003) "Communications and Politics in the Age of Information" In David O. Sears, Leonie Huddy, and Robert L. Jervis, eds., *Handbook of Political Psychology*. London: Oxford University Press.

is just not right," or, "our hair standing up on the back of our neck" – are all evolutionary adaptations to focus our attention on key information at critical moments. Emotions can be functional.

But we will also see that emotions can undermine more profound and critical elaboration and introspection. Often this is called "hot cognition" – the process by which emotions short-circuit reasoning.[12] It can skip deeper consideration and reflection: for example, "I don't like Trump. Therefore, any policy out of his administration is bad."

One such partisan emotion-driven example is the reaction of Americans to the infrastructure agenda. Ostensibly, everyone should be in favor of it at one level or another – it generates jobs, leaves tangible assets behind, and so on. But it too can be partisan.

As we will outline below, polling shows that Republicans will react negatively to an infrastructure bill associated with a Democratic messenger, but more positively to an infrastructure bill that creates jobs or is linked to a Republican. Here, emotions are central – if the information is tinged "red" (i.e., sponsored by a Republican leader) the Republican likes it; if "blue" (i.e., a "Biden bill"), Democrats are more positive toward it.

Certain cues ultimately determine whether we process the information more fully or simply discard it. Republicans will automatically reject "a Biden infrastructure bill" and not objectively, or more deeply, consider its merits because it is associated with a Democrat.

Memory Is Organized in Networks

Let's unpack this further. Memory is also organized in networks of concepts. We understand the world through the association of information inputs, or associated concepts. Take, for instance, our example of infrastructure.

Figure 3.3 can be considered a typical memory network. See how in **memory network 1**, the concept of infrastructure is associated with jobs and roads and bridges. This suggests that when one memory is activated then the others associated with it will be too. So, a person hears infrastructure, they immediately think about jobs as well as roads and bridges. If they don't, the associated concepts can be easily primed, such as "infrastructure means jobs"; or, "our infrastructure plan will be realized through 'building back America's roads and bridges'." Moreover, our memory networks are usually paired with emotions, so we might feel varying levels of positive

---

[12] Defined as Robert Abelson, 1963; https://dictionary.apa.org/hot-cognition. See Lodge & Table (2013) *The Rationalizing Voter*. Cambridge University Press.

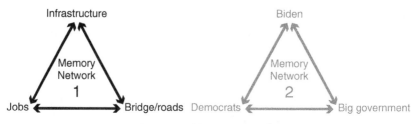

Figure 3.3 Memory networks

or negative emotion when a given memory network is tapped.[13] All in all, "memory network one" would produce a positive feeling or attitude.

In contrast, **memory network 2** shows a grouping for Biden, which includes the associated concepts of "Democrats" and "big government." In this case, the "infrastructure agenda" is conflated with Joe Biden to become the "Biden infrastructure agenda." For Democrats and independents, this has no material impact and therefore their reaction to "infrastructure" is most probably positive. But for Republicans such memory association is negative; this is because they are less likely to support any bill a Democrat puts forward. Perhaps most importantly, Republicans will be more likely to discard information about the bill even if it contains items they like. Why? It goes to the perceived credibility of the information. Think of how the Affordable Care Act got spun contemptuously as "Obamacare" and associated with alleged "death panels," setting the stage for it to be attacked by conservatives henceforth.

Ultimately, our opinions are conditioned by which memory networks are being tapped. *Again, packaging is key here. The central question for the pollster should always be: is the packaging credible or not?* Let's use the simple example of the infrastructure bill to reinforce our aforementioned points. Here, we conducted a randomized experiment with five conditions. The first asks support or opposition to the infrastructure bill with sponsorship from neutral experts. The others link it to a messenger or sponsor with a partisan tinge.

See how support for infrastructure projects depends on who endorses them (Table 3.2). The highest support is a bill sponsored by neutral experts (66%). Democrats are much more likely to be in favor if Charles Schumer and Nancy Pelosi back it (74% v. 46%). Republicans, in turn, are much more likely to be in favor if it is a Trump initiative (83% v. 41%). Here, we

[13] Nieuwenhius (2017) "Memory" in *Consumer Neuroscience*, edited by Moran Cerf and Manuel Garcia-Garcia. The MIT Press.

Table 3.2 *Support for infrastructure projects varies by partisan lean of sponsorship*

		Total (%)	Democrat (%)	Republican (%)
Condition 1	Donald Trump	59	41	83
Condition 2	Republican officials	50	37	78
Condition 3	Economists and transport experts	66	69	73
Condition 4	Democratic officials	60	74	50
Condition 5	Schumer and Pelosi	54	74	46

Source: Ipsos Poll 2018

can see how much of our belief in the merits of the bill depends on how it is packaged. Remember that nothing is mentioned about the specific aspects of the bill. No detail. Here, the meaning is derived from context.

In essence, the details of the bill are broad and generic. But when wrapped in partisan colors it becomes significantly more attractive to one side of the aisle or the other, undermining the more global support for infrastructure projects that exists absent of partisan cuing. Put simply, our prior assumptions about the world condition our attitudes toward it. And here the relative credibility of the information is key to understanding our attitudinal predispositions. In Chapters 11 and 12, we explore this in practical terms.

Online Processing Model

Again, the formation of our opinions goes on continually, often in a subconscious manner. We ingest and integrate information from our surrounding environment. Sometimes such inputs can change our attitudes or can reinforce them or just be summarily discarded. Information processing itself does not happen all at once but in stages. How does this happen? We take from the information processing literature and employ a **simplified online processing model.**[14] We will detail this next.

---

[14]   Taber (2003) "Information Processing and Public Opinion." In David O. Sears, Leonie Huddy, and Robert L. Jervis, eds., *Handbook of Political Psychology*; Kinder (2003) "Communications and Politics in the Age of Information" In David O. Sears, Leonie Huddy, and Robert L. Jervis, eds., *Handbook of Political Psychology*. London: Oxford University Press.

Stage 1: Attention and Exposure

We're constantly being bombarded with information from our environment. We mostly take in this information unconsciously, but sometimes we do pay attention. Our brains have evolved to ensure survival. When something is emotionally salient or threatening, it catches our attention, and we process it at a deeper level. This is known as bottom-up attention and is tied to our "fight or flight" system.[15] Take, for instance, a scream heard across the street. We would obviously look. Fear is a great motivator. It also contributes to the "cocktail party effect" where our brains are able to filter stimuli to decide which is most pertinent to them. It's what allows our brain to focus on a single conversation at a noisy party.

Stage 2: Interpretation

Everything we take in, consciously or unconsciously, gets filtered through the lens of our previous experience. We map new information onto our previous knowledge stored in our long-term memory. Mapping depends on the relative credibility of the information. If it is credible, the information will be more deeply processed; if not it will be discounted or discarded. Research shows that this is the moment where misinformation has its primary impact.[16] Here, misinformation can be seen as credible as well. False information can be seen as credible if packaged in a certain way.

Stage 3: Evaluation

At this stage, we ascribe a positive or negative value to the information considered. This process also operates as a two-way street where we update the knowledge and evaluations stored in our memories based on the new information. Given all this, we determine whether the object in question is positive or negative; safe or dangerous; good or bad. Remember our multi-attribute model. This can prompt a series of possible behavioral outcomes – call the police, help, run away from the scene, vote for a given candidate over another, and so on.

To conclude, we employ multiple models (online and memory) to understand how humans process information cognitively. As pollsters, we do pick and choose what makes most sense from a practical standpoint.

---

[15] Garcia-Garcia (2017) "Attention" in *Consumer Neuroscience*, edited by Moran Cerf and Manuel Garcia-Garcia. The MIT Press.

[16] Van der Linden (2022) "Misinformation: Susceptibility, Spread, and Interventions to Immunize the Public," in *Nature Medicine* Vol. 28, 2022.

Whether considering memory networks, credibility, emotion, words, or the interpretation stage – all are applied in our work. We detail the use of them in our case studies in Chapters 11 and 12.

BRINGING IT ALL TOGETHER

So how should we put all this together?

First, public opinion is also an individual level phenomenon. By understanding this, the pollster can decompose and recompose its fundamental elements to assess, predict, and engage it. We operationalize public opinion as an attitude as discussed in the last chapter.

Second, how do attitudes come to be? Generically, attitude formation can be defined as a function of prior beliefs and information. We operationalize such formation using two complementary models: the static process and the dynamic process.

Third, the static process, or model, sees attitude formation as a function of rankings and ratings. Our multi-attribute model in action. Such an approach is powerful, lending significant insight into the structure of public opinion. The caveat here is that the static model does not consider how information is processed by humans. Information is treated as a constant or at least an exogenous variable.

Fourth, our dynamic model incorporates cognitive processes into its framework and in turn details how humans ingest information. In our opinion, key here is the concept of credibility. Credible information is much more likely to be processed and more fully considered. The grist of credibility is words and symbols – some negatively trigger, others positively trigger, still others do nothing. Our memories are organized as networks of words and symbols – a veritable cognitive minefield. Pollsters must know these fields in order to navigate the contours of public opinion.

Ultimately, the pollster must understand public opinion as an aggregate and individual phenomenon. This is the package – *not* to understand this is to put the pollster at peril.

4

When Public Opinion Is Stable
and When It Is Not

Public opinion is not static. From the banal – like the popularity of movie stars – to the more momentous – such as same-sex marriage – public opinion is in a constant state of flux. But can public opinion be said to be "stable"? This is a core question that has been debated by philosophers, academics, and pollsters throughout the centuries. It matters because public opinion must be measurable and predictable to serve as a robust decision input for the pollster. If not, why would it be relevant to decision-makers?

By stable, we mean the perception that public opinion is consistent and predictable. From our perspective, this debate can be divided into two camps. The one camp, the "Yea's" holds that public opinion is a stable, measurable, and, ultimately, predictable phenomenon. The other side, the "Nay's," meanwhile, maintains that public opinion is ephemeral and whimsical because people are ill-informed and thus easily manipulated by the media, politicians, and other nefarious actors. As polling practitioners, we frequently encounter this perspective from clients and other stakeholders who doubt the soundness of public opinion as an analytical input. It is a perspective shared by many academics, decision-makers, as well as communications professionals. This school of thought holds that public opinion can be easily swayed if the right buttons are pushed at the right moment with the right tonality.[1]

It is true that we cannot expect every individual to be fully versed on all the fine points of public policy and the news. Indeed, even subject matter experts have to work to keep up with the latest development in their domains. So how can the public be capable of making a fully informed decision about the primary issues of the day?

---

[1] Illing (2018) "Intellectuals Have Said Democracy Is Failing for a Century. They Were Wrong," *Vox*, December 20, 2018.

We will unpack this dichotomy throughout this chapter. But to offer a preview, in truth, both sides have their points. Yes – public opinion is a measurable, predictable, and, for the most part, stable phenomenon. But under certain conditions, it can be more volatile. *It is key for the pollster to know when public opinion is stable and when it is not.*

In this chapter, we will first provide an overview of these two groups, the "Yea's," or those who believe that public opinion is stable; and the "Nay's," those who disagree. We will then cover conditionality, or the conditions under which public opinion appears to be more unstable.

THE YEA'S: ADVOCATES OF PUBLIC OPINION'S AGGREGATE STABILITY

According to the "Yea's," *stable* does not mean that public opinion never changes. Change occurs, but when it does, it happens in understandable ways. This is important because public opinion serves as the foundation of democracy and policy decision-making. If public opinion were ephemeral, then it wouldn't make much sense for political and economic actors to base their decisions on the public's preferences. Not only that, but it would be hard, if not impossible, to predict which policies would continue to receive support in the future or who would win the next election.

Aggregate Stability

Many public opinion trends show stability, and, indeed, rationality over the long term. In their seminal 1992 book, *The Rational Public: Fifty Years of Trends in Americans' Policy Preferences*, Benjamin Page and Robert Shapiro compared 1,128 identical policy questions over time (usually at least a year or two apart).[2] They found that 58% of the questions showed no significant opinion change. Domestic policy opinions were even more stable, at 63%, than foreign policy opinions (51%).[3] Among those opinions that did change significantly, the change tended to be modest. For instance, about half of these opinions changed by less than 10 percentage points.

---

[2] Page & Shapiro (1992) *The Rational Public: Fifty Years of Trends in Americans' Policy Preferences*. University of Chicago Press.
[3] Note that foreign policy is generally considered less important compared to domestic policy by Americans.

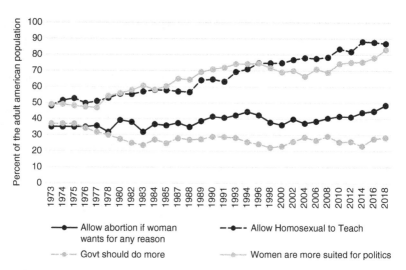

Graph 4.1 Examples of stable shifts in public opinion over the long term
Source: General Social Survey, NORC at the University of Chicago

When public opinion does change, it is understandable in the context of shifting demographics and values in society. For example, from 1938 to 1975, there was a 48% increase in the approval of a married woman earning a wage even if her husband was capable of supporting her. This would be expected given the increasing focus on women's rights and the entry of more women in the workforce over the past century.

As another example of public opinion's stability, look no further than the General Social Survey (GSS), which has been tracking core American attitudes around issues of public policy, civil rights, race and ethnicity, gender, and much else (Graph 4.1). First conceived of by James Davis in 1972, it now provides fifty years' worth of longitudinal data on trends in public opinion.[4] Consider the example shown in Graph 4.2. This depicts the percent of Americans, across generations, who were supportive of gay men teaching from the 1970's to today.[5] As you can see, the young people of the 1970s (today's older generations) are in lockstep with people under thirty-four today. Opinion has neatly coalesced at a near-total

---

[4] Davis (2001) "Testing the Demographic Explanation of Attitude Trends: Secular Trends in Attitudes among U.S. Householders, 1972–1996," in *Social Science Research* Vol. 30, pp. 363–385.

[5] The specific question text reads, "And what about a man who admits that he is a homosexual? Should such a person be allowed to teach in a college or university, or not?"

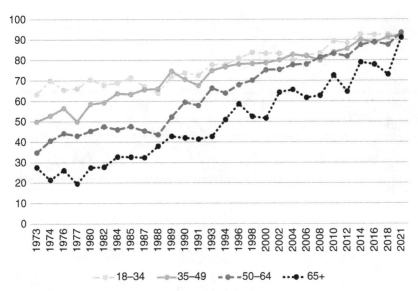

Graph 4.2 Percent allowing homosexual to be a teacher by age cohort
Source: General Social Survey, NORC at the University of Chicago

support as older Americans with less tolerant beliefs have left the population and younger ones with more tolerant perspectives have entered it.[6] But, at the same time, older Americans did become more progressive. Again, attitudes about social issues do change over time, but generally at a very gradual pace.

Public opinion does not always follow a linear trajectory. In response to extreme events, it can spike or change course abruptly. One of the classic examples of this is the sudden change in President George W. Bush's presidential approval ratings in the immediate aftermath of the September 11, 2001, terrorist attacks on the Twin Towers and Pentagon. Bush's approval ratings were at 51% before the attacks and spiked to 90% after (Graph 4.3). This is an example of a "rally around the flag" effect, in which people converge in favor of the party – or person – in power during times of crisis. While certainly not "stable" as one might traditionally conceive of the word, such shifts are nevertheless predictable and rational in their own way.

---

[6] In another measure of how public opinion has shifted, up until 1973 the American Psychiatric Association classified "ego-syntonic homosexuality" as a mental illness.

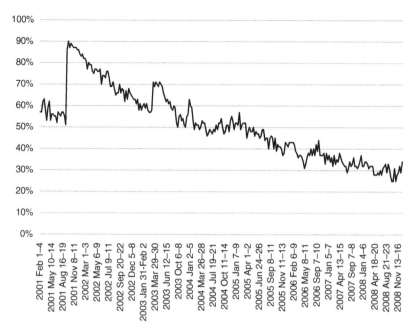

Graph 4.3 Trends in President Bush's approval ratings from 2001 to 2009
Source: Gallup Polling February 2001 to January 2009

Aggregate Enlightenment

One of the core critiques of public opinion is that is not necessarily well informed about current events or public policy. We saw this in Chapter 2 with Jay and Hamilton in the *Federalist Papers*. When it comes to elections, people might not even be able to name the candidates running for public office. Considering this, how can the collective viewpoint of a huge group of individuals of varying degrees of awareness and knowledge be expected to coalesce into anything remotely approximating stability?

The "Yea's" argue that public opinion is the aggregate of thousands – or indeed millions – of individual viewpoints, and not everyone within the group needs to be fully informed about an issue or hold an opinion about it. Just some within the group need to be.

This is a riff off of **the law of large numbers**, which maintains that aggregating all elements cancels out the random error of any one element.[7] While most individuals only know bits and pieces of a given issue, public

---

[7] The law of large numbers is a theorem in probability theory that posits: the greater the number of trails, the closer the average of the results is to the expected value.

opinion in aggregate has what it needs. Even if individuals have weak, poorly informed opinions that fluctuate at the individual level, aggregate public opinion is the average of all. Any errors that individuals make when forming their opinions will be canceled out so long as these errors are randomly distributed. ***There is collective wisdom in aggregate.***

THE NAY'S: THE PERCEIVED INSTABILITY OF PUBLIC OPINION

On the other side of the debate are the "Nay's." This group argues that at any given time, public opinion might change rather unpredictably because most people are ignorant and ill-informed. Walter Lippman memorably described the vagaries of public opinion as "the trampling and the roar of a bewildered herd" in *The Phantom Public*. As practicing pollsters, we often encounter anxieties about the seemingly fleeting nature of public opinion among our clients and other stakeholders.

There is a long lineage of such fears. You may remember from Chapter 2 that the American Founding Fathers were quite worried about an ill-informed citizenry and the instability of direct democracy. As John Jay put it, "Pure democracy, like pure rum, easily produces intoxication, and with it a thousand mad pranks and fooleries." Attempting to mitigate the public's underlying instability was the primary rationale behind the separation of powers and the creation of the Senate.

There is also empirical evidence of public opinion's underlying instability. One such thread in political science examines the public's relatively low levels of knowledge about politics – this is often referred to as the "ideal citizen" literature.[8] The mantra here is more or less, "An ill-informed citizenry makes for unstable public opinion and undermines a vibrant, healthy democracy."

The polling backs this up, at least in part. Many people – both in the United States and worldwide – are poorly informed about many issues, even including those that have a direct, material impact on their lives.[9] In the United States, Ipsos ran a series of polls with NPR testing true-false knowledge about issues like immigration, healthcare, and gun policy. These were animating issues with meaningful, and sometimes existential, implications for people's daily lives. Yet among the twenty-five

---

[8] See Villalobos et al. "What Is a Good Citizen?: A Systematic Literature Review," in *IEA Research for Education Series*. Sept 2021, FEAR, Vol. 2.

[9] Duffy (2018) *The Perils of Perception*. London: Atlantic Books; Carpini & Keeter (1996) *What Americans Know about Politics and Why It Matters*. Yale University Press.

true-false questions asked between 2018 and 2020, a majority of Americans only correctly answered eleven of them.

Non-Attitudes and Question Wording

Such arguments find further empirical proof in survey research outlined by Philip Converse in his 1964 article, "The Nature of Belief Systems in Mass Publics." In this, he examines three waves of the American National Election Study, finding that a large portion of respondents did not respond consistently wave over wave.

Converse coined the term **non-attitudes** which refers to responses from people who "lack [the] information about a particular dimension of a controversy [and thus] offer meaningless opinion that vary randomly during repeated trials over time."[10] *Non-attitudes have became synonymous with the instability of public opinion.*

Much of the subsequent work after Converse has focused on the level of issue salience, the education level of respondents, and question wording. In 2004, George Bishop unpacked the ways in which polling results can be suspect given the public's relatively low levels of knowledge about certain topics.[11] For instance, polls on the support for ACA (Affordable Care Act), or Obamacare, varied considerably in the first years – from 56.4% on the high end to 32.2% on the low end.[12] Why? Americans knew little about the policy, and question wording varied greatly from poll to poll.

Question wording is often one of the reasons that polls appear noisy. We will explore this sort of error in more detail in Chapter 5.

Non-attitudes are not just a charming oddity of public opinion. Instead, they can be linked to more nefarious phenomenon like misinformation. Ipsos found in a 2022 poll that more than half of Americans believed lies associated with January 6th and COVID.[13] Fiction becomes reality if it is seen as fact.

[10] Converse (1964) "The Nature of Belief Systems in Mass Publics," in D. E. Apter (ed.) *Ideology and Its Discontent*. New York: Free Press of Glencoe, pp. 206–261; Converse (1970) Attitudes and Nonattitudes: Continuation of a Dialogue. In E. R. Tufte (ed.) *The Quantitative Analysis of Social Problems*. Mass: Addison-Wesley.

[11] Bishop (2004) *The Illusion of Public Opinion: Fact and Artifact in American Public Opinion Polls*. Rowman & Littlefield Publishers.

[12] Holl et al. (2017) "Does Question Wording Predict Support for the Affordable Care Act? An Analysis of Polling during the Implementation Period, 2010–2016," in *Health Communication* Vol. 33, Issue 7, pp. 816–823.

[13] Newall, Jackson, & Lloyd (2022) "One Year after Jan. 6 US Capitol Riot, Concern about Misinformation Is High," *Ipsos Public Affairs, North America*, January 6, 2022. Retrieved

LOW INFORMATION RATIONALITY

One strong counter to "the Nay's" argument is how low information citizens make decisions in their best interests despite their informational limitations. Here, people use information from their environs to derive meaning and context. This coping strategy has been called different things by different researchers, including "heuristic-based reasoning," "low information rationality," and "bounded rationality."[14]

In our own experience, we see this play out all the time in our own work. Take inflation as an example. People may not be able to correctly cite the rate of inflation. But they are keenly aware of its impact on their pocketbooks – think about the price of gasoline, groceries, baby products, and so on. A typical comment goes: "I used to have 50 dollars at the end of the month; now I have nothing. I am barely making ends meet." Inflation is real and all around them. No need for a trivia test to assess self-preservation here.

This perspective provides powerful insights into opinion formation by showing the importance of contextual clues to derive meaning. In Chapter 3, we discussed information processing which is an interesting operationalization of the above-mentioned low information perspective.

MECHANISMS OF PUBLIC OPINION CHANGE

Change in public opinion typically occurs in response to external stimuli in the form of events, campaigns, the economy, and other paradigmatic shifts. Change can be momentary and fleeting – think, "the rally around the flag" effect on approval ratings in reaction to a terrorist attack or long-term and slow, like attitudes toward homosexuality. There are two primary types of change: within- and between-person.

Within-person change is what pollsters are most focused on. It can be used to answer questions such as:

- Who will win the next election?
- What is the winning message?
- Will the pandemic hurt the current administration's approval ratings?

from: www.ipsos.com/en-us/news-polls/one-year-after-jan-6-us-capitol-riot-concern-about-misinformation-high.

[14] See Popkin (1991) *The Reasoning Voter: Communication and Persuasion In Presidential Campaigns*. Chicago: University of Chicago; Sniderman et al. (1991) *Reasoning and Choice: Explorations of Political Psychology*. New York: Cambridge University Press.

Between-person change is slower moving but typically more durable. It takes decades to be fully detected. As such, this type of change is much less volatile and much more stable. Between-person change, rather than being used to interpret fleeting events, is associated more with underlying values, beliefs that often are crystallized at an early age. In such cases, pollsters typically use between-person change to answer longer-term questions such as:

- What will happen with climate change policy in ten years?
- Will the United States see a center-left, or center-right, party in the future?
- Is the tribalism we see today temporary or here to stay?

The overarching point here is that the pollster must properly identify the object of analytical focus. If the objective is short-term change, then we are talking about within-person change. If it is a long-term scenario construction, then it is most probably between-person change. Often, the answer to any given question is some mix of the two.

CONDITIONALITY

To sum up, we argue that the truth of public opinion's stability and reliability falls somewhere in the middle of the "yea" and "nay" camp. But, while public opinion is mostly stable, there are some conditions under which it is not. This instability takes the form of stark short-term changes. Here, we will review some conditions under which public opinion is more volatile.

External Events

Events such as wars, natural disasters, and economic downturns can significantly impact public opinion in the short term. Such change can be momentary and relatively fleeting. Table 4.1 shows the effect of highly disruptive events on presidential approval ratings and elections. However, as you will see, the effect varies across events. For instance, hurricanes and mass shootings have a net neutral effect on approval ratings. Why? People see these events as apolitical and so don't blame the government for these types of uncontrollable and unpredictable occurrences.

There are, of course, always exceptions to the rule. One notable example is Hurricane Katrina, which devastated New Orleans and led to over 1,800 fatalities. The public blamed the Bush administration for failing to respond

Table 4.1 *The impact of notable events on government and presidential approval ratings, voter intent, and election vote share*

Event type	Percent change in metric before and after the event in question	Metric
Currency devaluations	−17%	Presidential/government approval rating
Blackouts	−10%	Presidential/government approval rating
Spike in gas prices	−5%	Presidential/government approval rating
Floods and droughts	−1.5%	Election vote share
Hurricanes	–	Presidential/government approval rating
Mass shootings	–	Presidential/government approval rating
Sports games	+1.6%	Election vote share
Nominating conventions	+10%	Voting intention
Wars	+16%	Presidential/government approval rating
Terrorist attacks	+22%	Presidential/government approval rating

Sources: Young (2020) "Will Americans See the Impact of the Coronavirus as a Random Act of God or Government Ineffectiveness?," in Cliff's Take Ipsos POV March 2020

quickly to one of the worst natural disasters in modern US history.[15] But, in general, floods and droughts have only a slight negative impact and are generally construed as a randomly occurring event. This is because their impact is generally felt at the local level and thus does not spill over into sentiment at the national level.

Approval ratings drop the most after currency devaluations, blackouts, and gas price spikes. Why? The economy is frequently the public's top concern, and these events all have a direct and tangible impact on people's daily lives and pocketbooks. In bad economic times, the sitting government often takes a hit in their numbers; we will explore this in more detail in Chapter 9. But other events have the opposite effect, boosting approval ratings. Wars and terrorist attacks can unify the public, causing them to forget their differences and "rally around the flag" and their president. We mentioned this earlier when

---

[15] Healy & Malhotra (2009) "Myopic Voters and Natural Disaster Policy," in *American Political Science Review* Vol. 103, Issue 3, 2009.

discussing the change in George W. Bush's approval ratings after September 11th. At the local level, sometimes "feel-good" events, like a win for the local sports team, can boost perspectives on government performance.[16]

The bottom line here is that events can have an immediate impact on public opinion. This change is sometimes seen as capricious. But pollsters can account for the probable directionality of public opinion given the type of event in question.

ISSUE SALIENCE

As noted in our earlier discussion of George Bishop, low salience on an issue can lead to swings in opinion as people learn more. Elections are a good example of this. They are learning moments for the public, and as dark-horse candidates garner a bigger national profile, perspectives can shift.

Take the 2010 Brazilian presidential election. This pitted Dilma Rousseff against José Serra, who had been leading in the polls for two years up to the election. But ultimately, Dilma received 47% of the vote in the first round of elections to Serra's 33%. She decisively won in the second round (52% v. 39%). How did the tables turn so quickly? It was simply that Serra – the opposition candidate – was a known quantity. Rousseff, meanwhile, was a relative unknown as Lula's chief of staff. Yet once Brazilians learned that Rousseff was Lula's pick and her public profile grew sharper, support for her increased.

This is a classic case of *differential name recognition*[17] and how with greater exposure, public opinion can shift. More generally, public opinion polls at the beginning of an electoral season can be confused as false positives. In the case of the 2010 Brazilian election, many people thought Serra was a shoo-in. But, times changed. In Chapters 11 and 12, we will show the strong link between familiarity and favorability. There, we will learn one of the central precepts of communication – "you got to be known to be liked."

---

[16] Healy, Malhotra, & Hyunjung Mo (2015) "Irrelevant Events Affect Voters' Evaluations of Government Performance," the *Proceedings of the National Academy of Sciences* (107, 29), July 6, 2010; Fowler & Montagnes, "Reply to Healy et al.: Value of Ex Ante Predictions and Independent Tests for Assessing False-Positive Results," the *Proceedings of the National Academy of Sciences*, October 28, 2015.

[17] Typically, pollsters look at familiarity. The scale can vary, but it normally includes four to five categories from very familiar to never heard of. Name recognition is a subset of familiarity. Here, we define it as having at least heard of the given object.

Additionally, emergent issues often begin as low salience ones. This is because they are poorly understood at first. As such, public opinion can appear volatile as many people start off being unfamiliar with the issue. But as people become more familiar with it, opinions grow more stable. Some notable issues that began as low salience ones before rising to greater prominence include stem cell research and COVID-19.

Poor Question Wording

Variations in survey questions – including wording, context, and form – can create the illusion of public opinion's instability. Slight tweaks to question wording here and there might not seem like a big deal, especially if the questions are about the same topic. But even very slight changes in wording can alter the way that people interpret and respond. This is much of George Bishop's argument.

Take President Donald Trump's first impeachment in 2019 as an example. While a majority of Americans (57%) agreed that he had committed an impeachable offense, just 47% agreed that he should be impeached and removed from office. These variable question formulations were conflated by many pundits into "the public wants to remove Trump." As Joe Scarborough of *Morning Joe* said, there has been a "radical shift in public opinion in the past five, six days towards impeachment." As demonstrated, belief that Trump committed an impeachable offense is quite different than support for impeachment and removal.

Question framing is all-important (Graph 4.4).[18] And its misinterpretation leads to a sense that public opinion is capricious. We will examine this in more detail in the next part of this book, "The Data Scientist."

BRINGING IT ALL TOGETHER

So, what did we learn from this chapter?

First, public opinion is generally a predictable, stable phenomenon. This is critical for the pollster because without it, public opinion would be an unworthy decision input.

Second, non-attitudes demonstrate the potential ignorance of public opinion and corresponding volatility of it. But, people need not have all

[18] Young (2019) "The American Public Has Multiple Understandings of the Word 'Impeachment,'" *Cliff's Take* Ipsos, December 12, 2019.

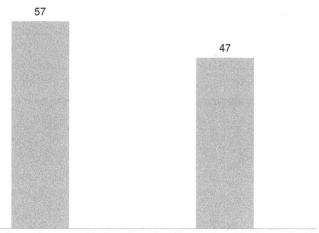

Graph 4.4 Two different ballot questions concerning impeachment
Source: Ipsos/FiveThirtyEight November 27 to December 2, 2019

the details to make sound decisions. Low information rationality plays out every day at the individual level. We derive meaning from bits and pieces of information in our environment. Ultimately, people need to just know enough to act in their own interests.

Does our collective ignorance lead to misaligned policy outcomes? There is evidence to suggest yes that there can be an alignment problem.[19] But this is a collective action problem that we *neither* contemplate *nor* resolve in these pages.

Third, under certain conditions, public opinion can appear to be unstable. It can be impacted by events, the salience of the issue, question wording, and other methodological anomalies. Each of these conditionalities is predictable or at least understandable in context. However, to the layperson's eye, public opinion may appear to be volatile. We provided a toolbox for the pollster to assess such uncertainty.

Finally, all of this is context for the practitioner. People often question why theory is important. Theory provides a conceptual framework for better understanding and meaning. Public opinion is many things; defined in many ways; still operationalized in even more ways. Pollsters must understand this.

---

[19] See Duffy (2018) *The Perils of Perception*. London: Atlantic Books; Hochild (2016) *Strangers in Their Own Land: Anger and Morning on the American Right*. New Press.

PART II

THE POLLSTER AS DATA SCIENTIST

"When you cannot measure your knowledge is meager and unsatisfactory."
—Lord Kelvin

It is the pollster's job to analyze public opinion data and arrive at an unbiased assessment of where the public stands on a given issue. To do this, we can look to both polling and non-polling inputs. But what happens when those inputs are flawed? All the best analytical capabilities will still fall short if the data are misleading.

Over the next three chapters of this book, we will focus our attention on the quality of public opinion data. The poll is the workhorse that brings public opinion data to the pollster, promising reliable results based on scientifically proven methods. There are from time to time high-profile polling misses, especially when it comes to elections. They shine more brightly than the innumerable times the polls are right.

The stakes are high. When there's an error in the polls, the reputation of the pollster, their polling firm and their media partner all take a hit. We would argue that confidence in the system is shaken; credibility is lost. Take the Landon victory over Truman in 1948. Wait, that was Truman over Landon. Or the universal preelection anointing of Clinton over Trump in 2016. Another rough moment for pollsters. Or the promised blue wave in the 2020 presidential election. In the latter two misses, the public's growing skepticism of the polls is justified. Of late, US election polling has been skewing Democratic while actual turnout reflects a subset of the GOP that simply isn't being captured in the lead-up.

While the polling problems have been particularly acute in the United States, such issues are not unique to any one country. It is a problem that pollsters everywhere must be fore-armed against. We find similar

Table II.1 *The three-hatted pollster as data scientist*

	Part II	Part III	Part IV
	The data scientist (to assess)	The fortune teller (to predict)	The spin doctor (to convince)
Primary client type	Media and all other clients	Private sector and financial sector	Politicians, governments, and private sector
Analytical focus	Maximizing accuracy	Forecasting outcomes	Developing the most convincing message
Typical question	Is my public opinion data bias?	Who will win the next presidential election?	What is the winning message?

challenges in places as diverse as Brazil, Colombia, France, the United Kingdom, Australia, and Argentina.

To be clear, the polling industry isn't standing idly by as the casualty list mounts. Pollsters everywhere are seeking to address the problem of accuracy by assessing their sample designs, 'likely voter models,' and measurement instruments.

In this part, "The Pollster as Data Scientist," we will tackle these challenges. Ultimately, one of the activities of **the three-hatted pollster** is to assess data quality. Here, we will deploy a simple framework to assess the robustness of public opinion inputs and to minimize – if not eliminate – such survey errors. *The intent of this book is not to train analysts in the science of polling, but to equip practitioners with the tools to assess the robustness of public opinion data.* Ultimately, problems might be local, but the solutions are universal.

Chapter 5 will cover the concepts of error and bias and their application in practice using an assessment framework. In Chapter 6, we assess data problems in preelection polling during the 2016 US presidential election. Here, our focus will be on problems with a single poll. In Chapter 7, the same concepts are applied to an aggregate of polls.

A POLLSTER'S TALE: BACK IN THE UNITED STATES

It's late on election night, November 4, 2008. I'm back in the United States, after ten years in Brazil. This is my first US election. The bulk of the returns have come in, and Obama is called the winner by the networks that night. But the returns are still trickling in; they keep getting closer and closer to our own results. We already know we picked the correct winner. We might even nail it to the decimal. Wow!

Obama trounced McCain by 7 points: Obama's 53 to McCain's 46. A landslide by US election standards. Our own polling? 53/46. Yes, we can! A little of skill and a lot of luck.[1]

For a few days, we basked in the glory of our achievement. Here, at thirty-seven years old, I had polled on Lula's monumental victory in 2002 and now that of Obama in 2008. I was unique in the world. Or so I thought.

Let's fast-forward to 2016. I'm at my office, watching the returns come in together with Ipsos nobility. I had come off a morning of TV interviews and would only be doing a little radio that night.

I always pay attention to Florida – as Florida goes so goes the nation. Specifically, I watched – the Tampa/Fort Lauderdale area – it was a bell-wether. But why was it flickering red then blue then back again? It should stay blue. Weird.

Other states started to show strangeness as the returns came in. Take North Carolina, which came in solidly red for Trump. Friends and family began to call, asking what the heck was up. All the polls, or at least most, had shown a Clinton victory. Ours as well. I kept on rationalizing what we were seeing.

It would be a very long night for all of us. My sparse radio plans turned into hourly interviews. I drew from our data and spoke a lot about how many Americans saw the system as broken, fueled by a nativist backlash. These were the reasons behind the votes. Context always matters.

I slept only two hours. The next day was spent explaining the polls and why they were off.

At the national level, the polling was within a point or two. But it was with the state polling that we all got it wrong. Our own polling followed this pattern. And it was in states like Wisconsin, Pennsylvania, and Michigan where Trump won. We were off; the market was off. Egg on our face; a very different experience than 2008.

I find these two cases telling.

We have the same pollster, same polling firm, and the same country *but* two completely different polling outcomes. Why? In 2008, we were able to account for the relevant error; in 2016 we were not. It's that simple. Correlated error killed us. We would later find out that nonresponse bias would be the silent killer in 2016 and beyond. Methods matter. This is why we argue in this book that the pollster as data scientist is the lynchpin of our profession. But we also see that in even in the worst moments, as in 2016, the pollster can still provide critical context. We matter not just as election forecasters.

---

[1] See www.ipsos.com/sites/default/files/news_and_polls/2008-11/mr081114-1DA.pdf.

Understanding Bias and Error

Rest assured – there will always be the potential for some form of error when capturing or collecting data. The key is to be aware of this pitfall and to be able to assess its relative impact. To wit, pollsters should ask two key questions:

- "Is our public opinion data unbiased?"
- "If not, can we still use the findings to draw credible conclusions?"

It is essential that the pollster can answer such questions. In this chapter, we'll cover the main types of errors and how such errors affect the quality of public opinion data. We'll then present a simple assessment framework that can be used to evaluate the quality of public opinion data. But first, a note about the difference between error and bias.

BIAS VS. ERROR

Although both bias and error help explain why there might be a difference between the true population value and the sample mean, they are distinct concepts, differing in their impact.[1] Take, for instance, Biden's approval rating during his first year in office (Graph 5.1). Here, we calculated the average of the polls for each month (dotted black line in Graph 5.1). And then we plotted that monthly average against a randomly selected poll from that same month (gray line in Graph 5.1). See how a single poll is more variable

---

[1] The true population value is what we would find if we collect data from the entire population without measurement error and calculate the average. The sample mean is when we take a sample from the population and calculate the average of the sample. Since we're not collecting data from the entire population, the sample mean will inevitably differ from the true population value.

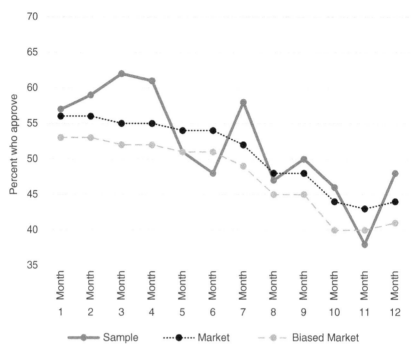

Graph 5.1 President Biden's weekly approval rating 2021: Market average versus single poll
Source: RealClearPolitics

than the market average of polls. Also, note how the single poll fluctuates up
and down against the market average. This is an example of error.

In contrast, bias is a systematic difference between the true population
value and the sample mean. In other words, it doesn't matter how large the
sample might be or how many times the poll is repeated; if it is biased, the
average will be off from the true population value.

Think again about Biden's job approval. If we excluded Democrats by
design or by omission, Biden's approval ratings would be lower in such a
poll. See gray dotted line. And it wouldn't matter how many times we conducted the poll or how large it was, it would always produce a lower Biden
approval rating than a poll without such bias problems.

BIAS AND ERROR DEPICTED MATHEMATICALLY

$$\text{Bias}\left(\hat{\theta}\right) = \left(E\left(\hat{\theta}\right) - \theta\right)$$
$$\text{where}\left(E\left(\hat{\theta}\right) - \theta\right) \neq 0$$

Bias and error can be depicted mathematically. Bias can be thought of as a nonzero difference between the estimate in expectation $E\left(\hat{\theta}\right)$ and the true population value θ .

$$\text{Error}\left(\hat{\theta}\right) = \left(E\left(\hat{\theta}\right) - \theta\right)$$

$$\text{where}\left(E\left(\hat{\theta}\right) - \theta\right) = 0$$

In contrast, error can be shown as a zero difference between the estimate in expectation and the true population value. We will refer to error and bias throughout the rest of this book. In this chapter, we discuss how to employ these concepts in a simple applied framework.

TOTAL SURVEY ERROR

Public opinion data are subject to two broad classes of error: sampling error and non-sampling error. We have developed a shortcut to think about these classes of error, as depicted in Figure 5.1 – a simplified version of a more complicated framework known as **total survey error**.[2] In our framework, sampling error and non-sampling error are unrelated – a

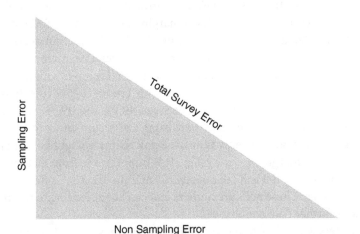

Figure 5.1 Total survey error triangle

[2] Groves (1989) *Survey Errors and Survey Costs.* Wiley & Sons; Groves & Lyberg (2010) "Total Survey Error: Past, Present, and Future," in *Public Opinion Quarterly* Vol. 74, Issue 5, pp. 849–879; Biemer (2010) "Total Survey Error Design, Implementation, and Evaluation," in *Public Opinion Quarterly* Vol. 74, Issue 5, pp. 817–848.

pollster can have a problem with one and not the other. Given their orthogonality, they are additive; we call this total survey error. The work of the pollster as data scientist is to assess error and to minimize it at both the pre- and post-survey stages.

Sampling Error

Sampling error – measured by margin of error (also known by its acronym, MOE) – is a function of the size of the sample and can be reduced with an adequate sample size. The margin of error is a function of the square root of the sample size $\left(\sqrt{n} \right)$, where the larger the sample, the smaller the error. Typically, the rule of thumb for pollsters is to use a 95% confidence interval, meaning that 95 times out of a 100 the true population mean will be found within the MOE. A margin of error using a 95% confidence interval and assuming a simple random sample can be displayed mathematically, as shown in the following equation, where p is proportion (here we assume p is .5), n is the size of the sample, and t is a 95% confidence interval with a t-statistic of 1.96:

$$\text{MOE} = \pm t^* \sqrt{\frac{p(1-p)}{n}}$$

As Table 5.1 illustrates, the margin of error decreases as the sample size increases. A sample size of 400 has a margin of error of +/−4.9%, whereas a sample of 5,000 has a margin of error of +/−1.4%. The margin of error on a poll of 400 assessing the vote share for Trump would be interpreted in this way: 95 times out of 100 the actual vote share for Trump is within +/−4.9% of the sample estimate. If we have a poll with Trump at 45% vote share, the true vote share ranges somewhere between 40.1% and 49.9% with a 95% confidence interval. Given that we are using a 95% confidence interval, this means that, one out of twenty times, the poll estimate might be completely outside of the margin of error range. It is important to note that, on average, 5 polls out of 100 will fall outside the margin of error – often well outside the range. These polls are outliers and can be misleading to the analyst without further data context.

Pollsters would like to increase their sample sizes as much as possible to reduce sampling error. However, there is a trade-off between size and cost. To strike a balance between managing the cost per interview and reducing sampling error, the rule of thumb in the United States for a nationally representative sample is to do 1,000 interviews, resulting in a margin of error of +/−3.1%. The industry standard for state- and local-level polling varies

Table 5.1 *Sample size and maximum margin of error (assuming* p = .5)

Sample size	Margin of error	Margin of error (DEFF of 2)
5,000	+/−1.4	+/−2.0
2,500	+/−2.0	+/−2.8
1,500	+/−2.5	+/−3.6
1,000	+/−3.1	+/−4.4
700	+/−3.7	+/−5.2
500	+/−4.4	+/−6.2
400	+/−4.9	+/−6.9
200	+/−6.9	+/−9.8
100	+/−9.8	+/−13.9
50	+/−13.8	+/−19.6

from 400 to 800 interviews with a margin of error ranging from +/−4.9% to +/−3.5%. In many countries, a sample size of 1,000 interviews is the norm, although this is not the universal standard. For instance, in Brazil, 2,000 interviews are the standard; while, in India, samples can be as large as 10,000 interviews or more.[3]

The margin of error typically is larger than the simple random sampling (SRS) formula we provided above. In practice, the poll has what we call a sample design effect or DEFF.[4] The DEFF accounts for aspects of the design including weights, the clustered natured of face-to-face samples, and the disproportionality of the design. The DEFF is calculated from question to question so any one poll will have a range – in our experience, design effects vary from 1 to 3. A DEFF of 1 is equivalent to an SRS. And a DEFF of 3 indicates an MOE that is about 73% larger.

Take our standard sample of 1,000 interviews in Table 5.1. If our sample is an SRS, it has an MOE of +/−3.1%, while, with a DEFF of 2, it comes to 4.4%. To adjust the MOE by DEFF, we must take the MOE and multiply it by the square root of DEFF known as DEFT. See the following equation.

$$\text{MOE} = \pm\ t^* \sqrt{\frac{p(1-p)}{n}} * \sqrt{\text{DEFF}}$$

[3] Note, mathematically, the size of the population only has a meaningful impact on the MOE when the population is less than 100 units or so.
[4] Kish (1965) *Survey Sampling*. John Wiley & Sons; Kish (1992), "Weighting for Unequal Pi," in *Journal of Official Statistics* Vol. 8. Issue 2, pp. 183–200.

Most public polls do not report DEFF adjusted MOEs. But it is important for the pollster to understand that poll variability is most likely larger than the reported MOE.[5]

NON-SAMPLING ERROR

While sample size and, thus, relative MOE are important starting points in assessing the robustness of a given survey, they do not encompass all forms of error that exist. It is a common misconception that they do. There are other forms of error that exist independent of sampling error. In practice, this means that while the sample may be large enough, other problems might exist that produce error-in estimates. Let's unpack the concept of non-sampling error into its constituent parts. These include:

- Coverage bias
- Nonresponse bias
- Measurement error
- Estimation error

COVERAGE BIAS

We begin our review of non-sampling error with coverage bias.[6] This can be distilled down to one simple maxim – who you interview is just as important as how many people you interview. For instance, a poll assessing presidential approval ratings that reached just Republicans would be much less favorable toward a Democratic president like Biden. Such a poll would also be far less accurate than one that included the perspectives of Democrats, Independents, and apolitical people. To be truly representative, a sample must reflect the characteristics of the broader population you are attempting to survey. To miss this key objective is known as coverage bias, which again occurs when eligible members of the population are excluded from or underrepresented in the sample frame. In technical terms, we might call this an **incomplete sample frame**. By sample frame, we mean the sample list from which a sample will be drawn. Often, sample frames are derived or combined databases. For instance, telephone frames often include geocoded census data with telephone lists or randomly generated numbers linked to the census data, or both.

---

[5] Rothschild & Goel (2016) "When You Hear the Margin of Error Is Plus or Minus 3 Percent, Think 7 Instead," *The New York Times*, October 5, 2016.

[6] Groves (1989) *Survey Errors and Survey Costs*. Wiley & Sons.

Table 5.2 *Voter intent, including and excluding Republicans*

	All respondents (%)	Excluding Republicans (%)
Donald Trump	40	17
Hillary Clinton	46	67
Other	6	7
Won't vote	2	3
Refused	5	7

Source: Reuters/Ipsos, October 2016

Coverage bias accounts for many electoral polling misses and single polls that deviate from the expected results. To minimize the problem of coverage bias, the pollster as data scientist asks, "Does my sample cover the intended universe?" Or, "Is it missing important subgroups?" Or, "Why are more affluent voters overrepresented in my poll? Or, where are the Trump-supporting Republicans?"

To further illustrate why coverage bias matters, we simulate an incomplete 2016 election sample frame that excludes Republicans. The question here is around voter intent – which candidate are respondents most likely to vote for in the 2016 election? When Republicans are missing, what happens? Table 5.2 answers this question. When GOP respondents are removed, Clinton holds a huge lead over Trump (67% vs. 17%). When Republicans are added back in, Clinton's lead over Trump narrows considerably (46% vs. 40%). Of course, coverage bias is rarely so blatant as the hypothetical example shown above. But remember the problem of coverage cannot be fixed by simply resorting to a larger sample or conducting more polls.

We will next outline simple steps to minimize the problem of coverage bias. One of the more common means of gauging coverage bias is to consider the mode of survey administration. Surveys are commonly conducted online, via telephone (mobile/landline) or mail or face-to-face. Look at Table 5.3. Mode of questionnaire administration can be used as a proxy for coverage bias. For instance, in the United States, both internet and telephone options are reasonable solutions given their high household penetration rates. By contrast, in India, both internet and telephone surveys would suffer from serious coverage bias as incidence rates are low. As such, face-to-face surveys are still the mode of choice in India.

Furthermore, coverage bias is strongly correlated with a variety of individual characteristics – most commonly socioeconomic status, educational attainment, income, age, urbanicity,[7] ethnicity, and political

---

[7] "Urbanicity" is defined as living in an urban, suburban, or rural area.

Table 5.3 *Internet, mobile phone, and landline coverage in select countries*

Country	Internet (%)	Mobile phone (%)	Landline (%)
Argentina	77	88	22
Australia	88	94	32
Brazil	64	87	33
China	63	98	13
France	89	70	59
Great Britain	96	83	48
Hungary	80	65	31
India	36	60	2
Malaysia	84	98	24
Mexico	61	79	42
Russia	80	97	21
South Africa	65	90	6
Turkey	74	61	14
The United States	90	97	37

Sources: Argentina Information Technology and Communications 2018; Australian Bureau of Statistics 2019; Canadian Radio-television and Telecommunications Commission 2019; Brazilian Regional Center for Studies on the Development of the Information Society 2017; Chilean Ministry of Social Development 2017; China Internet Network Information Center 2019; Eurostat 2018 and 2019; Saudi Arabia General Authority for Statistics 2018; Independent Communications Authority of South Africa 2020; International Telecommunication Union 2019; Internet and Mobile Association of India 2019; Internet World Stats 2019; Japan Ministry of Internal Affairs and Communications 2018; Korean Statistical Information Service 2019; Malaysia Department of Statistics 2019; Mexican National Institute of Statistics, Geography and Informatics 2017; Peru National Institute of Statistics and Informatics 2016; Pew Research Center; Statista 2018; US Centers for Disease Control and Prevention 2019; US Census Bureau 2018.

affiliation. Of course, how these variables intersect with coverage will vary from country to country. But the logic is strikingly similar worldwide – the more affluent, urban, and older an individual, the more likely it is that they will have access to phones and the internet. This means that they are easier to reach and therefore more likely to be overrepresented in the polls.

SAMPLE AND POST-SURVEY DESIGN DECISIONS

In today's world, it is less about the pedigree of the sample design (probability-based)[8] and more about how well a given sample represents the population of interest. This is a critical concern for the pollster.

---

[8] By probability-based, we mean a randomized selection process where every sampling unit in the population has a known probability of selection. The randomization mechanism can take on any number of forms, including a randomly generated number, pulling balls out of a hat, random walk or a randomly generated starting point with a systematic sampling interval.

Table 5.4 *Distribution of Educational attainment by Different Modes*

Educational level	Census Breakdowns	Landline +Cell telephone	Face-to-face
Primary School	47%	43%	54%
Middle School	36%	39%	36%
High school or more	16%	19%	11%

Sources: Eurasia/Ipsos Poll 2018; Brazilian PNAD 2017

Practically, we achieve this by minimizing coverage bias. How do we do this?

There are two options. First, we can assess and adjust the sample frame at the survey design stage. This can include "filling" the gaps with additional targeted list sample or greater effort to reach excluded subgroups (e.g., sending interviewers by boat to interview far off rural communities in the amazon rain forest). Pollsters also often combine survey modes. Second, pollsters can adjust the poll's results post-survey using some weighting scheme.

Take the example of Brazil. We knew that landline telephone polls in 2018 would most probably be biased against Fernando Haddad of Worker's Party in favor of the more conservative Jair Bolsonaro. Why? Poorer Brazilians who supported Haddad did not have landline telephones. Instead, such voters were more likely to have a cell phone. Given this, a combination of cell phone and landline frames was one solution. The alternative was to conduct more expensive but slower face-to-face surveys. See how the telephone poll overstates more educated Brazilians relative to census, while the face-to-face poll underestimates them. In Table 5.4, the telephone poll clearly shows coverage bias – it overstates more educated Brazilians. The face-to-face poll in turn understates more educated Brazilians which likely reflects some form of nonresponse bias. Different methodologies; different errors. This analysis suggests that the combination of the two modes – telephone and face-to-face – would most probably be the robust solution.[9]

It is also common practice to correct for coverage bias at the post-survey stage. Here, pollsters employ weights to adjust for demographic imbalances in age, education, income, race/ethnicity, and urbanicity, among other variables. Factors correlated with both coverage bias and the outcome variable have the greatest impact in reducing bias. The pollster should consider this when designing the poll and adjusting post-collection.

[9] Subsequent analysis in Brazil has shown that the combination of modes is optimal from a bias reduction standpoint. See El-Dash (2021) www.pollingdata.com.br/2022/07/qual-tipo-de-pesquisa-mede-melhor-a-opiniao-publica-brasileira-telefonica-ou-presencial/.

Table 5.5 *Hypothetical weighting table*

	Sample distribution (%)	Population distribution (%)	Weight factor	Approval rating (unweighted)	Approval ratings (weighted)
High education	50	20	0.40	50	50
Low education	50	80	1.60	35	35
Total	100	100		42.5	38

So, how do pollsters weight the data? Let's take the hypothetical example in Table 5.5. Here, we only weight by one variable – education. Ultimately, weighting is nothing more than adjusting the sample distribution back to that of the population. Note how the sample distribution on education (50/50) diverges from the distribution of the population (20/80).

See how the overall approval ratings shift depending on the distribution of education – 42.5% for the unweighted data and 38% for the weighted data. Pollsters often talk in terms of weight factors, or weight efficiencies. This gives an idea of the relative bump-up or down of the given demographic in questions. Notionally, higher education is weighted down (0.40) and lower education up (1.60). We could have employed other post-survey adjustments like MRP (Multilevel Regression with Post-stratification) and Calibration. See Table 5.6 for more details.

Nonresponse Bias

Nonresponse bias occurs when those who decline to engage with a survey are systematically different from those that do. To tackle this problem, the pollster might ask, "Do the groups who are unlikely to engage with a survey significantly different from those who are? Is the potential nonresponse correlated with my variable of interest?"

In the case of the 2020 US presidential election, the polls generally overstated Biden by five points over Trump. In some states, this deviation was even greater. So, what happened? In part, the evidence suggests that Trump supporters were less likely to respond to surveys.[10] His voters tended to be white, less educated, less engaged, and rural – all correlates of nonresponse in this context. Ultimately, the Trump brand was especially effective at attracting traditional nonparticipators – the politically disengaged, off-the-grid, nonconformists.

---

[10] Clinton et al. (2021) *AAPOR Task Force on Pre-election Polls*. www.aapor.org/AAPOR_Main/ media/MainSiteFiles/AAPOR-Task-Force-on-2020-Pre-Election-Polling_Report-FNL.pdf

Table 5.6 *Example of design decisions for the 2018 Brazilian election*

Steps	Consideration	Question	Description
1	Research question	What is my population of interest?	Our target is the Brazilian population.
2	Mode determination	What is the optimal mode of administration given our population of interest?	Telephone surveys have the quickest turnaround time and increasingly have greater access to people.
3	Hole assessment	Does my sample frame have holes or gaps?	In Brazil, poorer people do not have consistent access to landline phones. But have access to mobile phones.
4	Design solution	How can I fill in these holes?	Combined landline and cell phone frame
5	Design execution	How can I combine sample sources to build a complete frame?	1. Dual Frame. Combining two frames statistically at the individual level via the probability of selection. 2. Blended sample. Combining different sample sources modes into one sample list. More of a salad bowl approach. 3. Mean averaging. Combining at the aggregate poll level.
6	Post-survey considerations	Do I need to further adjust for coverage problems?	Assess poll estimate versus external benchmarks. Here, might weight. But weights increase the margin of error.
7	Post-survey adjustments	What is my best adjustment option?	1. Post-stratification. Simple demographic weights. 2. MRP. Hierarchical imputation-like model that takes into consideration data both internal and external to the poll. 3. Calibration. Using external benchmarks to adjust data. Considered a more heterodox solution as depends on analyst opinion and other inputs.

Table 5.7 *Response rates by party identification over six waves*

	Democrats (%)	Republicans (%)	Independents (%)
May	100	100	100
June	86	83	84
July	79	74	78
August	78	76	76
September	80	75	79
October	77	74	78

Source: FiveThirtyEight/Ipsos Panel Survey 2022

Nonresponse also can add variability to public opinion estimates. The classic case is party conventions in the United States. Historically, support for the nominee spikes after the convention and then typically regresses back to *status quo ante*. This is an example of *differential nonresponse*.[11] In essence, partisans become more energized after the convention and hence more likely to respond. Some pollsters weight by "past vote" to tamp down such noise.[12]

Scientific evidence suggests that nonresponse bias can be highly dependent on context and subject matter, making it difficult to detect and to fix. There is little data on those who don't respond; only special studies can get at nonresponders. But knowing the correlates of nonresponse bias helps the pollster tackle the problem conceptually.

Take the example in Table 5.7. See how party affiliation is correlated with nonresponse. Republicans are less likely to respond after multiple polling waves relative to Democrats. This shows empirically a **party identification nonresponse problem.**

The pollster can seek to address nonresponse at the pre- and post-survey stages. First, at the survey design stage, a common approach is to target potential nonresponders in order to convert them. This can involve multiple returns to the same respondent, incentives, invitation letters, or the use of credible messengers. Additionally, for face-to-face and telephone surveys, contact with respondents can vary by time of day and day of week. In the case of elusive Trump voters, targeted recruitment of respondents with culturally framed material has been shown to be effective.

Second, at the post-survey stage, weights can be employed to adjust for distortions in the demographic profile of a sample. Such weights typically include demographics and response probabilities. Other variables such as

[11] Gelman & Roshchild (2016) "Trump's Up! Clinton's Up 9!" in *Slate*, August 5, 2016.
[12] Lauderdale & Rivers (2016) "Why Polling Swings Are Often Mirages" in *RealClearPolitics*, November 1, 2016.

civic engagement, past vote, political engagement, and social isolation have been employed as nonresponse weight corrections as well.[13]

Ultimately, the pollster must be cognizant of this "silent killer." Best practices are key. But solutions can be hard to come by. The pollster should always be skeptical and validate.

Measurement Error

Measurement error occurs when a questionnaire, or other data capture instrument, produces biased data. In such cases, pollsters must ask themselves questions like, "Is the questionnaire capturing unbiased opinions?" "Is this question presented in a biased or misleading way?" "Were best practices followed?" Although there are many types of measurement error, in our experience, just a few account for the preponderance of public opinion measurement issues. We detail them next.

Context and question order effects: Significant empirical evidence shows that question order and questionnaire context impact how people respond to questions.[14] Take, for instance, Trump's approval ratings in Table 5.8. When a question about the economy or COVID precedes a question about presidential approval, it impacts how Americans rate his presidency overall. Performance on the economy was generally seen as one of Trump's strengths. Correspondingly, his approval ratings go from 40% to 44% when an economy-centric question precedes the standard presidential job approval question. In contrast, when questions about COVID in 2020 – arguably his greatest vulnerability – come before the approval question, his core approval numbers suffer. This is just framing by another name.

Table 5.8 *Trump approval rating varies by questionnaire context*

No preceding questions (%)	If approval is preceded by an *economy-related* question (%)	If approval is preceded by a *COVID-related* question (%)
40	44	37

Source: Ipsos July 2020

[13] Feldman and Mendez (2022) "Who Are the People Who Don't Respond to Polls," in *FiveThirtyEight*, October 26, 2022; Cohn (2022) "Will One Small Shift Fix the Polls in 2022," in *Upshot New York Times*. www.nytimes.com/2022/11/02/upshot/polls-2022-midterms-fix.html.

[14] See Sudman et al. (1982) *Asking Questions: A Practical Guide to Questionnaire Design*. San Francisco, CA: Josey-Bass; Sudman et al. (1996) *Thinking about Answers: The Application of Cognitive Processes to Survey Methodology*. Josey-Bass; Tourangeau et al. (2000) *The Psychology of Survey Response*. Cambridge University Press.

To avoid context and question order effects, it is best practice to begin with the most important questions at the top or near the beginning of the questionnaire. Often, there can be a few warm-up questions prior to the ballot question. If the poll in question has multiple purposes, often clear transition points are included in order to compartmentalize the respondent's questionnaire experience. Such strategies are easy to implement via questionnaire design. The public opinion analyst should keep this in mind when assessing the quality of data.

Response order in scale: Candidate name order on a ballot question impacts responses.[15] On average, the candidate that comes first has a 2–4% advantage over those candidates that come after. Given this, the most common practice is to randomize the response order in order to minimize this order effect. Here, the caveat is attitudinal scales – semantically speaking, humans think from positive to negative. In our experience, a reverse order scale sounds strange to respondents. Therefore, we like to keep them fixed, going from positive to negative.

Question wording – ambiguity and biased words: Poor question wording can often lead to biased public opinion estimates. Here, think Bishop and the "Nays" in Chapter 4. In our experience, there are two common types. The first is question ambiguity. This often happens when the question is too broad or abstract. Take, for instance, questions around "infrastructure." Our polling shows that people associate infrastructure with roads, bridges, and highways. But they also may link it to the internet, healthcare and social welfare system. Without further anchoring, a lack of specificity in the wording of a question can produce uncertain results.

The second includes biased wording in the question stem. We don't want our questions to push respondents in one direction or the other. Instead, they should be neutral or balanced. We see this clearly when we associate a politician with a given initiative; this then nudges responses in the direction of that politician's leaning. Take our infrastructure example in Chapter 3. Simply associating a Republican or Democratic messenger to a fictitious infrastructure bill affects responses on questions. At a very simplistic level, Republicans are likely to support a bill if it is associated with a figure like Trump; while Democrats will prefer one that is associated with Nancy Pelosi or Joe Biden. We now see how politically charged phrases – like "MAGA" or "Black Lives Matter" – or even more seemingly innocuous ones like "big government" or "social media," can trigger emotional responses depending on political affiliation. Ultimately, beware of charged words; they can skew results.

---

[15] Miller & Krosnick (1998) "The Impact of Candidate Name Order on Election Outcomes," in *Public Opinion Quarterly* Vol. 62, Issue 3, pp. 291–330.

"Don't know" and Don't-Know like options: Often, we provide "don't know" (DK) or similar options to respondents – such as "neither," "no opinion," "can't choose," or "no answer." There is no hard-and-fast rule whether to include or not include a DK option. For the most part, we like to minimize them – forcing the fence sitters to take a position. The mode of questionnaire administration can impact the level of such responses. Self-administered modes, including online and mail, show higher levels of DK responses than face-to-face and telephone options. Keep this in mind. The same question might produce significantly higher don't know rates for online surveys versus telephone or face-to-face ones. This complicates comparisons.

Other forms of measurement error exist, including interview effects, recall error, response scale format, and questionnaire format. Optimal measurement involves understanding such complexity. The pollster can assess and adjust for most forms of measurement error through a few simple best practices, as outlined earlier.

ESTIMATION ERROR

Estimation error occurs when the data does not accurately predict or depict the true value in question.[16] An estimate could be presidential approval ratings, the percent of Americans who favor abortion, or the proportion of the electorate who indicate that they will vote for Trump. These are all relatively straightforward cases where the poll question is the model.

Pollsters also are asked to estimate future outcomes. Here, data from a poll might be used as an input into a model (Figure 5.2). In such cases, the pollster might ask – is my model accurate? How has it performed in the past? How can I adjust it to improve performance? Keep in mind the data might be robust, but the model itself might be flawed.

Elections are the most common instance when pollsters model future behavior. One of the most important elements of election polling is determining who will vote and who won't. That's because not everyone votes; the

Figure 5.2 Estimation process with inputs and outputs

---

[16] By estimate, we mean an approximate calculation or judgment of value derived from a public opinion poll.

key therefore is to identify those that will.[17] But this is easier said than done. In our experience, many election flubs result from getting the voting population wrong.[18] In practice, pollsters employ a variety of models to predict who are likely voters. Such models are often black-box methodologies that polling firms hide from scrutiny. Here, we will shine a light on them.

Determining Likely Voters[19]

Why are likely voter models necessary? Well, again, not everyone votes. In fact, voting is not mandatory in many countries. Globally, an average of 65% of the eligible adult population votes in general elections. However, this varies greatly depending on the country, as Table 5.9 shows.

Turnout levels wouldn't matter much if voters and nonvoters were demographically, attitudinally, and politically similar. However, this usually isn't the case. Conventional wisdom holds that people who vote tend to

Table 5.9 *Percentage of voting-age population by country*

Country	Percent of voting-age population
Belgium	87
Sweden	83
Denmark	80
Australia	79
South Korea	78
The Netherlands	77
Israel	76
New Zealand	76
Finland	73
Hungary	72

[17] Kasara & Suyanarayan (2015) "When Do the Rich Vote Less than the Poor and Why? Explaining Turnout Inequality across the World," in *American Journal of Political Science* Vol. 59, Issue 3, pp. 613–627.

[18] See 2020 Pre-Election Polling: An Evaluation of the 2020 General Election Polls – AAPOR.

[19] The likely voter problem can also be thought of as one of coverage. The logic goes something like this: given that those who vote are a subset of the entire population, pollsters are essentially tackling an over-coverage problem. In our opinion, this is debatable as how can an unknown population (those who will vote) be known (screener in questionnaire) before the population can be known (fielding the poll)? Using a prior benchmark poll to derive a voter profile brings us closer to a coverage problem. But not all polls use this method and even using a prior benchmark survey requires a model. Chicken or Egg? This issue was brought up in a long, fascinating correspondence with Raphael Nishimura, Director of Sampling Operation, Survey Research Center, University of Michigan.

Table 5.9 *(continued)*

Country	Percent of voting-age population
Norway	71
Germany	69
Austria	69
France	68
Mexico	66
Italy	65
Czech Republic	63
The United Kingdom	63
Greece	62
Canada	62
Portugal	62
Spain	61
Slovakia	59
Ireland	58
Estonia	57
The United States	56
Luxembourg	55
Slovenia	54
Poland	54
Chile	52
Latvia	52
Switzerland	39

Source: Pew Research Center, 2018

be older, more affluent, and more educated than those who don't, although this can vary in practice.[20]

The 2016 US presidential election bears out this conventional wisdom. In Table 5.10, we see that the majority of 2016 voters had at least some college education, earning over $30,000, were middle-aged or older and white. Compare this to nonvoters who tended to be younger, non-white, having less than a college education and were making less than $30,000. This varies considerably from the standard demographic profile of those who voted.

Finally, some types of elections have lower turnout rates than the average. Take, for instance, primary elections in the United States.

[20] Kasara & Suyanarayan (2015) "When Do the Rich Vote Less than the Poor and Why? Explaining Turnout Inequality across the World," in *American Journal of Political Science* Vol. 59, Issue 3, pp. 613–627.

Table 5.10 *Demographic profile of voters and nonvoters in the 2016 US presidential election*

	Nonvoter (%)	Voter (%)
College+	16	37
Some college	33	34
HS or less	51	30
$75K+	15	33
$30K–$74K	28	38
Less than $30K	56	28
Age 50+	33	56
Ages 30–49	33	30
Ages 18–29	33	13
White	52	74
Black	15	10
Hispanic	19	10
Other	12	5

Source: Pew Research Center, 2018, www.pewresearch.org/politics/2018/08/09/an-examination-of-the-2016-electorate-based-on-validated-voters/

Such elections often see turnout levels that range from the low teens to mid-20s. Or, the US midterms that range in the low to mid-40s. This is important as such turnout elections skew even more partisan. Again, lower turnout would not matter if voters and nonvoters were the same. They aren't.

CONSTRUCTING A LIKELY VOTER MODEL

So, how do we avoid such problems? Pollsters employ a wide variety of solutions to account for who will vote, from the simple to the ultra-sophisticated (Table 5.11). At one end are naïve models that employ the general population as the voting population. This model assumes there's no difference between voters and nonvoters, thus no need for a model. It's simple and easy to use, but the least accurate. Other models include weighting by past elections, ranking respondents by summed likely voter indexes, using linked secondary and survey data to filter possible voters, logistic regression models to estimate the probability to vote, and so on.[21]

---

[21] Young and Bricker (2013) "Using Likely Voter Models to Estimate the Probable Electorate: Review of Approaches Pre-election Polls and Concrete Recommendations," in *Ipsos POV* 2013.

Table 5.11 *Summary of likely voter models and their details*

Models	Description	Questions	Strengths	Weaknesses	Articles
Naïve model	No filter is employed.	No questions used to filter likely voters.	Cost effective; easy to implement.	Big assumption that those who vote are like those who don't vote.	NA
Politico-graphic model	Weighting on past vote.	Voter profile of last election or typical election.	Does identify the profile of the typical likely voter.	Does not capture discontinuity elections where past behavior may not predict future behavior.	Green and Gerber (1996)
Traditional Gallup model	Summated index of 3 to 5 items.	Registered to vote Certainty/intention to vote Interest in Election Past voting behavior	Identifies both typical likely voters and atypical ones	Overstatement of enthusiasm; index can be clumpy, so precise cuts are difficult.	Perry (1960)
Derived intention model	Estimated probabilities of voting using logistic regression.	Variables in model can include demographic, attitudinal, and behavioral ones.	Identifies typical voters from atypical ones. Can make more granular cuts.	Still suffers from enthusiasm and can overstate intention to vote.	Voss et al. (1995)
Combinatorial models	Combination of past behavior from voter files with other variables.	Typically such models employ logistic regression to link the varied factors together.	Identifies the typical voter. Can make more granular cuts. And minimizes enthusiasm effect.	More computationally difficult and requires specialized staff.	Rogers and Aida (2013); Young and El-Dash (2013)

Source: See Young & El Dash (2013) "In Search of More Granular Likely-Voter Models for Low-Turnout Elections: The Case of the 2013 Florida and Ohio Primary Elections" Paper presented at the 67th AAPOR, Conference May 2013, Boston Mass; Rogers & Aida (2013) "Vote Self-Prediction Hardly Predicts Who Will Vote, and Is (Misleadingly) Unbiased," in *Faculty Research Working Paper Series*, Harvard Kennedy School, pp. 1–36.; Perry (1960) "Election Survey Procedures of the Gallup Poll," *Public Opinion Quarterly*, pp. 531–542; Voss, Gelman, & King (1995) "The Polls – a Review: Preelection Survey Methodology: Details from Eight Polling Organizations, 1988 and 1992," in *Public Opinion Quarterly* Vol. 59, pp. 98–132; Green & Gerber (2006) "Can Registration-Based Sampling Improve the Accuracy of Midterm Election Forecasts?" in *Public Opinion Quarterly* Vol. 70, pp. 197–223; Blumenthal (2004) *The Why and How of Likely Voters.* Online Blog.

WALKING THROUGH THE TRADITIONAL GALLUP MODEL

Most polling firms in the United States and around the world employ some variation of what the industry calls the "Traditional Gallup Likely Voter Model" (TG). Specifically, the TG model includes between three and five questions that vary but the simplest ones include: a past voting question, a question on the "probability" or "certainty" to vote in the upcoming election, and a question on interest in the election (see Table 5.12).

Typically, the questions are then summated into an index and respondents are ranked by their likelihood of voting: high scores indicating greater likelihood and low scores lower likelihood. In practice, pollsters often screen out respondents with lower scores or may inversely weight respondents by their likelihood to vote.[22] TG models suffer from two weaknesses. First, at most, such models only have between 12 to 18 points in the scale that makes very fine distinctions difficult. We like to say that such indices are "clumpy," which hinders precise cut points in some cases (Table 5.13).[23]

So, for instance, making a distinction between a 65% and a 72% turnout[24] becomes impossible (see Table 5.13). We unfortunately often find that

Table 5.12 *Examples of items in the Traditional Gallup likely voter model*

Question	Wording
Past voting certainty	Sometimes things come up and people are not able to vote. In the 2008 election for president, did you happen to vote?
Voting certainty	In November 2012, the next presidential election will be held. Using a 1–10 scale, where 10 means you are completely certain you will vote and 1 means you are completely certain you will NOT vote, how likely are you to vote in the upcoming Presidential election?
Interest in the election	How much interest do you have in following the news about the upcoming Presidential election?

[22] Voss et al. (1995) "The Polls – a Review: Preelection Survey Methodology: Details from Eight Polling Organizations, 1988 and 1992," in *Public Opinion Quarterly* Vol. 59, pp. 98–132; Murray et al. (2009) "Pre-election Polling Identifying Likely Voters Using Iterative Expert Data Mining," *Public Opinion Quarterly* Vol. 57, pp. 238–263.

[23] Young et al. (2011) "To Vote or Not to Vote: Are We Asking the Right Questions? Testing Different Likely Voter Models across 17 Midterm Elections," at the 66th AAPOR Conference May 2011. Phoenix Arizona.

[24] In the context of the TG model, turnout is estimated by the proportion of the sample that made the given cut. Different cut points produce different turnout levels.

Table 5.13 *Example of scale clumping
at different turnout assumptions*

Point of scale	Percent turnout (%)	Obama's lead
16	86	7
15	80	6
14	65	1
13	63	−1

a small difference like 5% in turnout can have a significant effect on pre-election poll results.[25]

Second, TG models suffer from momentary surges in optimism that can overstate likelihood to vote among certain segments.[26] Indeed, the strength of the TG models is also its primary weakness. On the one hand, it does minimize the primary fault of the past vote models by capturing those habitual nonvoters that ultimately vote. On the other hand, the "interest" or "certainty" questions are highly influenced by circumstances, often capturing "momentary voter enthusiasm," and not predicting real behavioral intent. Political events, or public gaffes can impact relative optimism and be magnified (temporarily) in the TG model. This can muddle preelection polls and pollster predictions.

As a response to the problems of the TG model, some pollsters use what we call the "Derived Intention Likely Voter Model" (DI). Such DI models are a derivation of the Traditional Gallup model. However, instead of summating a series of questions into an index, pollsters run a logistic regression on the "certainty" or "likelihood" question and then estimate probabilities of voting for each respondent.[27]

In practice, the DI model has two advantages. First, it does not suffer from clumping like the TG model: given that each respondent receives an estimated probability, finite distinctions can be made more easily (e.g., the aforementioned 72% versus 65% turnout). Second, such estimated probabilities can be

[25] Young (2012) "Spring Cleaning: Ipsos Polling in Ohio and Florida Republican Primaries," in *Ipsos Spotlight Blog*.

[26] Erickson et al. (2004) "Likely (and Unlikely Voters) and the Assessment of Campaign Dynamics," in *Public Opinion Quarterly* Vol. 68, pp. 588–601.

[27] Traugott & Tucker (1984) "Strategies for Predicting Whether a Citizen Will Vote and Estimation of Electoral Outcomes," in *Public Opinion Quarterly* Vol. 48, pp. 330–343; Freedman & Goldstein (1996) "Building a Probable Electorate from Pre-Election Polls: A Two-Stage Approach," in *Public Opinion Quarterly* Vol. 60, pp. 574–587; Petrocik (1991) "An Algorithm for Estimating Turnout as a Guide to Predicting Elections," in *Public Opinion Quarterly* Vol. 55, pp. 643–647.

used a priori (usually before an election season) to determine what combination of screener questions will produce an accurate turnout, reducing the overall cost of a poll by cutting its administration time. That said, DI models are not immune to momentary ebbs and flows in voter enthusiasm (similar to the TG model), which can throw off accurate prediction of those who will vote.

A DISCUSSION OF CUT POINTS: THE DIRTY
UNDERBELLY OF LIKELY VOTER MODELS

As detailed earlier, there are many variations on the likely voter model. The choice of any one specific method can depend on cost, timing, and the expertise of the polling firm. Once this choice has been made, a pollster then must consider their "cut-point" methodology. By "cut point," we mean how voters are defined and separated from nonvoters. We wanted to detail it here because it is critical pollster work unseen by the public.

Often, nonvoters are simply screened or filtered out of the effective sample. Cut-point approaches, however, can be broken down roughly into three distinct buckets (see Table 5.14).

We call the first bucket "No cut-point" approaches. Such methods make no specific decision as to who is a voter and who is a nonvoter. In the case of naïve likely voter models for instance, all respondents interviewed are considered voters. Politico-graphic likely voter models, in turn, weight the sample by the political profile of past elections. And no specific decision is made about voters and nonvoters. The central problem is that naïve methods take all the latitude away from the pollster to stress test their assumptions: for instance, what happens to voting preferences at different levels of turnout? We call the second bucket "a priori cut-point" approaches.

Table 5.14 *Likely voter cut points and their implications*

No cut points	Naïve and politico-graphic models	Fast and cheap	Can't stress test
A priori cut points	Determination of eligible respondents at screener stage of the poll	Fast and cheap	Only stress tested before election year
A posteriori cut points	Hard post-survey cut points; soft post-survey cut points	Can stress test turnout assumptions; greater flexibility to analyst	Need larger samples; more time and expertise at post-survey stage

Many polling firms use this approach. In practice, it is a two-step process: First, an initial benchmark survey is used to rank order respondents by their likelihood of voting. This is typically done at the beginning of the electoral calendar. And second, a predefined screener that is employed at the beginning of the questionnaire to identify eligible likely voters, and screening out nonvoters. Typically, the screeners range from one to four questions. The advantage of this approach is that it saves both time and money. First, it screens out nonvoters at the beginning. This is especially important for telephone surveys where the cost of a call is determined by the survey length. Second, no pollster time is required in determining who is a likely voter and who is not.

In contrast, such approaches suffer from two weaknesses. First, benchmark surveys are usually conducted well before the election (up to a year). As such, voter decision-making can change significantly in that time. And second, analysts have little flexibility in checking their turnout assumptions because the effective samples have already filtered out "nonvoters." This is a censored sample by another name.

Finally, we call the third bucket "a posteriori cut-point" approaches. These methods make the cut-point decision at the post-survey and adjustment stage A posteriori approaches can be further broken down into two sub-points: hard and soft cut points. In the case of hard cut points, pollsters will define an expected turn out level (typically from official statistics of past elections) and then make a cut-point decision based on the estimated turnout rate. A slight variation of this approach is a method that we call soft cut points. Here the analyst can assess voter preferences at different turnout levels. Using this approach, we employed this method to very good effect in the 2022 Brazilian election (see Table 5.15 as example).

The primary advantage of a posteriori cut-point methods is that they allow the analyst flexibility and for Bayesian-like approaches that take into consideration analyst opinion and external data. However, such methods do require larger samples. They also demand more

Table 5.15 *Vote share in 2022 Brazilian election by different turnout assumptions*

Turnout	100%	85%	80%	75%	70%	65%
Lula Vote	48	50	50	50	49	48
Bolsonaro Vote	43	46	47	48	50	51
Delta (Lula–Bolsonaro)	+5	+4	+3	+2	−1	−2

Source: Ipsos Eurasia Poll Brazil 2022

senior analyst time at the post-survey stage, and a very solid knowledge-base about elections and electoral behavior

FINAL CONSIDERATIONS ON ANALYST ASSESSMENT OF LIKELY VOTER MODEL

So, what should an analyst of public opinion do to assess likely voter models in polls? To the outsider looking at polling results, it's not always clear, as methodological detail often is not disclosed. The previous discussion shows just how technical likely voter model can be. However, the analyst does have a few options.

First, it is key to determine if the election in question is more likely to have higher or lower turnout. This will help determine potential exposure to estimation, or likely voter, problems. Australia typically is a high turn-out country – it is less likely to suffer likely voter problems than the United States, which is a lower turnout one. Keep this in mind.

Second, are political outcomes associated with turnout? Again, if there is no difference between those who vote and those who don't vote, then any likely voter problem is probably minimized.

Third, when analyzing the polls, it is critical to assess what universe they represent. Most polling firms will designate their poll as "all adults," "registered voters," or "likely voters." Focus on the likely voter polls as the election nears.

Fourth, for any given election, try to determine the likely voter methodology being employed by polling firms. Remember that likely voter models rest on certain assumptions, and each has its own foibles and flaws. Sometimes enough detail can be found in the poll's methodological note; however, often it is not included in any detail. In such cases, direct contact with polling firms may be required.

Finally, the previous discussion allows the analyst to ask the right questions. Likely models are as varied as they are complex.

SENSITIVITY ANALYSIS OF WEIGHTS AND LIKELY VOTER MODEL IN THE 2022 BRAZILIAN PRESIDENTIAL ELECTION

Let's apply the assessment of likely voter models to a real-world example: the 2022 Brazilian presidential election. The first round of the 2022 Brazilian presidential election was hotly contested. Bolsonaro beat expectations and

Table 5.16 *First-round results by different weighting schemes*

	Lula vote	Bolsonaro vote	Delta (Lula–Bolsonaro)
Actual election results	48	43	5
Unweighted polling results	43	45	−2
Polling results with demographic weights	45	42	3
Demographic weights + past vote weight	47	38	9
Demographic weights + past vote weight + likely voter model	45	41	4

Source: Eurasia/Ipsos Poll Brazil 2022

came within five points of Lula. The polls came under serve scrutiny as a result. Accurate polling was at a premium.[28]

Table 5.16 is a typical one used by pollsters to assess polling results. We show the raw data and different weight adjusted scenarios. Note the raw data is very Bolsonaro (−2). Why? Here, we are looking at a telephone poll (cell/landline combined) – more affluent people are more accessible and thus overrepresented. This is a great example of coverage bias. Our first weight is a demographic one to correct for such bias (+3). Then, we deploy a "past vote" weight to correct for nonresponse bias (+9). That is a brute force correction for nonresponse (and coverage) bias. Some evidence suggests that such adjustments might over-correct for the problem.[29] Pollsters should be cautious when employing such corrections.

Finally, we deploy a "likely voter model" that filters those who are likely to vote from those who aren't. Abstention is about 20% in Brazil. We employed a modified-Gallup model here that included four items in a summated scale. See how the poll estimates based on the demographic, past vote, and likely voter model comes close to the actual results (final results +5 versus Ipsos polling estimate +4).

---

[28] Young & Garman (2022) "Pesquisas-Mitos E Ajustes Adequados," in *Estadao* OpEd October 29, 2022.

[29] Feldman & Mendez (2022) "Who Are the People Who Don't Respond to Polls," in *FiveThirtyEight* October, 26, 2022;

THE CONCEPTS OF VALIDITY AND RELIABILITY

Up to this point, we have focused on bias and error and not talked about **validity** and **reliability**. But they too are key scientific concepts and help the pollster in assessing data quality. By validity, we mean a measure that captures what it should be capturing. For instance, that IQ tests indeed capture intelligence; that approval ratings are measuring support for government; or that mental health diagnostics accurately diagnosis mental conditions.

Validity and bias are related concepts. Only in the rarest of circumstances can you have a biased, *but* valid measure. A measure that is significantly off from the true value (bias) is more than likely not capturing what it should be (validity). Ultimately, validity is a concept used in measurement, while that of bias in statistics.

In this book, we will discuss **triangulation**, which is a form of **validation**. Fundamentally validation is comparing or contrasting the data with other external benchmarks. **Convergent validity** is when a given measure aligns with an external benchmark as expected. **Divergent validity** is when the measure and the benchmark misalign but in the expected direction. And finally **predictive validity** is when a measure predicts what it is expected to predict.

Take the example of COVID vaccine uptake. During the dark days of the pandemic, public health officials argued that wholesale vaccination was the only way for the world to get back to normal. The measurement of vaccine adoption was thus critical. However, this was made difficult by the lag of official vaccination data relative to the evolving public health needs. So, in the place of official statistics, public health officials widely employed surveys. But were surveys valid instruments to capture vaccine uptake?

To answer this question, we validate the Axios-Ipsos measure of vaccine uptake using official statistics from the CDC as the benchmark (Table 5.17).

Table 5.17 *Correlation between the Axios-Ipsos vaccination questions and CDC administrative vaccination data (monthly figures January to July)*

	Axios-Ipsos survey	CDC administrative data
Axios-Ipsos survey	1	**
CDC administrative data	0.99	1

Source: Axios-Ipsos Polls January to July 2021; CDC Administrative Data January to July 2021

Table 5.18 *Gallup 2010 US midterm election results*

Date	Republican	Democrat	Difference
September 26	55	40	15
October 3	55	41	14
October 17	56	39	17
October 24	56	39	17
October 31	56	38	18

Source: Gallup Polling 2010

Note the extremely high correlation between the survey vaccination rates and official statistics (r=.99). Such a correlation suggests that the vaccination question on the Axios-Ipsos poll was measuring what it should be measuring.[30]

By **reliability**, we mean measurement consistency over time or across multiple trails. A measure might be reliable *but not* valid. Take the example in Table 5.18. The generic ballot question for the 2010 midterms was reliable – see the consistency! But the polling was off relative to the election results (18-points in the polling versus 7-point election result). Consistent *yet* not valid.

BRINGING IT ALL TOGETHER

It is the nature of the polling business to contend with error. But, luckily, the pollster as data scientist has the solutions to deal with it. So, what did we learn?

First, we have a framework for assessing error and bias in polls. Remember the triangle! The pollster must manage both sampling error and non-sampling error. We have the tools to do just this.

Second, sampling error, measured by the MOE, only accounts for one type of survey error. All other types of error – coverage bias, nonresponse bias, measurement error and estimation error – fall outside its prerogative. This means that an MOE of 3.1% as generally seen in the methodological statements that accompany 1,000-person surveys is part of the story but not all of it.

---

[30] Bradely et al. (2021) "Unrepresentative Big Survey Significantly Overestimated US Vaccine Uptake," in *Nature* Vol. 600, pp. 695–700.

Third, it is in the non-sampling error where a pollster's headache lies. Let's reiterate our points.

- Many polling misses result from **coverage bias**, or the over- or under-representation of certain sub-populations in the polls. We detailed the tools required to assess and account for this.
- **Nonresponse bias** is an ever-present threat *but* elusive and difficult to measure, although post-survey weights have been shown to account for nonresponse problems. That said, a pollster should be ever vigilant because at any moment it can rear its ugly head.
- With a handful of best practices, the pollster can account for **measurement error**: context, order, "don't know" options, biased wording, and question ambiguity. These are not the only types of measurement error, but these account for most of a pollster's problems.
- **Estimation error** is polling's dirty little secret. In our opinion, pre-election polls are often wrong because likely voter models incorrectly attribute who will vote. In other words, the polling data might be robust, but the model itself is flawed.

Fourth, we also addressed the concepts of **validity** and **reliability**. These are concepts from measurement but are also critical tools for analysis and prediction. Human beings validate information continually by comparing and contrasting evidence to allay doubts. Pollsters should do this too. Reliability is the silent killer of validity. We saw that a reliable measure is not necessarily a valid one. Beware.

As demonstrated in this chapter, the pollster does have the tools to reduce error and bias in their public opinion data. We detailed here a total survey error framework to do just that. Ultimately, a large part of the activity of the pollster is to check, re-check, and check the data again. Comparing public opinion data to benchmarks and external measures is "the meat and potatoes" of polling. In the next two chapters, we will show this in detail.

6

Assessing a Single Poll during the
2016 US Presidential Election

We now have a framework for assessing the quality of public opinion data. Let's apply it in practice to the 2016 US presidential election, a high-stakes, transformative political event. The election pitted Hillary Clinton, a well-known establishment Democrat, against Donald Trump, an outsider who had just overturned the Republican Party by winning the GOP nomination.

Beginning in early June 2016, the Reuters/Ipsos horse race poll began showing a 10-point lead for Clinton, while the market average showed a narrower 4- to 5-point gap. This persisted for a month. Given the high salience of the election, the deviation was concerning enough to prompt us to reframe the ballot question itself, a fairly drastic move.[1]

It was not a decision we arrived at lightly. At first, we thought that the difference between the Reuters/Ipsos survey and the market was just a random error. But the team became increasingly concerned as the difference persisted. Ultimately, a rigorous assessment was conducted of the polling and ancillary data to unpack what was happening. Let's now employ our **total survey error** framework discussed in the preceding chapter to the problem of the original Ipsos 2016 ballot question.

SAMPLING ERROR

In such situations where we have data at variance with expectations, our first question is always, "Is the observed difference due to sampling error?" Again, assessing sampling error comes down to whether the sample size and the corresponding margin of error are large enough to be discriminatory

[1] Young (2016) "The Rationale behind the Redesign of the Reuters/Ipsos Presidential Ballot Question." July 28, 2016. *Ipsos POV* Retrieved from: www.ipsos.com/en-us/knowledge/society/reuters-ipsos-presidential-ballot-question.

or not. This is why pollsters often aggregate surveys from multiple firms to obtain a larger sample size. As discussed in Chapter 5, a larger sample size increases analytical robustness and reduces sampling error.

To operationalize our analysis, we need to determine if the two spreads overlap or not. By spread, we mean the difference in the vote share between the two candidates, that is, Clinton and Trump. This is a commonly used metric in election polling. If the two spreads overlap and this can be accounted for by the margin of error, then the difference is due to sampling error. If they can't be, then the observed difference probably results from non-sampling error.

For this exercise, we will rely on forty-nine polls in the months of June and July. To do this, we take a simple average of the polls as shown below. In this case, $\hat{a}_i$ is the vote share of the individual poll, n is the total number of individual polls, and $\underline{a}$ is the average vote share of all the polls.

$$\underline{a} = \frac{1}{n} \sum\nolimits_{i=1}^{n} \hat{a}_i$$

We can calculate the "spread" $(\underline{s})$ of our polling estimate. This is calculated simply by subtracting the vote share results for "Clinton" $(\underline{a}_{\text{clinton}})$ from that of "Trump" $(\underline{a}_{\text{trump}})$. The spread can be negative or positive.

$$\underline{s} = \underline{a}_{\text{clinton}} - \underline{a}_{\text{trump}}$$

To measure sampling variability, we need to calculate the margin of error for both the Ipsos polls and the market average. Remember our margin of error equation in Chapter 5. Here, we riff on it and calculate the MOE of the "spread" by adjusting it by standard error of two proportions of the same sample, where p_1 is the proportion of the vote for Clinton; p_2 is the proportion of the vote for Trump and t is a 95% confidence interval with a t-value of 1.96. See the following equation.

$$\text{MOE} = t^* \sqrt{\frac{1}{n} * \left[(p1 + p2) - (p1 - p2)^2 \right]}$$

We first aggregate the polls between June 1 and July 24, 2016 (Table 6.1). Again, we do this to ensure a larger sample size and smaller margin of error. In total, we assess five Ipsos polls with a total sample size of 7,926 and a corresponding margin of error of +/−2.19%. And for the market average, or "all other polls," we examine forty-nine polls with a total sample size of 133,182 and a margin of error of +/−.55.

Table 6.1 *Election polling conducted June–July 2016*

	Spread (Clinton–Trump)	Number of polls	Total sample size	Margin of error
Ipsos	9.6	5	7,926	2.2%
Online	3.6	15	95,512	.63%
All polls	4.3	49	133,182	.54%

Source: **Pollster.com**; polls conducted between June 1 and July 24

So, do the spreads overlap? The short answer is, "No, they don't." For the Ipsos polls which have a margin of error of +/−2.2%, we would expect to find the true population value between 7.4% and 11.8%. For "all other polls" which have a margin of error of +/−.54%, we would expect the true population value to fall between 3.76% and 4.84%. Note how the upper bound of "all other polls" (4.84%) and the lower bound of the Ipsos polls (7.4%) *does not overlap*. This means that the observed difference does not result from sampling variability. Instead, our problem is likely due to non-sampling error. But what type of non-sampling error might account for the observed difference? Further analysis is required.

NON-SAMPLING ERROR

Coverage Bias

Let's start with coverage bias. Remember that coverage bias occurs when a sample frame – or the representative complement of all the various demographic groups we want to capture – is incomplete. We know that under-coverage tends to disfavor the less affluent, rural, and less educated. In other words, a voter profile that just so happens to be more sympathetic to Trump.

We typically start our analysis by looking at the mode of administration, or how the polls were conducted (online, by phone, or in-person). Mode of administration is a good proxy for coverage problems. Here, our main questions are, "Did the Ipsos poll employ an adequate mode of administration?" "Did it cover the universe in question?"

In 2016, the Ipsos election polling was conducted online. Could this be a problem?

At first blush, online polling is probably not the reason for the observed difference. In the United States, most people (circa 90%) have access to the internet, as opposed to more limited access in countries like India or Brazil.

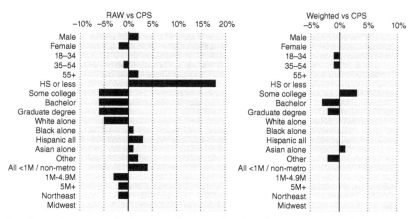

Graph 6.1 Comparing deviations in demographic distributions in raw and weighted data
Source: Reuters/Ipsos July 2016

That said, even in the United States, online polls deserve a closer look. Many online polls employ non-probability designs.[2] The primary concern here is that respondents are not randomly selected but opt into panels or come in via river sampling.[3] An additional concern is that such designs may suffer from incomplete sample frames given the haphazard nature of construction.

But does the empirical evidence bear these concerns out? No, it doesn't. For US elections, such online polls had performed well relative to other methodologies employed in the 2012 election.[4] Moreover, other online polls in July 2016 with similar methodologies produced results much closer to the market average. Our table bears this out. So, nothing to see here.

Perhaps the observed difference was a coverage issue idiosyncratic to the Ipsos poll? To gauge this, we conducted an in-depth demographic analysis. Here, we put together an analysis (Graph 6.1) with the distribution of results across key demographics, and then compare it to population numbers from official sources.

---

[2] Baker et al. (2013) *Report on the AAPOR Taskforce on Non-Probability Samples Nonprobability Taskforce.*

[3] By river sampling, we mean the recruitment of respondents via website pop-up ads and other forms of enticement; typically, these are one-off engagements. By panel, we mean the recruitment of respondents who are interviewed multiple times using incentives and other mechanisms of enticement.

[4] See Silver (2012) "Which Polls Fared Best (and Worst) in the 2012 Presidential Race," in FiveThirtyEight. https://fivethirtyeight.com/features/which-polls-fared-best-and-worst-in-the-2012-presidential-race/amp/.

See how the frequency distributions on the raw data seriously deviate on certain demographics, such as education. This is a classic under-coverage example. The less educated, less affluent and less plugged-in are less likely to be online even in the United States. In contrast, when we compare the weighted to the US current population (CPS) by gender, age, education, and ethnicity, observe how well the weighted and population proportions line up. This makes sense since the population figures are used as the weight factors to adjust the sample. This is a good example of how to correct for coverage bias.

Such raw data is not always available to third parties. For this reason, public opinion analysts often use methodological statements like the following one to assess coverage bias. ***This is an imperfect approach but is better than nothing.*** From the statement, the Ipsos polls appear to be employing best practices, such as weighting by demographic variables.

Example of Methodological Statement

"The data were weighted to the U.S. current population data by gender, age, education, and ethnicity. Statistical margins of error are not applicable to online polls.[5] All sample surveys and polls may be subject to other sources of error, including, but not limited to coverage error and measurement error. Figures marked by an asterisk (*) indicate a percentage value of greater than zero but less than one half of one per cent. Where figures do not sum to 100, this is due to the effects of rounding."

All told, it does not seem like coverage bias is the reason for the observed difference. Here, we should understand that such assessments are tentative at best. In our experience, we should never assume that we can weight our problems away. This said, this is a process of elimination often testing with incomplete information. With this in mind, let's check coverage bias off the list.

So, might it be nonresponse bias?

NONRESPONSE BIAS

As mentioned in Chapter 5, nonresponse bias is very difficult to assess. As compared to the other sources of non-sampling error – namely coverage bias and measurement error – we have the most difficult time in observing nonresponse bias. The best way to assess from afar this is to look at the methodological statement provided by the polling firm to ensure proper

---

[5] In the case of nonprobability opt-in online polls, we employ Bayesian credibility intervals, which in this case are equivalent to the MOE adjusted by a design effect.

post-survey weighting. Did Ipsos do this? Yes, it did. A quick look at the aforementioned methodological statement suggests that such methods were indeed employed. So, it doesn't look to be a nonresponse issue. **But, as already indicated, we should never make a strong assumption on non-response. This is the silent killer of polls.**

As a side note, subsequent analysis has suggested that there has been a roughly 3-point bias in 2016, 2018, and 2022 in favor of Democrats over Trump and Republicans due to differential nonresponse. This bias is tricky to detect and to minimize; however, such corrections at both the design and post-survey stage are increasingly being deployed by pollsters.[6]

ESTIMATION ERROR

Could the observed difference come down to estimation error – a faulty likely voter model? Remember when it comes to election polling, the population of interest is *not* the population as a whole, or even registered voters, but of those who will vote in the election. Determining this universe is the central challenge for pollsters leading up to election day, pushing them to employ likely voter models in their assessments of polling results. Such models can take on many forms as detailed in the last chapter.

However, the observed difference does not appear to be a likely voter problem. Critically, in July 2016, forty-four of forty-nine polls had registered voters – not likely voters – as their target universe. In the United States, pollsters typically employ likely voter models only after the Democratic and Republican national conventions. This is when most people begin to pay attention to the election. In other countries, a similar rubric is often used where such models are employed only four to six weeks out from the election. Again, given that most of the polls at the time only surveyed registered voters, including Ipsos, we cannot attribute the discrepancy to an estimation, or likely voter, problem.

That said, often pollsters conduct **sensitivity analyses** on their likely voter models. Here, we assume different turnout levels in order to assess their impact on results. In Table 6.2, we conducted such an analysis on an Ipsos poll that ran in late July. Remember that Ipsos, like other polling firms in the United States, uses a modified-Gallup model as discussed in Chapter 5. The

---

[6] Young & Jackson (2022) "Plugging the Dike," at AAPOR 77th Annual Conference; Feldman & Mendez (2022) "Who Are the People Who Don't Respond to Polls," in *FiveThirtyEight*, October 26, 2022.

Table 6.2 *Vote spread by different voter turnout assumptions (Clinton–Trump)*

	General population	Assumed turnout		
		High	Medium	Low
Spread (Clinton–Trump)	10	8	6	6

Source: Ipsos Poll July 2016

results are quite clear – the spread in favor of Clinton is consistently greater than that of the market. And this is the case across turnout assumptions. The takeaway is clear. Some other form of non-sampling error is at play.

MEASUREMENT ERROR

So, could the observed difference be a result of some type of measurement error? Is it some issue with questionnaire construction or question wording? As we have learned, there are a few key elements to look for when assessing measurement error. These range from question context and order to wording and scale order to the use of don't know and undecided-like response categories. The Ipsos questionnaire is a short electoral instrument with eight questions, plus standard demographics. Let's examine the questionnaire in detail. Note the full questionnaire can be found at the end of this chapter in Table 6.5

First, best practice dictates that ballot questions should come at or near the beginning of the questionnaire, so as to minimize the effect of question order and context. In the case of the Ipsos poll, the ballot question was placed near the beginning of the questionnaire. Only neutral likely voter; right/track wrong track and presidential approval questions preceded it. This is quite standard in the field. Hence, questionnaire order and context do not seem to be the culprits.

Second, a quick look indicates that no biased words or wording were employed in the question stem. Remember that "hot button" words can have a biasing effect. The Ipsos questionnaire employs all standard conventions. And it is quite comparable to other ballot questions employed by other polling firms. Nothing problematic can be found here either.

Ballot Question

"If the 2016 presidential election were being held today and the candidates were as below, for whom would you vote?" [Rotate candidates]

- Hillary Clinton (Democrat)
- Donald Trump (Republican)
- Neither/Other
- Wouldn't vote
- Don't know/Refused

Third, pollsters should also rotate the order of response categories as best practice. This reduces recency or primacy effects by ensuring that participants don't automatically pick the first or last response. For the 2016 US presidential election, this meant rotating Trump and Clinton as a first choice. Examination of the above question shows that scale rotation was employed. Again, this is best practice.

Finally, **a look at the "other" option shows a possible variation from what would be considered the standard ballot question.** As indicated earlier, the Ipsos poll asked about the election in the same way as other polling shops (e.g., "If the 2016 presidential election were being held today and the candidates were as below, for whom would you vote?").

However, while Ipsos included a combined "Neither/Other" option, other polling firms did one of two things: (1) they provided a pure "Other" option (without the word "Neither") or (2) they did not provide any "Other" option at all, allowing only three response options ("Clinton," "Trump," and "Undecided" – or a variation on "Undecided"). Ipsos was the only polling firm with such a question formulation. This is noteworthy. Here, we might have the answer to why the spread was at such variance from the market average.

So, was the use of "neither" the reason for the observed difference? Thus far, it seems to be the most probable culprit. But before rushing to a conclusion, Ipsos conducted an **experiment** to determine the impact of the question wording. In practice, we tested three different ballot questions:

- Ballot 1: The original question wording.
- Ballot 2: The Ipsos question wording minus the "neither" option.
- Ballot 3: The three-category question with no other option.

Respondents were randomized to one of three ballots with a sample of approximately 940 respondents per condition, as indicated in Table 6.3. We also broke the data down by different universe definitions (e.g., the level of turnout on election day). These included all adults, high turnout, medium turnout, and low turnout.

Table 6.3 *Three vote ballot questions by different voter turnout assumptions*

	Response items	Medium turnout (70%)	Medium turnout (60%)	Low turnout (50%)	All adults age 18+	All adults age 18+, unweighted
Ballot 1	Hillary Clinton (Democrat)	46	45	45	42	41
	Donald Trump (Republican)	38	39	39	32	34
	Neither/Other	10	10	10	12	12
	Wouldn't vote	2	2	1	7	6
	Don't know/ refused	5	5	5	7	7
Ballot 2	Hillary Clinton (Democrat)	43	44	43	41	43
	Donald Trump (Republican)	42	43	44	37	34
	Other	5	5	5	7	7
	Undecided	8	7	6	9	10
	Not voting	2	2	2	6	5
Ballot 3	Hillary Clinton (Democrat)	43	43	43	41	41
	Donald Trump (Republican)	44	45	44	38	39
	Undecided	13	12	12	20	20

Sources: www.reuters.com/article/us-usa-election-poll-reutersipsos-idUSKCN10910T
www.ipsos.com/en-us/knowledge/society/reuters-ipsos-presidential-ballot-question

Reviewing these results, we find substantively significant differences across ballot conditions. Specifically, the Ipsos ballot approach (ballot one) maintains a consistently larger spread than do ballots two or three. The "neither/other" option in ballot one is five percentage points higher than that of ballot two. Both ballots two and three behave in ways that make intuitive sense: the spread declines with decreasing turnout. The unweighted data for ballots one and two look almost identical. Only when the data is weighted are ballot one's results at odds with what we would otherwise expect.

These trends strongly suggest that the "neither" option was attractive to a specific subgroup of prospective voters with a distinctive demographic profile. When we break the results down by demographics, we see that this is indeed the case. Respondents selecting "neither/other" are older and whiter than those selecting "other," and are also slightly more educated (Table 6.4).

Table 6.4 *Demographic analysis of "neither and other"*
respondent categories

Variable	Category	"Neither/Other" (Ballot 1)	"Other" (Ballot 2)	Difference
Age	18 through 24	22	40	−18
	25 through 34	11	10	+1
	35 through 44	13	10	+3
	45 through 54	14	17	−3
	55 or more	40	24	+16
Education	College or more	22	32	−10
	No college	42	40	+2
	Some college	36	29	+7
Race and ethnicity	Black/African American	3	3	−
	Hispanic	11	26	−15
	Others	14	17	−3
	White only	72	54	+18
Sex	Female	61	62	−1
	Male	39	38	+1

Sources: www.reuters.com/article/us-usa-election-poll-reutersipsos-idUSKCN10910T
www.ipsos.com/en-us/knowledge/society/reuters-ipsos-presidential-ballot-question

The substantive question is why the "neither" option would appeal to the distinct subgroup. We hypothesize that the inclusion of "neither" adds a layer of ambiguity that may appeal to voters sitting on the fence. Particularly in the 2016 election, there might have been "soft Trump supporters" who preferred not to make a choice in June and July of 2016.[7] Americans who were more likely to choose "neither" fit the average profile of a Trump supporter.[8]

Ultimately, faced with these results, Ipsos opted to modify ballot's response options, dropping "neither" from the "neither/other" option. This helped address the measurement error and brought Ipsos in line with the standard response options used in other polls.

In the previous case, we employed a simple framework to assess sampling and non-sampling error. Remember our triangle. We now have shown how

[7] Enns et al. (2017) "Understanding the 2016 US Presidential Polls: The Importance of Hidden Trump Supporters," in *Statistics, Politics, and Policy* Vol. 8, Issue 1, pp. 41–63.
[8] Young & Clark (2016) "What an Actual Trump Voter Looks Like," in the *Daily Beast*, June 2016.

Table 6.5 *Questionnaire except for 2016 polls*

Question number	Question System	Question responses
Q1	Sometimes things come up and people are not able to vote. In the 2012 elections for president did you happen to vote?	Yes No Don't Know/refused
Q2	For whom did you vote for President in 2012? [Randomize First Two Responses]	Barack Obama (Democrat) Mitt Romney (Republican) Other Unsure/Refused
Q3	Did you happen to vote in any of these other elections?	2008 presidential election 2010 midterm congressional election 2014 midterm congressional election
Q4	Using a 1–10 scale, where 10 means you are completely certain you will vote and 1 means you are completely certain you will NOT vote, how likely are you to vote in the next presidential election in November 2016?	Scale 1 to 10
Q5	Generally speaking, would you say things in this country are heading in the right direction, or are they off on the wrong track?	Right Direction Wrong Direction Don't know
Q6	Overall, do you approve or disapprove about the way Barack Obama is handling his job as president?	Approve Disapprove Don't know
Q7	If the 2016 presidential election were being held today and the candidates were as below, for whom would you vote? [Rotate Candidates]	Hillary Clinton (Democrat) Donald Trump (Republican) Neither/Other Don't Know/refused

Source: Ipsos Poll July 2016

this can be applied in practice (see Ipsos questionnaire Table 6.5). Here, it is important to note that such an analysis is often more of a process of elimination than the identification of a smoking gun. To close, the total error framework is an important tool for the pollster as data scientist.

7

The Case of Grexit and Assessing
the Polls in Aggregate

INTRODUCTION

We now know more about the ways in which a single poll can go awry. But how can the pollster protect themselves in situations when multiple polls are biased, leading to flawed forecasts?

As mentioned in earlier chapters, one of the more common methods for reducing sample variability is **poll aggregation**. The rough idea is that by assessing the results of multiple polls together, the effective sample size will be increased and thus the margin of error minimized.[1] Aggregators all have the same technical objective of minimizing noise and maximizing signal. But does this work in practice? This is what we will explore in detail in this chapter.

Before we dive in, let's take a look at what poll aggregation looks like in its simplest form – that is to say, as a simple average. Table 7.1 aggregates the polls conducted during the last two days of the 2016 US presidential election cycle. This results in a total sample size of 17,677 interviews, with a corresponding margin of error of 0.7%. In contrast, as we learned in Chapter 5, any single poll with a sample size of around 1,000 interviews has about an +/−3.1% margin of error. See how the individual polls are more variable relative to each other and their margin of errors are larger. Ultimately, the market average came close to the actual election results (+3.2 versus +2.1).

As we move through this chapter, remember that the margin of error is a measure of sampling error. Non-sampling error also contributes to polling misses.

---

[1] Jackman (2005) "Pooling the Polls over an Election Campaign," *Australian Journal of Political Science* Vol. 40 Issue 4, pp. 499–517; Jackson (2018) "The Rise of Poll Aggregation and Election Forecasting," in *Polling and Survey Methods*. Eds. Atkeson and Alvarez. Oxford Press.

Table 7.1 Poll results published in the last two days of the 2016 election

	Date	Sample size	Margin of error (MOE)	Percent support Clinton	Percent support Trump	Spread
Bloomberg	11/4–11/6	799	3.5%	46	43	Clinton +3
IBD/TIPP Tracking	11/4–11/7	1107	2.9%	43	42	Clinton +1
The Economist/ YouGov	11/4–11/7	3669	1.6%	49	45	Clinton +4
LA Times/USC Tracking	11/1–11/7	2935	1.8%	44	47	Trump +3
ABC/Wash Post Tracking	11/3–11/6	2220	2.1%	49	46	Clinton +3
Fox News	11/3–11/6	1295	2.7%	48	44	Clinton +4
Monmouth	11/3–11/6	748	3.6%	50	44	Clinton +6
NBC News/Wall Street Journal	11/3–11/5	1282	2.7%	48	43	Clinton +5
CBS News	11/2–11/6	1426	2.6%	47	43	Clinton +4
Reuters/Ipsos	11/2–11/6	2196	2.1%	44	39	Clinton +5
AVERAGE		17677	0.7%	46.8	43.6	Clinton +3.2

Sources: Bloomberg, Reuters/Ipsos, CBS News, NBC News/Wall Street Journal, Fox News, ABC/Wash Post, Monmouth, LA Times/USC, The Economist/YouGov, IBD/TIPP

Not all aggregators are created equal. Some report a simple rolling average over a given time period. Others use sophisticated algorithms, such as *Monte Carlo Markov Chain* models, to account for outliers and sparse data. Still others utilize additional inputs like economic data or historic election results to "smooth" their estimates.

The aggregate is only as good as the individual polls that underpin it. Biased individual polls lead to biased aggregates. The "market of polls" can also have a gravitational force of its own. Polling outfits will closely watch the market average and in some cases seek to adjust their own results to reflect the general consensus. This is known as "herding" and can push the polls toward an artificial standard. We will discuss herding in more detail in Chapter 8.

In the preceding chapters, we detailed and then employed our **total error framework** to assess the quality of a single poll. As we saw there, many election misses come down to failing to correctly identify the voting population or accounting for coverage bias. We also saw how other forms of error, such as poor question formulation, can lead to significant analytic uncertainty.

In this chapter, we will apply our total error framework to the polls in aggregate. Such analysis is typically done retrospectively in order to determine why the polls did not predict a given outcome.

However, aggregate assessment can also be done in real-time to assess the polls against models, economic data, social media activity, and the like. In these instances, we seek to probe why the polls are at variance with other evidence, and to detect whether there is some systemic bias in the polls that is sending the wrong signal.

We most commonly assess the performance of polls relative to elections. But we can apply this to non-electoral cases as well, such as referenda, impeachments, and reform bills. The primary characteristic of all these instances is that they are distinct outcomes, bounded with some degree of discreteness. In this chapter, we will conduct a retrospective analysis of one of the most astonishing polling misses in recent memory, the 2015 Greek referendum, or Grexit.

2015 GREEK REFERENDUM: GREXIT

Context

In the summer of 2015, the Greek sovereign debt crisis had reached a breaking point.[2] The Greek government missed its $1.7 billion debt payment

---

[2] Council on Foreign Relations. Greece's Debt Crisis: 1974–2018. Retrieved from: www.cfr
    .org/timeline/greeces-debt-crisis-timeline.

due to the International Monetary Fund (IMF). As a result, banks closed, and Greek citizens scrambled to withdraw cash from ATMs. The IMF, the European Commission, and the European Central Bank offered Greece a bailout with certain austerity conditions. The specter of Greece's exit from the Eurozone and a return to the drachma loomed. Prime Minister Alexis Tsipras, who had been elected on an anti-austerity platform, opposed the bailout and called a last-minute referendum allowing the citizens to vote on whether or not to accept said conditions. Tsipras and his Syriza party argued that a "no" vote on the referendum would strengthen Greece's negotiating position as it would show that Greece wasn't willing to accept the austerity terms without some kind of push back.

Yet the Greeks were not wholly in favor of a "no" vote. In opposition, the grassroots movement Menoume Europi (Stay in Europe) arose, which advocated for a "yes" vote, reflecting their eponymous desire to stick with the European Union. In the lead-up, EU leaders affirmed that they would read the "no" vote as a rejection of Europe, although Tsipras denied this.

The Greek referendum was announced just eight days before it was held. In the interim, Greece defaulted on its debt payment to the IMF. To make matters worse, the question on the ballot asked voters if they approved of a by-then-outdated proposal, made on June 25, 2015, by Greece's creditors. These terms were already invalidated because, as mentioned, Greece has just defaulted on its debt.

Complicating this matter, the proposal to Greek voters was one of bureaucratic verbiage about tax changes and pension rules. Difficult stuff for the average citizen to comprehend, and with just eight days to study up on it, very little time to unpack it.

Meanwhile, the global financial markets, international leaders, and political pundits were nervously eying the referendum as the day approached. Tsipras rallied his supporters, exhorting them in fiery terms, "I call on you to say a big 'no' to ultimatums, a 'no' to blackmail. Turn your back on those who would terrorize you." On the other side, the opposition emphasized to the public that this was really a vote of whether to stay in the EU or not.

At the time, Aristos Doxiadis, an economist and adviser to To Potami, an opposition, pro-Europe party, commented, "Once the banks closed, the whole game, or point of the referendum, changed completely. How on earth were we going to have functioning banks again? The referendum was never going to be about specific agreements. It is about whether we stay in the Eurozone or not." Needless to say, the polls took on an outsized importance leading up to this high-stakes event.

Table 7.2 *2015 Greek referendum, polling, and actual results*

	Votes for "Yes"	Votes for "No"	Spread (No-Yes)	Number of polls	Sample size	Margin of error
June 27–29, 2015	34.3	53	–17.7	6	6,052	2.5%
July 4–5, 2015	46.9	50.2	–3.3	5	5,000	2.8%
All polls	41.7	47.3	–5.6	31	31,325	1.1%
Actual referendum results	38.7	61.3	–22.6	N/A	N/A	N/A

Sources: Greek Ministry of the Interior, MRB, MARC, Metron Analysis, Alco, GPO, Ipsos, PAMAK, Public Issue[3]

The Problem

Unfortunately, events would reveal that not only were the polls wrong, they were significantly off. The final vote gave a 22.6-point advantage to the "no" vote over "yes," as Table 7.2 shows. Interestingly, at the beginning of the week, the polls did show a substantial margin for "no." Early polls were closer to the final results (17.7 versus 22.6) than the later polls. But over the course of the week, amid the bank closings and generalized chaos, many thought the narrowing gap shown by the polls made complete sense. Ultimately, the polls suggested a much closer race of around 5 points for "no." The polls sent all the wrong signals to markets and other decision-makers.

Grexit was a major upset, seemingly defying the logic of the times.

Assessment

So, what went wrong? To assess, we will employ our total survey error framework here. As in Chapter 6, we will use the spread as our primary evaluative statistic. It is simple to calculate and intuitively appealing. However, many analysts use other statistics to evaluate the polls. The most common of which is the Average Absolute Difference (AAD).[4] To calculate the AAD, we take the actual election result (AR) for candidate i minus the poll result (PR) for candidate i and divide that by the number of candidates

---

[3] The polling results shown in the table are based on thirty-one phone-based polls conducted prior to the referendum.

[4] Mitofsky (1998) "The Polls – Review: Was 1996 a Worse Year for the Polls than 1948?" in *Public Opinion Quarterly* Vol. 62, pp. 230–249.

(c) in a given race. One benefit of the AAD is that it can be used in three-way races or more. See the following equation:

$$AAD = \left(\sum |AR_i - PR_i| \right) / c$$

But, shifting gears back to our thought experiment, we will set aside the AAD and focus our analysis on **the spread**. As we dive in, remember that there are two broad classes of error – sampling and non-sampling error. For this exercise, we will rely on thirty-one polls conducted leading up to the referendum. The equation to take a simple average of the polls is shown as follows. In this case, $\hat{a}_i$ is the vote share of the individual poll, n is the total number of individual polls, and $\underline{a}$ is the average vote share of all the polls.

$$\underline{a} = \frac{1}{n} \sum\nolimits_{i=1}^{n} \hat{a}_i$$

We can then calculate the "spread" $(\underline{s})$ of our polling estimate. This is calculated simply by subtracting the vote share results for "no" $(\underline{a}_{no})$ from that of "yes" $(\underline{a}_{yes})$. The spread can be negative or positive.

$$\underline{s} = \underline{a}_{no} - \underline{a}_{yes}$$

Alternatively, we could have weighted the results by the sample size of each poll (a larger poll would get a larger weight) or some other criteria. Jackman's equation is the industry standard for aggregating polls in this way.[5] To do this, all we need is the vote share and sample size for each poll. From there, we then:

- Calculate the standard deviation (s) for each poll based on the vote share $(\hat{a})$ and sample size (n) using this equation: $s = \sqrt{\hat{a}(1-\hat{a})/n}$
- Calculate the "precision" of each poll, which is based on the standard deviation and used to weight the poll based on the sample size. We calculate the precision (p) using this equation: $p = 1/s^2$

Now we have all of the pieces for the individual polls to combine them. For simplicity's sake, let's say we're just combining two polls: one from organization A and the other from organization B. We need the precision (p) and vote share (a) from A and B and we combine them like this:

$$\hat{a}_{AB} = \frac{p_A \hat{a}_A + p_B \hat{a}_B}{p_A + p_B}$$

[5] Jackman (2005) "Pooling the Polls over an Election Campaign," in *Australian Journal of Political Science* Vol. 40, Issue 4, pp. 499–517.

Here, we have what's called a "precision-weighted average" vote share. Polls with larger sample sizes are given more weight. Additionally, analysts often take into account the "house effects" of each individual polling firm. This is done to account for the systematic bias of any given polling firm. We opted **not** to make these additional adjusts for the sake of simplicity.

Now, as we move on to our error assessment, keep these key points in mind:

- The spread (No-Yes) of the actual referendum results was −22.6 points.
- The spread (No-Yes) shown in the polls was −5.6 points.
- The margin of error of all the polls included in this analysis, which produced a sample of 31,325, was plus or minus 1.1%.

SAMPLING ERROR

First, could the miss have been due to sampling error? Taking into consideration the margin of error, the spread of all the polls could reasonably have been as high as −4.5 points and as low as −6.7 points.[6] Yet clearly, at −22.6, the actual spread was far outside these bounds. The polls conducted at the end of the week, or July 4 and 5, are outside the margin of error as well (−6.1 versus −22.6). While the polls published at the beginning of the week (June 27 to 29) are closer to reality (−20.2 versus −22.6), the spread of these polls still falls outside the margin of error.

In other words, no matter which way we slice it, the difference between the polls and the referendum itself was much larger than chance variability already baked into the polls. As such, we can't chalk the miss up to random noise. Something else is at play. By definition, if not sampling error, then the polling problem in Greece must be the fault of non-sampling error. But which one?

NON-SAMPLING ERROR

As we turn our attention to non-sampling error, let's first consider the problem of **measurement error**.

---

[6] Here, we calculate the MOE of "the spread" by adjusting it by standard error of the difference of two proportions of the same population, where P_1 is the proportion of the vote for "No"; P_2 is the proportion of the vote for "Yes" and t is a t-value of 1.96 for a 95% confidence interval.

$$\text{MOE} = t^* \sqrt{\frac{1}{n} * \left[(p1 + p2) - (p1 - p2)^2 \right]}$$

Divergent polls can result from questionnaire construction, the wording of specific questions, or the way in which we administer the questions to the respondent, all forms of measurement error. We also learned some best practices for constructing unbiased questions, or the way in which we administer the questions to the respondent. These are useful rules to assess public opinion polls.

In particular, we focus on three aspects of the ballot question:

- It should be at or near the beginning of the questionnaire in order to avoid unintended influence from questions. Such influence can come from the general context of the question, or more specifically to the sequence of the questions.
- It should be as neutral as possible to minimize biased responses. Here, we want to stay away from hot button words that might elicit a strong emotional response, inadvertently influencing responses.
- The response options should be randomized in order to ensure that the order of the responses do not influence the way people answer.

In the case of the Greek referendum, very few of the polling firms published their questionnaires and more detailed methodological statements. This complicates the assessment of measurement error. That said, in our experience, referenda ballot questions often are difficult to understand because they deal with technical or esoteric topics. The case of the Greece referendum was no different. See the following referendum. As you can see, it is quite vague, difficult to understand and only makes tangential reference to key documents with little additional detail.

The Greek Referendum Question

The Greek people are asked to decide with their vote whether to accept the outline of the agreement submitted by the European Union, the European Central Bank and the International Monetary Fund at the Eurogroup of 25/06/15 and is made up of two parts which constitute their unified proposal:

The first document is entitled: Reforms for the completion of the current program and beyond and the second is Preliminary Debt Sustainability Analysis.

Whichever citizens reject the proposal by the three institutions vote: Not Approved/NO

Whichever citizens agree with the proposal by the three institutions vote: Approved/YES

The Grexit question was met with bemused astonishment by experts worldwide. What the Greek citizens themselves actually thought is harder to parse, although polling leading up to the referendum suggests that perspectives on what the fallout would be were split. The vast majority of "no" voters believed that their vote would not lead to Greece's exit from the euro zone. Meanwhile, more than half of the "yes" voters believed that Grexit would likely result from a "no" vote.[7]

Additionally, there are obvious political motivations in how referenda questions are framed. In this case, Tsipras and Syriza controlled the wording of the ballot question. Again, they were in favor of a "no" vote.

Consider the construction of the referendum question above. Notice how the "no" option precedes the "yes." This construction runs counter to how humans think, which is typically from positive to negative, not the contrary. This construction makes the question appear to be an obvious attempt from the "no" camp to take advantage of the response order to influence voters. Ultimately, the opaque wording and biased question construction raises doubts about whether the true wishes of Greek voters were captured.

However, further evidence will show that a confusing ballot question was not the primary reason for the polling miss. Often, such an assessment is a process of elimination.

NONRESPONSE BIAS, COVERAGE BIAS, AND ESTIMATION ERROR

Could the Grexit polling miss have resulted from other forms of non-sampling error, such as coverage bias, nonresponse bias or estimation error? As we indicated in Chapters 5 and 6, **nonresponse bias** is not easy to assess directly. We often make the simplifying assumption that post-survey weighting will correct for any issues with nonresponse. This is a significant assumption. But for simplicity in this case, let's remove it from the list.

In our experience, **coverage bias** is a common reason for polling misses in elections and other election-like events. It might be a strong culprit for the Grexit polling miss. Is this the case? The data suggests no. See in Table 7.3 how those in favor of "no" were more educated than those in favor of "yes." People with this profile typically are less likely to have access to a telephone. So, our proxy coverage variable – education – is negatively correlated with no. If there were coverage bias, "no" should be more pronounced, not less.

Additionally, remember that all thirty-one polls leading up to the referendum were conducted by phone, many of which deployed some mix of landline and cell phones. As you might recall from Chapter 5, pollsters may use mode of survey administration (face-to-face, telephone, mail, or

---

[7] Walter (2015) "What Were the Greeks Thinking? Here's a Poll Taken Just before the Referendum." *Washington Post.* July 9, 2015.

Table 7.3 *Those who are likely to vote by education*

Q8: Intention of vote in the referendum	All respondents (%)	<10 Years (%)	12 Years (%)	University (%)
Accepting (YES)	38	48	36	41
Rejecting (NO)	55	45	58	51
White/invalid	1	1	1	1
Haven't decided	3	5	2	2
Abstention	1	1	1	2
Don't know	0	0	0	0
Don't answer	2	1	2	3

Source: Eurasia/Ipsos Tracking Poll June 29 to July 4

online) as a quick proxy for coverage bias in the absence of other evidence. Again, as public opinion analysts, we normally don't have access to the raw data from polling firms. We know that the rate of telephone ownership in Greece was high at the time (circa 90%). So, looks like the polling miss was not a result of coverage bias.

Alternatively, could the Greek miss have resulted from **estimation error**, or more specifically, from incorrectly identifying who would vote in the referendum? Determining what the voter population will look like is oftentimes the single most difficult task for pollsters. Likely voter models are equally, if not more, challenging for third-party analysts to interpret because outside observers don't have access to the raw polling data or know what elements were considered when constructing the model.

As mentioned in Chapter 5, pollsters employ a variety of likely voter models in order to separate out those who will vote from those who won't. Remember that from an international perspective, participation in elections is generally not obligatory. As a result, not everyone who is eligible to vote actually does so. Globally, the average turnout in national elections is around 65% among the voting age population.[8]

In the case of the 2015 Greek referendum, 63% of the voting population turned out, which was on par with parliamentary election turnout at the time. But the question is, did the pollsters in Greece get the right subset of voters, that is, did they correctly identify who would show up to vote?

To get at this, we will take an Ipsos tracking poll conducted from June 29 to July 4, 2015 (Graph 7.1). The poll consisted of a daily sample of 800

---

[8] DeSilver (2020) "In Past Elections, US Trailed Most Developed Countries in Voter Turnout." Pew Research Center, November 3, 2020.

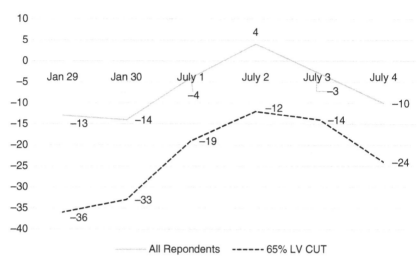

Graph 7.1 Greek referendum polling ("No" responses minus "Yes" responses)
Source: Eurasia/Ipsos Polling, June 29–July 4, 2015

interviews; it aggregated the daily sample into a three-day rolling average of 2,400 interviews to minimize sampling error. To assess different turnout scenarios, we employed a modified-Gallup likely voter model based on a summated index of multiple items.

We ranked respondents by their likely voter scores. We, then, made likely vote cuts at different levels of turnout (65% to all adults). The "all adults" scenario represents a naïve model utilized by most pollsters at the time; the 65% scenario represents a likely voter model that approximates the actual turnout levels (65% versus 63%).

As the graph would indicate, the pollsters did not correctly identify who would vote. At a turnout of around 65%, close to that of the referendum, we replicate the final election results (−24 as opposed to −22.6). In contrast, the naïve model (100% turnout) closely mimics the polling results at the time with an average spread of around −7 points. Here, it is worth noting that there was a trend toward "yes" over the course of the week. But, after taking the likely voter population into account, we see that this never put "no" at risk. These are important insights lost to decision-makers at the time. ***The polling miss looks to be a likely voter problem.***

CONCLUSION

In this chapter, we applied our **total error framework** to the case of the 2015 Greek bailout referendum. This polling miss had profound market consequences and was a black eye for the polling industry. But there are ways to assess what went wrong, in Greece and other instances where the polls whiffed, as demonstrated in this chapter. Often such assessment is far from cut and dry but instead is a process of elimination and empirical conjecture. The total survey error framework is essential for thinking through such problems.

As discussed, the evidence strongly suggests that the problem in Greece resulted from a likely voter problem; more specifically, incorrectly identifying who would show up on election-day. So, why did pollsters not utilize likely voter models at the time? This is a complex question to answer.

Many didn't; some did. The most common approach at the time was to weight the data by the results of the last parliamentary election. This is a brute force method for determining the profile of who ends up voting on referendum day. Yet, it does not measure likelihood to vote directly and makes a strong assumption that the past will predict the future. Some electoral events follow a completely different logic than past ones. We only have to think of the 2016 US election, as seen in Table 7.4, to see the risks of assuming that the voting patterns of the past will play out in the future.

Remember the Greek case was a referendum **and not** a parliamentary election. This means that the patterns **would not necessarily** map to those traditionally seen during the latter. Ultimately, the methodological approach was a serious blind spot for pollsters as it reinforced already preexisting beliefs in favor of "yes" – as mentioned, many elites and more educated Greeks were pro-EU and pro-yes. Such cognitive biases together with their own experiences of the chaos on the ground only validated the polling data coming in. We will learn more about such problems in Chapter 8.

Some argued that the polling miss resulted from "herding" as pollsters adjusted their results in response to other polls and what seemed most intuitively "correct" given the circumstances.[9] This might have been a secondary or tertiary culprit, but would be very difficult to ascertain directly. The more likely explanation was that pollsters were using the same or similarly faulty approaches for identifying likely voters, as detailed earlier.

Finally, the Grexit question was also marred by the biased construction of the referendum wording itself. Generally, voters are given more straightforward options at the polls. While Grexit is an extreme case, precedent tells us that even when question wording is perfectly clear, the polls may still be off in aggregate. The lessons of Grexit still offer useful insights that apply to

---

[9] Silver (2015) "The Polls Were Bad in Greece. The Conventional Wisdom Was Worse," in *FiveThirtyEight* July 7, 2015.

Table 7.4 *Some examples of election misses*

	Actual margin	Projected margin based on polling	Picked correct winner	Issues at play
2016 US presidential election	2.1	3.2	No	Rural white voters were missing in the polls; the polls themselves favored Clinton over Trump; Swing states mattered most. State polls overstated as well
2019 Argentinian PASO election	14	4	Yes	The polls overestimated Macri relative to Fernandez. Online and telephone polls failed to adequately cover lower SES voters. They were untested methodologies.
2018 Columbian referendum	−0.4	30	No	Coverage bias and silent refusals or "no's"
2015 Greek referendum, Grexit	−22.6	−3.3	Yes	Polls in the last two days were particularly off. Some analysts pointed to herding or coverage bias. Others point to pollsters not using likely voter models.
2016 Brexit	−3.8	2	No	The polls missed soft Brexit voters, those who were struggling with economic issues. Differential nonresponse also might have been a culprit.
2020 US presidential election	1.7	4.3	Yes	Post-election analysis suggests that there was an issue of nonresponse bias among Trump voters, particularly those who do not typically vote

Sources: RealClearPolitics, AP, UK Election Commission, *Financial Times*, *The Telegraph*, Greek Ministry of the Interior, MRB, MARC, Metron Analysis, Alco, GPO, Ipsos, PAMAK, Public Issue, ToThePoint,

more neutrally worded ballot questions as well as contexts in which voters seemingly act in contradiction to their own interests.[10]

As a final note, poll aggregation sites have become ubiquitous around the world. We use them frequently as data sources and for additional analytical insight. However, aggregator sites are not the only source. Wikipedia entries and desk research also make polling data accessible with a bit of legwork. The pollster of today does not lack for data.

---

[10]   Walter (2020) "The Mass Politics of International Disintegration." *Center for Comparative and International Studies*. Working Paper No. 105. June 2020.

PART III

THE POLLSTER AS FORTUNE TELLER

"I beseech you, in the bowels of Christ, think it possible that you may be mistaken."
—Oliver Cromwell

One of the primary functions of the three-hatted pollster is to utilize public opinion to predict future events. This is the pollster as fortune teller. To generate forecasts, we use public opinion either as a single decision input or together with others. This part includes three chapters, each covering a different aspect of prediction. First, we'll look at cognitive biases that limit our ability to produce accurate forecasts. We detail approaches to minimize such shortcomings that we call **triangulation**.[1] This is an important issue that typically gets little attention. We want to give it an extended look here.

Second, we'll look at public opinion as an input in predicting elections. We will start here because elections can be understood as a special case of a broader class of predictions derived from interpretations of public opinion. Often, we think of public opinion prediction in the context of elections. Many decision-makers will pay top dollar to handicap them. The typical client in these cases could be political parties, politicians, the media, private sector companies, or the financial sector.

Elections are easily defined from an analytical perspective. For instance, they have a set day of occurrence; a known consideration set of candidates and are highly salient events. Our comparison sample is also large given the sheer number of elections that have occurred and for which we have usable data.

---

[1] Triangulation is often referred to as *aggregation*; see Kahneman (2011) *Thinking Fast and Slow*. Farrar, Straus, and Giroux; Tetlock & Gardner (2015) *Super Forecasting: The Art and Science of Prediction*. Broadway Book. New York.

Table III.1 *The three-hatted pollster as fortune teller*

	Part II	Part III	Part IV
	The data scientist (to assess)	The fortune teller (to predict)	The spin doctor (to convince)
Primary Client Type	Media and all other clients	Private sector and financial sector	Politicians, governments, and private sector
Analytical Focus	Maximizing accuracy	Forecasting outcomes	Developing the most convincing message
Typical Question	Is my public opinion data biased?	Who will win the next presidential election?	What is the winning message?

We will also discuss means of predicting other political outcomes like presidential impeachments, referenda, or bills, such as healthcare reform. The fuzziness in these cases comes from the level of issue salience that is typically low. Generally speaking, people are not highly tuned in to these issues. Given the low levels of public awareness, public opinion is a less robust predictor. The pollster should tread carefully in such cases.

Third, we will take a close look at presidential or governmental approval ratings. These are vital to understand as key predictors of elections and other political outcomes. An important aspect of the pollster's job is to assess the relative impact of events, actions, and policies on approval ratings. Commonly asked questions by pollsters include "Will the improving economy have a positive impact on the president's job approval numbers?" Or, "Will COVID help or hurt the sitting government's approval ratings heading into the election?" Or, "Will the economic relief package materially alter the administration's sagging approval numbers?"

Such analyses are more directional in nature. They help us interpret whether a given event or action is good or bad for the administration. Often directionality – up or down – is all that is needed for decision-making.

Finally, we will examine context-based analysis. This is when pollsters look at broader societal outcomes, such as the effect of long-term demographic change on attitudes and politics. Topics of analysis can include the rise of populism and its effect, the importance of a growing middle class in emerging markets, or the impact of tribalism on society. Here, pollsters can elucidate the general context for decision-makers. This often sets the stage for greater understanding of events.

Ultimately, our forecasting models and corresponding inputs are driven by the question at hand. As a fortune-teller, the pollster might seek to divine who will win the next election, or which countries are most likely to have populist political outcomes. Or, they might attempt to determine the most pressing issues facing society over the next few years.

In order to make these forecasts, the pollster must rely on the assumption that there is link between public opinion and those who govern. Think about it, if the behavior of decision-makers did not reflect the will of the people how could public opinion shine any light on the future?

A POLLSTER'S TALE: WHY THE PAST MATTERS FOR THE FUTURE

My first presidential election working as a pollster was in 2002. It pitted Luiz Inácio Lula da Silva, the perennial opposition candidate, against José Serra – the sitting president Fernando Henrique Cardoso's Minister of Health.

The early 2002 polls showed that Lula had a substantial lead over Serra. This was met with both disbelief and consternation. Narratives to counter the polls abounded. These ran the gamut from, "There is no way someone like Lula could be president," to "He doesn't even have a college degree" to "He doesn't have the right upbringing," to "He lost the last three elections; he will lose this one," to, "He will not keep inflation in check."

In my naivete, I began asking some very simple questions. Are candidates with early leads in the polls favored? How might this election be similar or different to past ones? I thought we could find something more structural to help us navigate the uncertainty.

The answer, "Every election is different. There is nothing to learn from the past."

This seemed odd to me. I was after all a trained quantitative social scientist and understood that past behavior does typically predict future behavior. But I hadn't been trained as a political scientist with its literature on election forecasting. The internet was at its infancy so no quick look up. I didn't have the requisite years of experience to have built up a solid knowledge base at the time. So, I tucked these questions away to investigate at a future date.

Ultimately, Lula won; Serra lost. A shock? I would later learn that it shouldn't have been. In fact, there is a clear pattern to elections, expressed almost perfectly in the contest between Lula and Serra.

The key contours of this pattern are as follows: successors like Serra have lower probabilities of victory, particularly when approval ratings of the sitting government are low. And candidates that are strongest on the main issue also tend to win. In Brazil, social mobility was the issue of the day. Lula dominated on this point. Income growth had stagnated under FHC's administration. The promise of the Real Plan never materialized.

No matter which way you sliced it, Lula appeared to have the upper hand. The past has much to say about the future. I didn't know this at the time. But hopefully you will.

8

Cognitive Biases in Prediction

Predictions often falter because of human error. Most misses have much more to do with our own human shortcomings than with the technical sophistication of the method at hand. In our experience, forecasting errors occur when we discard or misinterpret evidence right in front of us. The clues are there, but we are blinded by our own filters. This is why it is essential to tackle such biases and discuss corresponding solutions. In this chapter, we'll look at studies on the forecasting prowess of experts. Then, we'll focus on cognitive biases that skew predictions. Finally, we'll present an applied approach to minimize such biases.

ARE EXPERTS GOOD AT PREDICTION?

Beware the next time you tune in to what the experts have to say about the upcoming election cycle. There may very well be more noise than substance there. We tend to assume that experts, being experts, can accurately predict the future and explain the past. The public generally feels that expert opinion is by definition insightful, privileged, and accurate information. But is this really true?

Unfortunately, the empirical evidence suggests that experts do not have the best track record at predicting the future. In a seminal 2005 study by Philip Tetlock, titled *Expert Political Judgment: How Good Is It? How Can We Know?*, 284 political and economic pundits were asked to offer probabilities that certain events would occur in the near future. These included events both within and outside their wheelhouse. Tetlock gathered over 80,000 expert predictions overall, with questions centering around highly salient issues, such as "Would the US go to war in Iraq to protect Kuwaiti sovereignty?" What he found was astonishing. ***Experts were no better at predicting the future than a coin toss!***

Not only that, but subject matter experts were no better at predicting the future in their area of expertise than the nonexperts. One-quarter of respondents said that events would absolutely happen that never occurred, while 15% said that certain events had no chance of happening that ultimately did occur.

Taking a step back, is this not something we can all identify with? How many times have we seen a talking head on TV make a prediction and later noted that it never came to pass? Many, indeed.

TEST CASE: THE 2016 US PRESIDENTIAL ELECTION

The fallibility of our so-called experts should humble all of us, including pollsters. Let's take the 2016 US presidential election as a real-life example. Most experts expressed high confidence that Clinton would win the election over Trump.

As you likely know, however, Trump beat Clinton. His victory resulted from a few key swing states breaking his way: Michigan, Wisconsin, and Pennsylvania. These gave him the electoral advantage over Clinton – 304 to her 227 electoral college votes. That said, he did not win the popular vote, which broke in Clinton's favor at 48.2% to Trump's 46.1%. But Trump still won the presidency, contrary to what the experts said would happen.

Before we dive into the specifics of the 2016 election, let's consider some of the broader reasons why election polling can go awry, despite the veneer of analytic objectivity that surrounds election forecasters and other experts.

In our experience, three interrelated human shortcomings undermine our ability to predict the future: (1) an orientation toward single input styles of learning; (2) confirmation bias; and (3) thinking in binary terms. The scientific literature reinforces our own experience.[1] Ultimately, there are other biases as well. But, in our experience, addressing the aforementioned three can improve our predictions and our ability to navigate uncertainties.

SINGLE INPUT LEARNING STYLES:
HEDGEHOGS VERSUS FOXES

Our individual, innate cognitive idiosyncrasies put all of us at an advantage, or disadvantage, when attempting to predict the future. We are not

---

[1] See Tetlock (1995) *Expert Political Judgment: How Good Is It? How Can We Know?* Princeton University Press. Kahmeman (2011) *Thinking Fast and Slow.* Farrar, Straus, and Giroux; Tetlock & Gardner (2015) *Super Forecasting: The Art and Science of Prediction.* Broadway Book. New York.

the first to make this observation. Tetlock notes that while expert prediction might be no better than a flip of a coin, a subset of experts are very good at forecasting.

He identified two forecasting archetypes: the hedgehog and the fox. This is derived from a 1951 Isaiah Berlin essay on Tolstoy, "The fox knows many things, but the hedgehog knows one big thing." Hedgehog pundits tend to be worse at forecasting than foxes. Unfortunately, the former tend to be the majority. Let's consider the profile of the typical hedgehog and fox.

HEDGEHOGS

Most pundits fall into the hedgehog camp. They know a lot about one thing and use one strategy for prediction. This expertise becomes their undoing because they get overconfident in their ability to predict. They resist admitting to being wrong and blame failed predictions on timing or unforeseeable events. Interestingly, Tetlock found that the more famous the pundit, the more overconfident and bombastic their forecasts. In the context of public opinion forecasting, we see hedgehogs as those who only use a single data input. Take elections as an example. A hedgehog-like orientation would be a reliance on polling as the sole forecasting input. In many election cycles, this approach might work. However, as we learned, the polls can be biased. In such cases, the hedgehog will fail. An overreliance on a single strategy can betray the analyst.

FOXES

A small minority of pundits can be described as foxes. Foxes know a little about many things and have multiple strategies for prediction. They are complex thinkers and recognize that many different factors come together and interact – often in unexpected ways – to produce a given outcome. They are not wedded to one ideological framework and thus are more comfortable with uncertainty and nuance.

As a result, they tend to be more cautious and more willing to admit mistakes in their predictions. Foxes were the most accurate forecasters in Tetlock's study. Another way to think about the fox's strategy for prediction is **triangulation**. They take information from multiple sources, incorporate ideas from different disciplines, and employ varied strategies to solve problems. In the case of elections, this might mean using polls in addition to other inputs shown to be correlated with election outcomes, such as economic growth, incumbency, approval ratings, or candidate adherence to voter priories.

In a practical sense, the fox and hedgehog analogy gets at how individuals instinctually process information when approaching a given problem. Some utilize information from a variety of sources when making a summary judgment about an outcome, while others will draw on one source or perspective. The advantage of the use of multiple inputs, or triangulation, is that our summary judgment does not depend on any one set of assumptions. The hedgehog's success rests on the relative strength of a single input, while the fox's does not.

THE 2016 US PRESIDENTIAL ELECTION AS A SINGLE-INPUT FAILURE

Let's get back to the specifics of the 2016 US presidential elections. The failures at play were characterized by a hedgehog orientation. Many analysts were confidently declaring a Clinton victory as early as 2015.

As Dana Milbank wrote in the *Washington Post* on October 2, 2015, "I'm so certain Trump won't win the nomination that I'll eat my words if he does. Literally: the day Trump clinches the nomination I will eat the page on which this column is printed in Sunday's *Post*. I have this confidence for the same reason Romney does: Americans are better than Trump."

Or, take University of Virginia forecaster Larry Sabato's assertion: "We've favored Hillary Clinton as the 45th president of the United States ever since we did our first handicapping of the Clinton vs. Donald Trump matchup back in late March."

Even statistically oriented forecasters gave incredibly high probabilities to a Clinton win. Nate Silver of FiveThirtyEight estimated that Clinton had a 71% chance of winning, *Huffpo*'s Pollster.com estimated her chances at 98%, and *The New York Times*' Upshot had her at 85%.

Sam Wang, a Princeton professor, was quite bullish, tweeting on October 18, 2016, "It is totally over. If Trump wins more than 240 electoral votes, I will eat a bug." That is confidence for you.

As wildly off-base as these predictions now seem with the benefit of hindsight, their confidence appears more reasonable if we were just looking at the polling results in isolation. And of the aforementioned prognosticators, even those with the most sophisticated models, were relying almost exclusively on polls. Of the 136 national polls in the final month leading up to the 2016 election, 128 put Clinton in the lead. More importantly, of the 385 polls in the six swing states, 295 had Clinton ahead.

But, what if the polls were wrong? Such a single input strategy was a blind spot for all involved. This was a clear instance of hedgehog behavior.

So, where were the foxes during all this? They were present, but their warnings were drowned out amid the onslaught of positive polling for Clinton. Take, for instance, the filmmaker Michael Moore's prescient warning that Trump was likely going to win. In July 2016, he told Bill Maher:

I lived in Michigan and let me tell you. It's going to be the Brexit strategy. The middle of England is Michigan, Wisconsin, Ohio and Pennsylvania.... All he has to do is win these three states. I was there during the primary, he went down and said, "They moved the factory down to Mexico, I'm putting a tariff on cars," and it was music to peoples' ears.

This was a qualitative or anecdotal piece of evidence but worth paying attention to nevertheless. Unfortunately, it was an insight that largely fell on deaf ears.

In a similar vein, the polls did display contradictory signals. Some underscored the importance of rising nativist, populist, and antiestablishment sentiment to Trump's ascendancy in the United States.[2] Think about it. How well would a creature of the establishment, such as Clinton, fare in a context ripe for an outsider candidate? Few analysts took this to its logical conclusion, that such sentiment could – and would – carry Trump to the White House. Do not forget this point. We will discuss context-based analysis in Chapter 10.

Yet, there were some quantitative analysts paying heed to the warning signals. Take, for instance, Helmut Norpoth, a political scientist at SUNY Stony Brook. His "Primary Model," which is based on candidate performance in primary elections, found that Trump had an 87% chance of winning. Or, take Alan Abramovitz, whose "time-for-change" model forecasted Trump as the winner. Or, the Young/El-Dash "salad bowl" model that put the odds of a Clinton victory at 53%.[3] As Young and Clark put it in June of 2016, employing the salad bowl model, "we think this is a near-even election, with Clinton having a slight advantage."

Both the "time-for change" and "salad bowl" models were based on approval ratings and the incumbent's length of time in office, among other variables. The latter model employed elections from multiple countries and contexts, while the former just those from the United States.

---

[2] Young & Clark (2016) "Even Odds for Trump & Clinton: Is Trump a 'Spoiler' or a 'Game-Changer'?" *RealClearPolitics*. June 3, 2016.

[3] Young & Clark (2016) "Even Odds for Trump & Clinton: Is Trump a 'Spoiler' or a 'Game-Changer'?," *RealClearPolitics*. June 3, 2016.

At the time, Young and Clark, like good foxes, argued that all should take heed given the contradictory signals were all around us. "…[L]et's be wary of pundits or pollsters making definitive predications at this point in time. Regardless of their experience or expertise, they are seriously understating the uncertainty of this electoral cycle. We believe a healthy dose of skepticism is fundamental right now."

The evidence was there. Yes, Clinton led in most of the polls. But some election-based models pointed to a Trump victory. Additionally, the polls showed Trump leading Clinton on the most important issue – the economy. These very basic indicators should have given everyone pause. But, this is not to say that all analysts ignored the full sweep of evidence before them. For instance, Nate Silver's model gave Clinton a relatively low victory probability, at 71%, compared to most other forecasters. This was a step in the right direction. Yet it still sent the wrong signal about Trump's chances.

Instances like the 2016 US elections are where the fox's ability to synthesize and process disparate data inputs into a summary judgment is vital. Beyond the fundamental warnings signs just mentioned, such as election modeling and Trump's strength on the economy, there were other pieces of evidence to integrate. A fox would have recognized that this was a disruptive election, that a large swathe of the population believed that the system was broken, and that they no longer believed that parties and politicians were much concerned about people like them.

Think about it. Analysts were confronted with contradictory evidence and a context that favored the outsider candidate. Setting aside the nuances of how a fox might have interpreted the aforementioned evidence, it is difficult to see in retrospect how Clinton could ever have been deemed a 99% absolute favorite. She simply was not strong enough on all the most important inputs. Triangulating the evidence would have been far more instructive than just looking at the polls.

CONFIRMATION BIAS AND CHERRY-PICKING

Pundits can get predictions wrong for reasons other than relying on a single input. They can also go astray because they introduce bias into their selection or assessment of the data. We often call this confirmation bias, or rationalizing data to fit our beliefs to justify the outcome we expect.

Confirmation bias can be difficult to overcome. In fact, presenting counterarguments can actually make people cling to their erroneous beliefs that much more tightly. Research shows that partisans become more entrenched in their world view when confronted with contradictory facts.[4] In some cases, people only see what they want to see.

To illustrate what confirmation bias looks like in practice, let's once again consider the 2016 US presidential election. As we already mentioned, the polling evidence strongly suggested that Clinton would beat Trump, but other evidence contradicted this thesis. Take, again, Abramovitz, Young/El Dash, and Norpoth's models suggesting a Trump victory.

And yet, the perception that Trump couldn't win held on stubbornly. This despite the fact that the arguments against his chances were more subjective than objective, centering around his appearance and provocative persona. The core argument boiled down to sentiments like, "He is just a TV personality," or "He has no experience in politics," or "He looks ridiculous," or, "He is not presidential." In contrast, Clinton's public personality and her gravitas, particularly as compared to Trump's frequent buffoonery and coarse manner of speech, corresponded far better with the traditional profile of an American president.

Even Abramovitz cast doubt on the results of his own statistical model, telling *Vox* on August 17, 2016, "What the model basically says is that if both parties had nominated mainstream candidates, the GOP would be a slight favorite. ***But, of course, Donald Trump is far from a mainstream candidate.***" This is the power of confirmation bias. The pundits too were incredulous that someone like Trump could win.

GQ editor Jim Nelson perhaps put it best, opining on October 18, 2016: "He [Trump] will lose this election badly, by which I mean poorly. Exceedingly poorly. The bad news: After he does so, he will take his wounded pride and his seething, tiny-fingered resentment to war against this country."

Many Republicans could not conceive of a Trump victory. As an unnamed GOP insider told *Politico* in August 2016, "Trump is underperforming so comprehensively.... It would take video evidence of a smiling Hillary drowning a litter of puppies while terrorists surrounded her with chants of 'Death to America.'" Such cognitive cherry-picking happens all the time. We often take data and force fit it to our desired narrative.

Even one of the authors of this book (Clifford Young) responsible for the "salad bowl model," which gave near 50/50 election odds, could not resist the onslaught of the polls at the time. Here, the tone of his analysis increasingly became more Clinton the closer to election day.

[4] Lodge & Tabor (2013) *The Rationalizing Voter*. Cambridge Press.

TEST CASE: 2019 ARGENTINA PASO ELECTION

Take another example – the 2019 Argentine Open Simultaneous and Mandatory Primaries (PASO). The Argentine presidential PASO election is not dissimilar to the US primaries, the distinction being that every candidate runs on the ballot at the same time. This case shows that even when the polls tell the correct story directionally, the experts can still miss the mark.

Mauricio Macri, then the sitting president, was considered the favorite. He looked and sounded the part, he had studied at all the right schools, circulated in all the right circles and was the market darling. As president, he had implemented market-friendly policies, ending economic uncertainty. From a utilitarian market perspective, what was there not to like?

In contrast, Macri's primary challenger, the populist Alberto Fernandez, was the new face of the Justicialist Party, or the main branch of the influential Peronist Party. But, he was a relatively unknown, as a chief of staff closely linked to Nestor Kirchner, the former populist party president. Fernandez did not "look" like the ideal candidate. Yet, despite this, the PASO polls leaned slightly in Fernandez's favor. But the official narrative held that Macri could eke out a win nevertheless and was in fact narrowing the gap. On the PASO election day, however, Fernandez won by 16 points. Later, Macri became the first Argentine incumbent to lose their bid for reelection.

Disbelief followed in the aftermath of this upset. Jimena Blanco, research director and chief analyst at the global risk intelligence company Verisk Maplecroft, captured the general sentiment by telling CNBC, "There is total shock on both sides." The markets agreed. The peso closed 15% weaker at 53.5 cents per US dollar after plunging 30% to a record low earlier in the day.

So, what happened? Well, the analysts cherry-picked the data points that suited their views and discarded the ones that didn't. Yes, it's true that the polls showed a tightening race and that historical precedent favored the incumbent. But all the hard evidence pointed to an opposite outcome. First, there was the floundering economy, paired with the fact that the economy was the number one issue of the day. Then there was Macri's poor performance on the economy in the polls and his declining approval ratings. All these signaled that Macri might be in for a loss on election day.

But, as mentioned earlier, Macri fit the stereotype of the "ideal" candidate better than Fernandez. This led the analysts to give an outsized weight to the narrowing gap in the polls as it mapped to what they wanted and expected to see.

AVAILABILITY AND HERDING BIAS

Here, we want to address two additional biases that can affect the pollster's ability to make accurate forecasts. Both are related to confirmation bias *but* should be thought of as distinct.

The first is availability bias. We tend to over-rely on the information that's readily available in our memory. Information that's easier to recall has greater bearing on our perceptions and decisions. This means that more recent information, such as the latest news story, can have an outsize impact on our opinions. In addition, we judge the frequency, likelihood, or typicality of an event based on how easily it comes to mind. For example, people tend to overestimate the probability of plane and train crashes when they've recently heard about it in the media or when they've personally experienced it.[5] In reality, plane and train crashes are relatively rare, but they can seem more frequent when every crash is covered by the media.

Take the example of the 2016 US election. Most of the polls had Clinton in the lead, and, in real-time, it seemed that every day another poll showed the same results. A media environment saturated with the seeming inevitability of Clinton's win was the context in which the pundits were operating. There was a strong gravitational force pulling analyses toward a Clinton victory. We know; we felt it too. Even we who had the benefit of a 50/50 election model felt the pull. The onslaught of the polls was too much to stay the bold outlier. By the last week, we had Clinton as a strong favorite.

The second is "herding bias." On an individual basis, we tend to imitate what others are doing and adopt consensus views while ignoring or discarding information that conflicts with established opinions.[6] There is strong social pressure to conform in daily life. When forming their opinions, people will generally look to opinion leaders, or people that they regard as experts or reliable sources, assuming that these people are better informed than they are. For example, evidence indicates that if a politician shifts her views on a policy, her followers will also shift their views, rather than change their preferred leader.[7] Think of our infrastructure example in Chapter 3. The herding behavior has also been studied extensively among financial investors. Investors will follow the lead of other investors.[8]

---

[5] Baddeley et al. (2015) *Memory*. Psychology Press.

[6] See Baddeley et al. (2015) *Memory*. Psychology Press; Banerjee (1992) "A Simple Model of Herd Behavior," in *The Quarterly Journal of Economics* Vol. CVII, Issue 3, pp. 797–817.

[7] Lenz (2012) *Follow the Leader?: How Voters Respond to Politicians' Policies and Performance*. University of Chicago Press.

[8] Bikhchandani & Sharma (2000) "Herd Behavior in Financial Markets: A Review," in *IMF Working Paper* March 2000.

Herding bias affects pollsters as well, and particularly so during election season. No one wants to be the one polling outfit who was wildly off the mark. Pollsters will often watch the market average and, if their findings are at variance, will put their "thumb on the scale" to ensure that their results generally reflect what other pollsters have found.[9]

However, when pollsters choose to adjust their findings, they are doing so in response to past results that, by definition, are retroactive. Public opinion can evolve in the weeks and days leading up to an election. By adjusting polls to match the rest of the herd, pollsters produce "statistical artifacts" as Bishop would say. Herding can distort the true picture of an election. This especially is the case when certain reputable pollsters become the herding reference even though they are biased themselves.

Herding is one of the reasons why some analysts think the polls got the PASO election wrong. Others suspect that pollsters in the 2016 US presidential election were also guilty of regressing to the mean of the market. Proving that herding has occurred, however, is difficult to do. That's because few pollsters will admit to having fiddled with their results.

BINARY AND PROBABILISTIC THINKING

Binary thinking and probabilistic thinking can be summarized as the difference between thinking in black and white, and thinking in shades of gray. At a certain level, binary thinking can be advantageous. We need to be able to make quick, snap, either/or decisions. Without this ability, we would be too paralyzed by indecision to perform basic activities, like buying groceries or choosing which shirt to wear for the day.

But with issues that call for greater analytic complexity, thinking in a black or white manner leads to errors in judgment and prediction. It replaces uncertainty with absolutes, even though there are always contingencies and various shades of gray.

For instance, a binary thought process might lead to absolute statements like, "Trump will win the election"; or, "Russia will win the war in Ukraine"; or "Trump will not be impeached." In reality, outcomes come down to conditions and context.

The opposite of binary thinking is probabilistic thinking.[10] When engaging in probabilistic thinking, we ascribe a range of likelihoods

[9] Silber (2014) "Here's Proof Some Pollsters Are Putting a Thumb on the Scale," in *538*, November 14, 2014.

[10] Johansen (2020) *Full-Spectrum Thinking: How to Escape Boxes in a Post-Categorical Future.* Berrett-Koehler Publishers.

to outcomes. As example, pollsters will apply probabilities to a given election.

Probabilistic thinking is important for a few reasons. First, it allows decision-makers to plan for various contingencies. If, in the 2016 election cycle, Clinton was thought to have had only a 60% chance of winning, then one would have begun planning for the possibility of a Trump presidency as well. A 40% chance is still quite high. By contrast, there is a lesser need to prepare for a Trump administration if Clinton has a 90% chance of winning. Second, uncertainty forces the analyst to consistently stress test their assumptions. If something appears to have a high level of certainty, there is less incentive to seek new evidence or alternatives explanations. In moments of uncertainty, human beings become much more vigilant. As analysts of public opinion, we too should be vigilant by continually challenging assumptions in the face of new evidence.

Do people think in probabilities? This has long been a worry of political risk and intelligence experts.[11] In our experience, people do a pretty good job of understanding qualitative likelihood categories (see Table 8.1). Here, we see that people ascribe higher probabilities to the "very likely" label and lower probabilities to "not at all likely" label. But there is a high degree of variability around the mean. The pollster should keep this fuzziness in mind when communicating to decision-makers. Humans are imprecise predictive thinkers.

Such probabilistic thinking is now commonplace among election forecasters. It also has utility for the intelligence community, political risk firms, business, science, financial institutions, and many other domains. And probabilistic thinking has applications for a wide range of sociopolitical outcomes. Ultimately, thinking about the world in shades of gray is

Table 8.1 *Respondent declared numeric probability for each qualitative level of likelihood*

	Mean (%)	Standard Deviation (%)
Very likely	61	30
Somewhat likely	54	24
Not very likely	34	23
Not at all likely	27	25

Source: Ipsos Poll October 11, 2022; sample size of 1,028.

[11] See Friedman & Zeckhauser (2014) "Handling and Mishandling Estimative Probability: Likelihood, Confidence, and the Search for Bin Laden," in *Intelligence and National Security*, Routledge.

a virtue. It more accurately captures the full spectrum of possibilities and allows us to adjust accordingly.

BRINGING IT ALL TOGETHER

So, how do we minimize the aforementioned biases in our thinking? We need to take a page from the fox's playbook and **triangulate** – a strategy that incorporates multiple data sources and approaches.[12] Relying on a single source of data is a recipe for prediction disaster.

Let's take a hypothetical election. In this case, triangulation may incorporate political and economic variables (e.g., GDP, incumbency, consumer confidence, approval ratings) with multiple polls that have been aggregated. We'll cover this in more depth in the next chapter on election prediction. While these models tend to be more complicated, they overcome the weaknesses of relying on a single data input.

Table 8.2 is a good example of triangulation, and a hypothetical example of an exercise that public opinion analysts might perform when attempting to assess the full range of possible outcomes. First, see how we combine different inputs into one visual perspective. This allows us to see the variability in the outcome. Second, observe how we assign probabilities to each of the inputs. Pollsters commonly consider a number of inputs to predict future outcomes. See how the probabilities vary according to the input. This captures the degree of uncertainty in the face of various contingencies. The key here is that we are not falling prey to binary thinking **but** recognizing that the world is complex.

Table 8.2 *Hypothetical triangulation – Clinton's probability of winning relative to Trump based on key inputs*

Weight factor	Input 1 Model (%)	Input 2 Polls (%)	Input 3 Economy (%)	Input 4 Heuristic (%)	Predicted probability (%)
Equal weight	40	90	52	40	56
Unequal weights	40	90	52	40	69

---

[12] Tetlock & Gardner (2015) *Super Forecasting: The Art and Science of Prediction.* Broadway Book. New York; Silver (2012) *The Signal and the Noise: Why So Many Predictions Fail – but Some Don't.* Penguin Books.

Beware of confirmation bias and triangulate! Knowing that such bias exists can help check it as we look for alternative explanations and new evidence. As shown in Table 8.2, some of the four hypothetical inputs favor Clinton more; others less. Ultimately, we must come to a summary judgment. To do this, we simply averaged the four inputs. But, in practice, pollsters often weight the inputs differentially given their confidence in the actual input.

For instance, when weighted equally, our predicted probability of a Clinton win comes to 56%. In contrast, in the unequal weighting line, we give the polls a weight of .55; all other inputs received a weight of .15 each. With this, see how the predicted outcome changes to 69%.

But which weighting scheme is the right one? That is where the pollster needs to make a judgment call. We suggest playing around with the table, ascribing different weights to different inputs and treating the range of results as a **sensitivity analysis**.

A triangulation table should have the last word on the matter, even if it contradicts the analyst's expectations. Too often, analysts will put their "thumbs on the scale" to align results with personal expectations. **Doing this only re-introduces your bias!** Let the triangulation table have the last word. Pollsters should take heed and remember to set their own biases aside.

9

Triangulating Election Prediction

Now that we better understand the effect of cognitive biases on prediction and have methods to minimize them, let's focus on elections as a special case of public opinion–based prediction. ***Here, it is all about convergence.*** Candidates must be aligned with the needs of public opinion if they are to have any chance of winning. It really is that simple conceptually.

Forecasting elections is a high-risk, high-reward endeavor. Today's polling rock star is tomorrow's has-been. It is a high-pressure gig. Public opinion polls have been a staple of election forecasting for almost ninety years. But single-source predictions are an imperfect means of forecasting, as we detailed in the preceding chapter. One of the most telling examples of this in recent years is the 2016 US presidential election. In this chapter, we will examine public opinion as an election forecast input. We organize election prediction into three broad buckets: (1) heuristics models, (2) poll-based models, and (3) fundamentals models (see Figure 9.1).

The focus here is not on the specific statistical techniques used in prediction, but on analytic frameworks that are easily accessible to all. Throughout, we will use the 2016 US presidential election to illustrate our methods.

HEURISTIC MODELS

By heuristic, we mean a shortcut or practical method to solve a problem. Pollsters often use such assumptions as a "rule of thumb" when handicapping elections. Some examples of heuristic lines of thinking include:

- "A sitting president must have an approval rating of at least 45% in order to be reelected."
- "A bad economy is bad for the incumbent."
- "This is a 'throw the bums out' year."
- "This is the year of *the common touch*."

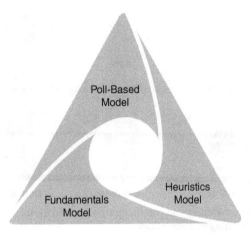

Figure 9.1 Election prediction triangle

Considering the above examples, one might feel an impulse to discard heuristic thinking as merely anecdotal. But, in our experience, these seemingly impulsive, purely intuitive insights actually do have roots in empirical reality. However, relying on heuristics alone is unwise. We typically employ them in conjunction with other models in order to stress test our assumptions. But, such simplifying rules do in fact serve as important analytic context for the pollster.

Change Election Heuristic

Perhaps the most common heuristic employed by pollsters is a simple framework that classifies elections as **change, continuity,** or **middling** (Graph 9.1). We can think of elections as existing on such a continuum.

Continuity elections are ones in which the electorate wants "more of the same." These can be characterized by high government or presidential approval ratings, belief that the country is on the "right track," a relative dearth of scandals or an economy that is doing well. Such elections are more likely to favor the government candidate, or the party of the candidate who already holds office. In these instances, the government candidate has a high likelihood of winning, generally 90% or more.

In change elections, people are seeking to "throw the bums out." Here, things are going poorly, whether on the political or economic front, or both. In such scenarios, the government candidate only wins about one in five times. Finally, middling elections sit somewhere between change and

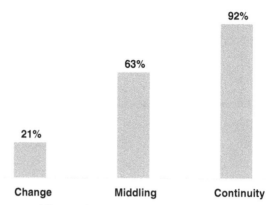

Graph 9.1 Change, middling, and continuity elections and the likelihood of a government candidate winning by election type
Source: Estimated from model detailed in Young and El Dash 2015.[1]

continuity. Other factors, such as incumbency and campaign effectiveness, have a larger role to play here. In these cases, the government wins about 63% of the time.

The 2016 US presidential election fell into the middling camp. The economy was growing at 2.9%, Obama's approval ratings hover at around 45% and just over 30% of the public believed that the country was headed in the right direction (another commonly asked polling question to gauge public opinion). So, by these metrics, 2016 was a middling election, one in which other factors like incumbency and campaign effectiveness would hold greater weight. No slam dunks for Clinton.

Approval Heuristic

Approval ratings are yet another commonly used heuristic. The logic goes something like this, "If the approval numbers are strong, a sitting government has a good chance of winning." Approval ratings in the high 40s often are thought of as the rubric for success. But is there merit to this? The short is answer is "yes," approval ratings are strongly correlated with electoral success. We know this both academically and empirically. Take Table 9.1 as a proof point.

---

[1] Here, we define change elections with an approval rating of 0 to 39; middling elections from 40 to 54; and continuity elections from 55 or more. The data comes from 267 elections in 35 countries. See Young & El-Dash (2015) "Election Forecasting in Low Information Environments," at the 70th Annual AAPOR Conference in Hollywood Florida.

Table 9.1 *Likelihood of a government candidate winning by level of approval rating*

Approval rating	Probability of victory (%)
41	42
42	45
43	48
44	51
45	54
46	57
47	60
48	63
49	66
50	69

Source: Estimated from model detailed in Young and El Dash (2015)

Here, two important takeaways. First, the higher the approval rating, the greater the likelihood that the government candidate will win. And second, an approval rating of 44% is the tipping point. Above this threshold, the odds become more robust for the sitting government. Below, less so.

Leading up to the 2016 election, Obama hovered in the mid- to high-40s for most of the year. By this metric, Clinton had a better than 50/50 chance but was never the absolute favorite. This gives us a very different perspective on the election than what was being signaled by the polls.

The Economy Heuristics

The performance of the economy is often used as a proxy for future electoral success. The logic is simple. Given the importance most people ascribe to their fundamental economic well-being, they will pivot with the relative strength of the economy. If the economy is doing well, the government candidate should do well on election day. But if the economy is suffering, the opposition is favored. A large body of scientific literature reinforces that there is a positive correlation between economic performance and electoral success of the party-in-power.[2] By our estimate, economic variables account for between 20% and 30% of the variance in electoral outcomes.

---

[2] Lewis-Beck & Stegmaier (2000) "Economic Determinants of Electoral Outcomes," in *Annual Review of Political Science* Vol. 3, pp. 183–219.

However, the pollster typically employs this heuristic in a more qualitative, ordinal way. Much of the analysis focuses on GDP growth, but metrics like unemployment, inflation, gas prices, the cost of basic foodstuff, and exchange rate fluctuations can be used to handicap elections. In this book, we are not looking to use statistical models to predict future elections, although there is a vast scientific literature on them. Instead, when it comes to economic performance, the pollster is most concerned with directional "cause and effect." Distilled down to its simplest form, this sort of line of inquiry might look like, "Is the economy doing well or not". If the answer is yes, then the sitting government stands to benefit.

Take Table 9.2. Here, we have identified the key economic metrics that are shown to have an impact on electoral outcomes. The scientific evidence shows that economic turbulence will have a strong, negative impact on perceptions of an incumbent government. Meanwhile, a good economy will help *but* less so than a downturn hurts.[3] Drastic changes in prices and exchange rates typically translate quickly to depressed electoral chances. This effect is especially strong in emerging markets. GDP growth and unemployment rates are slower moving but can set the context for an election, that is, one that is more or less favorable for the incumbent.

In 2016, the economy was on a steady, if unremarkable, course. Inflation was low, unemployment had been declining since the Great Recession in 2009, and GDP growth was at 2.9%. In light of this, the economy would in theory have been neither a significant help to Trump nor a hindrance to

Table 9.2 *Economic indicators in 2016*

Economic metric	Short-term impact	2016 context	Relative to benchmark
GDP	Low	2.9%	Average
Inflation	High	1.3%	Average
Unemployment	Medium	4.7%	Average
Gas prices	High	$2.22	Average
Exchange rate fluctuation	High	Dollar stability	Expected

Sources: BLS, EIA, BEA

---

[3] Mueller (1970) *War, Presidents, and Public Opinion*. John Wiley & Sons; Lewis-Beck & Stegmaier (2000) "Economic Determinants of Electoral Outcomes," in *Annual Review of Political Science* Vol. 3, pp. 183–219.

Clinton. But, as we will explore in the next section, perceptions of the candidate's relative strength on the economy had a part to play in determining the ultimate outcome of the election.

Main Problem Heuristic

The main problem heuristic is another pollster standby. Remember our **multi-attribute model** in Chapter 3. Here, the logic goes that candidates strongest on the main issue are much more likely to win the election than those who aren't. This is typically the battle cry of any campaign – "We must own the agenda." And if the campaign finds itself weak on the most important issue, this shifts to – "We must change the narrative."

Why? Because, as discussed, what the public wants largely defines politics in democracies. Table 9.3 lays this out.

Concretely, in 1,000 simulations of 10 US presidential elections from 1972 to 2008, Armstrong and Scott found that the candidate strongest on the main issue wins about 87% of the time.[4] The predictive power of the main problem increases when taking incumbency into consideration. To simplify things, we employ a more intuitive 85% number. There is always a lot of judgment in what pollsters do. We will examine its application later in this chapter.

Table 9.3 *Some examples of the main problem heuristic*

Election	Main issue	Candidate perceived as strongest on the main issue	Winner
US 2020	COVID	Biden	Biden
US 2016	Economy	Trump	Trump
Brazil 2018	Corruption	Bolsonaro	Bolsonaro
Brazil 2022	Social inequality	Lula	Lula
Mexico 2018	Corruption and crime	Obrador	Obrador
Argentina 2019	Economy	Fernandez	Fernandez

Source: Ipsos Polling

---

[4] See Graefe & Armstrong (2011) "Predicting Elections from the Most Important Issue: A Test of the Take-the-Best Heuristic," in *Journal of Behavioral Decision Making* Vol. 25, Issue 1, pp. 41–48.

The main problem of the day can be identified via most political tracking polls. A standard question might read as, "In your opinion, what is the most important problem facing the nation today?" **Given the utility and predictive ability of this question, we often say that if a pollster were only to have one question on their poll, it should be this one.**

From a forecasting perspective, main problem questions have two interesting properties. First, the rankings of issues or attributes generally are stable over time.[5] This is important to note because priorities can be treated as fixed in the short to medium term. Of course, as already mentioned in this book, events like terrorist attacks, pandemics and economic downturns can alter the public agenda. But extreme events tend to be the exception, not the rule. And once they have occurred, their effect can be roughly anticipated.

Second, main problem questions are correlated with real-world outcomes. For instance, whether it is thriving or ailing, the economy is often seen as one of the topmost issues of the day. But when it flounders, it becomes all the more salient of an issue. Meanwhile, a more secondary issue, like terrorism or national security, can spike in importance following an attack, and so on. Knowing this is important because it allows the pollster to anticipate changes to the issue agenda as the reality on the ground shifts. We saw this with the ebb of COVID as the main issue and the onset of the inflationary regime in 2022.

In our opinion, main problem questions are critical to understanding where public opinion stands at any given moment in time and to what extent political and economic actors are convergent with those needs. Again, political actors must meet public opinion where it is if they are to have any hope of success at the ballot box. Given the importance of the main problems, pollsters spend a considerable amount of time and energy ensuring that they have the correct rank ordering. Normally, inputs from multiple polls are collated and compared. Such vetting might also include the administration of different main problem questions and engaging with focus groups to ensure consistency and stability of the rank order.

In 2016, the main issue was the economy (Table 9.4). This had been largely the case since the Great Recession. But on this measure, Donald Trump was perceived as stronger than Hillary Clinton, both at the national level and, critically, in the key swing states. Although the economy was humming

---

[5] Young & Zeimer (2018) "Understanding the Decision-Making Process: The Multi-Attribute Model" in Ipsos Cognitive Battlefield Series; Wlezein & Jennings (2011) "Distinguishing between Most Important Issues and Problems?" in *Public Opinion Quarterly* Vol. 75, pp. 545–555; Krosnick (1988) "The Role of Attitude Importance in Social Evaluation: A Study of Policy Preferences, Presidential Candidate Evaluations, and Voting Behavior" in *Journal of Personality and Social Psychology* Vol. 55, Issue 2, pp. 196–210.

Table 9.4 *Main problem and priority
leader, 2016 preelection polling*

	Main problem	Leader	Trump–Clinton spread
Arizona	Economy	Trump	+12
Florida	Economy	Trump	+4
Michigan	Economy	Trump	+4
North Carolina	Economy	Trump	+5
Pennsylvania	Economy	Trump	+2
Ohio	Economy	Trump	+5
National average	Economy	Trump	+2

Source: Reuters/Ipsos 2016

along just fine under Obama, Republican candidates have historically been perceived as stronger on the economy. Advantage here to Trump.

Poll-based Models

Single Polls

The preelection poll has been the workhorse of election prediction for almost a century. Polls are used to determine relative support for each candidate in a given race. The most common approach is to ask respondents their voting or behavioral intent when it comes to a list of candidates. Pollsters often call this a ballot, trail-heat, or horse race question. The Ipsos 2016 post-convention question reads:

If the presidential election were being held today and the candidates were [rotate candidates], for whom would you vote?

- Hillary Clinton and Tim Kaine, the Democrats
- Donald Trump and Mike Pence, the Republicans
- Gary Johnson and Bill Weld of the Libertarian Party
- Jill Stein and Ajamu Baraka of the Green Party

At its most basic level, the ballot question itself is a model, one linked to the stated behavioral intent of the respondent. Behavioral intent questions are employed in many domains to predict future behaviors.[6] But such models

---

[6] Fishbein & Ajzen (1975) *Belief, Attitude, Intention, and Behavior: An Introduction to Theory and Research.* Reading, MA: Addison-Wesley; Ajzen (1991) "The Theory of Planned Behavior," in *Organizational Behavior & Human Decision Processes* Vol. 50, Issue 2, pp. 179–211.

make two key assumptions. First assumption is that stated intent is correlated with actual behavior. Second assumption is that the poll is robustly measuring the phenomenon in question. Let's investigate these assumptions.

Assumption One: Intent versus Practice

Behavioral intent questions assume that there is a link between intent and behavior.[7] But in our experience, there are two cases when this link can be attenuated or broken. The first is when barriers impede or block the intent–behavior link. In this instance, a given behavioral outcome is a function of three variables: intention, barriers, and attitudes.

By intention, we mean an inclination to take a certain action. In the case of the 2016 election, intention would center around voter preference for Clinton or Trump. Pollsters measure this via the ballot question, as detailed earlier. Attitudes would consist of the favorable or unfavorable opinion of each candidate. Meanwhile, barriers are physical or psychology limitations that might impede an otherwise willing actor from engaging in a given behavior. Examples of barriers include "I've never voted for a Republican in my life." Or, "I don't have transportation to the polling station." Or, "I can't get time off work." Or, "I have to cross dangerous territory to vote."

Here, we believe that the likely voter model, as described in Chapter 5, represents a special case of "the barriers to action problem." Empirically, we find that those who vote have greater motivations to do so than those who don't. This stands to reason. In practice, utilizing likely voter models implicitly captures these barriers and provides a better scale of probable outcomes given certain contingencies. Likely voter models are not a cure-all for the problem of barriers. But they can help minimize surprises come election day for the pollster.

The second fatal flaw of the ballot question are timing effects. The further out from an election, the less accurately such questions capture behavioral intentions. Early polling can be muddled. Consider the US primaries, in which many Americans may not have even heard of some of the candidates on the ballot. For many people, elections simply seem too abstract and distant, at least until election day draws closer. At which time, people start paying closer attention. We call this phenomenon "reduced issue salience," or "diminished election salience" regarding elections specifically.

As a proof point, see Table 9.5. The polling error is about five larger time larger (7.9% vs. 1.7%) a year out as compared to one week before election

---

[7] Ajzen (1991) "The Theory of Planned Behavior," in *Organizational Behavior & Human Decision Processes* Vol. 50, Issue 2, pp. 179–211.

Table 9.5 *Accuracy of poll prediction as a function of time from the election (measured by average absolute difference)*

Time before election	Absolute average difference	
	US presidential (%)	International executive (%)
One week	1.7	3.2
One month	2.7	3.6
Two months	3.8	4.0
Three months	4.8	4.8
Six months	5.8	5.8
Nine months	6.9	6.4
One year	7.9	6.8

Source: Young (2020) "Beware of Horse Race Polls," in *Cliff's Take.* Ipsos. August 2020

day. Time matters when it comes to polling accuracy. Why? As discussed, the intent–behavior link becomes stronger as people gain more information about their choices. People are just not as motivated to become informed about a distant event as they are to learn about one that is right around the corner. Reduced issue salience can often lead to polls being more variable and noisy at the early stages of an electoral cycle. Observers should be cautious when attempting to interpret the early polling. In practice, pollsters worth their salt tend to give less weight to the earlier polls and more to the later ones.

Navigating the polling cycle comes down to the importance of assessing multiple pieces of evidence and then determining how confident we can be about each of them. Hold this thought. We will come back to it in greater detail later in this chapter.

Assumption Two: Failing to Account for Error and Bias

Assuming that a given poll is flawless is yet another trap that the pollster can fall into. Polls are subject to both sampling and non-sampling error, as we discussed in the second section. On the non-sampling side, any given poll might be biased due to coverage bias, nonresponse bias, measurement error, or estimation error. The pollster employs a variety of methods to minimize such errors. When considering sampling error alone, the margin of error of a standard 1,000 respondent survey will be plus or minus 3%. And five out of every hundred polls are complete outliers. This, however, does not account for other forms of bias and error that can be introduced into polling results.

The pollster can overcome the statistical limitations of the polls in a number of ways. As we discussed in greater detail in Chapter 6, poll aggregation is one such approach. Its principal benefits include providing a larger sample, thus minimizing sampling error. It also incorporates a broader range of methodologies as aggregators typically include polls from multiple polling firms, all of whom bring their own "special sauce" to the process. We often call the biases of a single poll or cluster of polls conducted by a single polling firm "house effects."[8] These can arise from any number of pollster decisions regarding sampling design, weighting, questionnaire design, interviewer protocols, and so on.

Simple aggregation of the polls can wash out these effects. Forecasters might also use statistical techniques to account for the unique effect of a given polling firm in order to smooth out the data further. But polling aggregation also has its limitations. It can fail due to systemic, market-wide polling errors as already detailed in Chapter 6.

We've already discussed the Greek referendum polling miss, but consider also the 2016 US election. This miss was attributed to an underrepresentation of Trump's supporters in the polls, a demographic that tends to be more rural, white, and less likely to be college-educated.[9] Other recent polling misses indicate similar biases among key constituencies. But the main takeaway here is that wholesale deviations can, and often do, happen. This is why the triangulated approach beats out a single input.

Turning Aggregated Polls into Probabilities

Single polls are only able to capture candidate vote share, which is a very deterministic summary of the situation – Like Clinton will beat Trump. Building from aggregated polls, however, can provide an opening for pollsters to assess the win probability for each candidate. This is only possible when there are many polls to aggregate.

Let's take a look at the aggregate polling leading up to the 2016 US presidential election. In Graph 9.2, we estimated the relative probabilities of a Clinton or Trump victory using a technique known as *Markov Chain Monte Carlo Simulation* (MCMC). Many forecasters, including the leading

---

[8] Jackman (2005) "Pooling the Polls over an Election Campaign," in *Australian Journal of Political Science* Vol. 40, Issue 4, pp. 499–517.

[9] Kennedy et al. (2017) "An Evaluation of 2016 Election Polls in the U.S.," in APPOR Ad Hoc Committee on 2016 Election Polling.

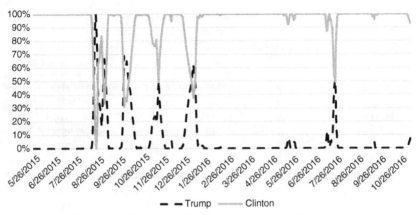

Graph 9.2 Probability of Clinton and Trump victory using poll-based aggregation
Source: Polls from RealClearPolitics

lights of the field, such as Nate Silver, Nate Cohn, G. Elliott Morris, and Neale El-Dash, employ similar methods.

The grey solid line represents Hillary Clinton's odds of winning and the dotted black Donald Trump's odds of winning. As the chart shows, the probabilities bounce around, but Hillary has a clear advantage over Trump in the year and a half leading up to the election. By August, Clinton's chances of winning hovered in the 90s.

Does this mean a pollster needs to hire a statistician or their equivalent to estimate the win probabilities? Our response is, "No, not necessarily." The aforementioned example is a fancy way of doing simple counts. The logic to poll-based probability estimation is very simple.

$$\Pr(v) = \frac{\sum_{i p_i^C > p_i^T}^{N} 0}{n}$$

Here, let's think of each poll as a trial heat, or clinical trial. First, we need to determine how many polls were conducted, and, of these, how many had Clinton in the lead. Put mathematically, the probability of victory of a given candidate $\Pr(v)$ is a function of the total number of polls in favor of that candidate ($p_i^C > p_i^T$) over the total number of polls (n). Let's walk through a concrete example (Table 9.6).

In 2016, there were a total of 136 polls in the months of August to November at the national level. Of these, 128 were in favor of Hillary. Put differently, 94% of the polls had Clinton in the lead. Pollsters take this

Table 9.6 *Polls in the months of August to November 2016*

	Polls with Trump lead	Polls with Clinton lead	Total number of polls	Percent with Clinton lead (%)
National	8	128	136	94
Arizona	24	21	45	47
Florida	19	61	80	76
Michigan	1	48	49	98
North Carolina	15	54	69	78
Pennsylvania	4	67	71	94
Wisconsin	0	44	44	100
Total	71	423	494	86

Source: RealClearPolitics

frequency and think of it as a probability; this is a Bayesian heuristic.[10] If we were to rely on this logic alone, we would have believed that Clinton had a 94% chance of winning. Many of the aforementioned swing states showed a similar likelihood of a Clinton victory. At Ipsos, we have employed such simple counts in a number of instances. Some examples include the 2016 Republican primary, the 2016 US presidential election, and the 2020 US presidential election.[11] Again, pollsters can arrive at a rough probability simply based on the poll count without the employment of sophisticated statistical models. But, even just using the example of the 2016 US election alone, we can see how widely the poll-based model can swing off the mark.

FUNDAMENTAL MODELS

We can't let statisticians off the hook entirely, however. Another common approach used by pollsters are fundamentals models to predict elections. Such models aggregate past elections and correlate their characteristics with future electoral outcomes. Many of these models employ linear regression or other similar statistical techniques.

$$Vote = Political + Economic$$

---

[10] McElreath (2007) *Statistical Rethinking: A Bayesian Course with Examples in R and STAN.* CRC Press.

[11] Young & Jackson (2016) "Math: Donald Trump Has 90-Percent Chance of Winning GOP Nomination," in Reuters Opinion 2018 February; Young & Clark (2016) "Even Odds for Trump & Clinton: Is Trump a 'Spoiler' or a 'Game-Changer'?" in RealClearPolitics, June 2016; Young (2020) "Contradictory Signals," in *Cliff's Take* Ipsos September 2020.

Fundamentals models can be depicted as vote (V) being a function of political (P) and economic (E) variables. Table 9.7 shows that both political and economic variables can be quite varied from model to model. Political variables may include the party-of-the president, approval ratings, incumbency status, or the number of years in power. In contrast, economic variables may include unemployment, consumer confidence, personal finances, inflation, or GDP. As a whole, fundamental models use a combination of public opinion and non-opinion inputs. As such, they are less subject to the inherent noise of the polls.

In Table 9.7, we detail some of the more prominent models employed in the United States today. There are a number of key takeaways to be gleaned from them. First, as noted earlier, the models employ a variety of economic and political inputs. Some use non-survey inputs exclusively; others use public opinion inputs exclusively and most some combination of the two. The use of multiple models together is a form of triangulation. Ultimately, pollsters should think of the fundamentals model as a kind of triangulation in that it combines public opinion and nonpublic opinion inputs.

Second, such models do a good job of accurately forecasting election outcomes. What's more, they arrive at such forecasts faster than the polls or polling aggregation models. For instance, using political and economic data from the second quarter of the election year has a strong record of accurately predicting election results. Compare this to the single input trail-heat poll that only becomes more accurate the closer it gets to the election.

Third, these models assume that past behavior will predict future behavior. But this isn't always the case, as in the case of disruptive elections. Fundamental models are limited in their ability to predict disruptive elections as past behavior is not indicative of future behavior in these cases.

Fourth, fundamental models are very context dependent. Yes, we see that six of the nine models picked Clinton as a winner and were close to the actual vote share. But, remember that Clinton actually won the popular vote by 2.9 million votes, capturing 48% of voters nationwide to Trump's 46%. So, in a sense, these models were "right," though they missed a certain fine-grained nuance. That's because this outcome reflects just the composite picture, not outcomes at the state level. Due to the quirks of the Electoral College, the national vote is not the deciding factor in the US presidential elections. Indeed, a handful of swing states generally carry the day. Ironically, Norpoth and Abramovitz had the right call for the wrong reasons. Both their models predicted a popular vote victory for Trump.

Table 9.7 *Summary of fundamental models, their details, and the 2016 US elections estimates*

	Variables	Comments	Estimated winner 2016	Diff (C-T)
Norpoth 1996	Primary Results, Party Vote, GNP, Inflation	US elections from 1912 to 2012	Trump	−2.5
Abramowitz 2016	GDP in Second Quarter, Approval Rating, Time in Office	US elections from 1948 to 2012	Trump	−3.4
Fair 1978	GNP, Time in Office, Incumbency	US elections 1912 to 2012	Clinton	1.1
Lewis-Beck and Tien 1996	Approval Ratings, GNP	US elections from 1948 to 2012	Clinton	1.1
Wlezien and Erikson 1996	Consumer Confidence, Approval Ratings	US elections from 1948 to 2012	Clinton	2.1
Campbell 1996	Trail Heat Poll, GDP	US elections from 1948 to 2012	Clinton	0.7
Holbrook 2012	Trail Heat Polls, Index of Approval Ratings, Satisfaction with personal finances	US elections from 1948 to 2012	Clinton	2.5
Linzer 2013	Trail Heat Polls, GDP, Incumbency, Time in Office	US elections from 1948 to 2012	Clinton	2
Young and El-Dash 2015	Approval Rating, Incumbency	267 elections in 35 countries	Trump	NA

So, how do we navigate this wrinkle? In the case of the US, the correct strategy would have been to run models for each state. To be parsimonious, this can be limited to the six or seven key swing states. Polling can get expensive and some states are a foregone conclusion. Remember that context really matters. *How the pollster might forecast one election might be different from another.* As always, the right tool should be used for the right job.

Lastly, these models are built on the aggregation of previous elections. However, the amount of data tends to be limited since most countries only have a handful of elections. For instance, polling data is available for just 18 of the past US presidential elections (since 1948 as this is the year of the advent of the modern poll). This results in a small sample size as well as the risk that outlier elections can have an outsized effect. In fact, fundamentals models tend to have an error rate of 20% in large part because of the small sample size.[12] This problem is only overcome by triangulation.

Fundamentals models have been employed in other countries such as France, the United Kingdom, Germany, New Zealand, and Mexico.[13] They use similar variables but are again context specific. To sidestep the inevitable pitfalls, the pollster should always do their homework before an election. This includes both an assessment of the context on the ground and the existing academic research.

CONTEXT-INDEPENDENT FUNDAMENTALS MODELS: THE SALAD BOWL

There are fundamentals models that do not depend on context or country. One such model, **which we call the salad bowl**, is based on 267 elections in 35 countries.[14] In this model, two variables are employed to predict the likelihood of the government candidate winning an election ($\Pr(v)$). They include – incumbency (I) and approval ratings (AR). Note that both variables are easily collected independent of context, that is, time and place.[15]

$$\Pr(v) = Incumbency + Approval\,Ratings$$

What can we learn from this model? First, that incumbents have almost a threefold advantage over successors. See how much lower the win probabilities are for the successor versus the incumbent. Second, the tipping point for a sitting president is an approval rating of 40%. This is where the odds become

[12] Young & Bernd (July, 2014). "The Rise of the Forecaster-Pundit: Big Data, Data Aggregation and the 2012 US Presidential Election." *Understanding Society*. Ipsos MORI.

[13] See Lewis-Beck & Dassonneville (2015) "Forecasting Elections in Europe: Synthetic Models," in *Research and Politics* January–March 2015, pp. 1–11; Belanger et al. (2022) "Which Historical Forecast Model Perform Best? An Analysis of 1965–2017 French Presidential Elections," in *PS: Political Science and Politics* Vol. 55, Issue 4, pp. 692–696; Stoetzer et al. (2019) "Forecasting Elections in Multiparty Systems: A Bayesian Approach Combining Polls and Fundamentals," in *Political Analysis* Vol. 27, Issue 2, pp. 255–262.

[14] See Young & El Dash (2015) "Election Forecasting in Low Information Environments," at the 70th Annual AAPOR Conference; Kennedy et al. (2017) "Improving Election Prediction Internationally," in *Science* Vol. 355, Issue 6324, pp. 515–520.

[15] The model can be depicted as a mathematical function where $\log(p\,/\,1 - p) = -10.06 + (3.11 * Incumbent) + (0.18 * Approval\,Ratings)$.

Table 9.8 *2016 US presidential election: Win probability, approval rating, and incumbency*

Government approval rating (%)	Incumbent win probability (%)	Successor win probability (%)
35	34	2
40	56	5
45	76	12
50	89	26
55	95	46
60	98	68

Source: Estimated using model from Young and El-Dash (2015)

Table 9.9 *Swing states in the 2016 US presidential election, approval ratings, and win probability*

	Approval rating of Obama (%)	Probability of a Clinton win (%)
Arizona	52	33
Florida	55	46
Michigan	48	19
North Carolina	51	29
Pennsylvania	55	46
Ohio	40	5

Source: Estimated using model from Young and El-Dash (2015)

better than 50/50. In the run-up to the 2016 election, Obama's approval ratings were in the high 40s. All this indicated rough waters for Clinton. As she was a successor not an incumbent (Table 9.8)

But, the national vote does not define the election in the United States. Instead, we need to look at metrics in the swing states. Here, Clinton's chances become vanishingly small. And this, ultimately, is what matters. In no swing state does the win probability break 50% (see Table 9.9).

PUTTING IT ALL TOGETHER

Now that we have learned about different election models, let's triangulate our evidence for the 2016 US election. Remember we have three families of models: (1) heuristics models; (2) poll-based models; and (3) fundamental models. It is important to bring them together to form a summary judgment (Table 9.10). As discussed earlier, the US election is not national in nature. Instead, it should be thought of as fifty separate state elections. To be successful, the pollster must employ the right tools to the problem. For this reason, we focus on the states. And, to keep our analysis even more targeted, we zero in on the swing states where the election will actually be decided.

We normally use the change heuristic as our initial gauge. This rule of thumb serves as an umbrella framework for both the approval and economy heuristics. As already discussed, the 2016 election was a middling election. This was an election that favored neither Clinton nor Trump, at least according to our change versus continuity criteria.

Once we get an initial take, we then look specifically at the main problem heuristic. Again, the candidate strongest on the main issue wins the election around 85% of the time. In the case of the 2016 elections, the main problem was the economy. For most of this electoral cycle, Trump led Clinton on this metric. As we noted, this lead was found nationally and in the key swing states. Here, the advantage goes to Trump.

Now on to our poll-based model. Here, we aggregate the polls and then turn them into a probability based on a simple count. Should we take the polls at the national level? Or the state? Or a combination for the two? This requires a judgment call. But given that the presidential race in the United States is effectively a series of state races via the electoral college, we will focus on the six swing state races. In total, there were 494 polls, 423 of which favored Clinton. This gave her an 86% chance of winning.

While the polls were decidedly in Clinton's favor, the fundamentals models told a more mixed story. As we saw earlier in this chapter, six out of eight fundamental models showed a Clinton victory. But this was at the national level. Remember the election was decided by a handful of swing states. Alternatively, we could employ a model that is context independent. As noted, using such a method, Trump is shown to be a clear favorite in six of the eight states. Just Florida and Pennsylvania were toss-ups.

Again, the practitioner builds a triangulation table to minimize the effect of their own biases. In table 9.10, we use the three primary inputs to handicap the 2016 US presidential election. And quickly we see that they tell a divergent story. On the one hand, the polls indicated that Clinton would win. On the other hand, both the main problem heuristic and the fundamentals models show Trump in the dominant position. Such divergence should signal uncertainty to the analyst. The fox

Table 9.10 *Triangulation table – probability of a Clinton win in the swing states*

	Heuristic (%)	Fundamental (%)	Poll-based (%)	Average (equal weighting) (%)	Average (unequal weighting) (%)
Arizona	15	33	47	32	38
Florida	15	46	76	46	58
Michigan	15	19	98	44	58
North Carolina	15	29	78	41	52
Pennsylvania	15	46	94	52	67
Ohio	15	5	25	15	16
Average	15	30	70	38	48

Source: Reuter/Ipsos Polling, RealClearPolitics

in us needs to be hypervigilant given this evidence and continually validate our working assumptions.

So, what is our summary judgment?

At first blush, we can take a simple average of the three inputs. Note how we first do it by state and then take the average of the states. Here, we find that Clinton has a probability of winning at 38% to Trump's 62%. The odds trend in Trump's favor. This gives us a very different perspective than the prevailing wisdom at the time.

What if we made the polls more important in our forecast? Here, pollsters can weight the data in any way they see fit. We often do this as a form of **sensitivity analysis** to understand the range of possible outcomes. Here, we gave a weight of .50 to the polls; .40 to fundamentals models; and .10 to the heuristic model. By doing this, we get a 48% probability of a Clinton win (Table 9.10). An improvement for Clinton but still an even election.

Alternatively, we could just take the average of the fundamentals and poll-based models. This is a common approach in election forecasting.[16] Here, we get a Clinton win probability of 50%. We are starting to see a pattern. It looks like a 50/50 election – one leaning Trump. In short, both our change and economy heuristics showed a toss-up or middling election.

---

[16] Linzer (2013) "Dynamic Bayesian Forecasting of Presidential Elections in the States," in *Journal of American Statistical Association* Vol. 108, Issue 501, pp. 124–134.

This is additional validation that the election would be closer than the polls alone suggested.

Additionally, an analysis of the broader context shows that it was an election defined by antiestablishment and nativist sentiments.[17] This broader context favored Trump, as he styled himself an outsider who would disrupt the status quo. Again, this is an important counterpoint to the narrative of Clinton as an absolute favorite. We will talk more about such broader scenario analysis in the following chapter.

Once we probe a little deeper, all the evidence suggested a tossup election. This underscores the risk of relying on a single-source prediction. It is critical to consider an election from multiple angles and keep the broader perspective in mind. In the United States, this means remembering that whatever the national polls might show, the election is most often won in a few swing states. Ultimately, the pollster should be aware of the electoral rules of the game; this will condition the way the election is analyzed.

OTHER ELECTIONS AND DISCRETE OUTCOMES

We focused on national elections for the chief executive in this chapter. However, the same logic can be applied for subnational, legislative, primary, and special elections, cited in Table 9.11. Such elections can also include elections beyond the chief executive called "down ballot" races: for instance, attorney general or secretary of state races in US elections. Ballot initiatives and referenda also can be lumped into this broad category. Here, all these cases employ ballot questions as the primary polling inputs. Take the generic congressional ballot used in the United States. But context really matters. As such, fundamentals and heuristics models can vary considerably. Finally, the aforementioned elections tend to be low salience, which makes predictions that much more difficult. The pollster should understand this when working on them.

Lastly, we do use public opinion to predict other discrete outcomes. Some examples include legislation, impeachments, and regime stability. These outcomes tend to be less salient. The public-decision-maker link is more attenuated. As such, the pollster should tread lightly. But like a presidential election, the same best practices should be employed including triangulation, the use of multiple inputs, and a healthy bit of skepticism. Take

---

[17] Young & Clark (2016) "Even Odds for Trump & Clinton: Is Trump a 'Spoiler' or a 'Game-Changer'?" in RealClearPolitics, June 2016.

Table 9.11 *Some other types of elections covered by pollsters*

State/province	Ballot initiatives
Municipal	Referenda
Congressional	Special
Senate	Judicial
Down Ballot Races	Primary

the impeachment of Donald Trump. We employed polling and a modified fundamentals model.[18] Or, the Arab Spring where we used consumer confidence to gauge regime stability. Or, the ACA, commonly referred to as Obamacare where we used question probes to identify soft support.[19] Such predictions also employ the best practice of triangulation.

[18] Young (2019) "Impeachment in Global Context." Cliff's Take Ipsos, October 2019.

[19] Young & Burles (2009) "A Pollster's View of Obama's Healthcare Reform Missteps" in *OpEd McClatchy News.*

10

Decision Inputs

Approval Ratings and Context

ADDITIONAL FORECASTING INPUTS

This chapter tackles two additional activities of the pollster as fortune teller. The first is the assessment and prediction of government approval ratings. As we have already seen in Chapter 8, approval ratings are extremely important in predicting elections. There is both an art and science to the analysis of such measures. Here, we want to lay out an analytical framework that will allow pollsters to assess both structural and policy factors related to approval ratings and then how to utilize multiple methods to triangulate future outcomes. We will focus on the Biden administration circa August 2022. Ultimately, a large component of a pollster's workload is the continual assessment of government initiatives and their convergence (or not) with what people want.

The second is a discussion of context-based analysis. The pollster has an important role in helping decision-makers understand the bigger picture. Here, broader demographic and social trends help gird such analysis. In practice, it takes on two distinct forms. First, trends in main problems help provide context and meaning. In this section, we will look at Brazil from 2005 to 2013 and what we call *the rise of the quality-of-life agenda*.[1] This trend was a long-term shift in priorities that determined sociopolitical outcomes for almost a decade and ultimately ended in social unrest. Without such context, decision-makers would have been lost during this period of time.

We will also look at how values and beliefs can be important drivers of sociopolitical outcomes. Such trends are slower moving usually being

---

[1] Garman & Young (2013), "Brazil's Protests Are Not Just about the Economy," in Reuters, June 2013.

driven by generational replacement. Here, we detail the rise of the antiestablishment agenda from 2015 on and its importance in determining policy and political outcomes. This contextual variable is key for decision-makers and their understanding of global outcomes today.

GOVERNMENT POPULARITY AND APPROVAL RATINGS

Understanding how the public views the government is core to dissecting the overall direction of public opinion. Government popularity is ultimately the assessment, or score, given to those who govern by those who are governed. Remember the centrality of this concept in Chapter 3.

Popularity is often operationalized in terms of approval ratings. Such questions can be directed at the person in the position, such as Joe Biden, Donald Trump, Jair Bolsonaro, or AMLO. Alternatively, they can be treated generically, that is, centered around the government itself rather than the individual in charge. Approval ratings are typically linked to presidents, but they have their analogues in parliamentary systems as well.[2]

Government or presidential approval ratings are some of the most ubiquitous opinion questions asked in polling. Some version of the approval question has been asked since 1937, first by Gallup, and has been administered in almost every country in the world.

The scale respondents are offered helps shape our interpretations, as noted in greater detail in Chapter 2. A rating of two points – approve vs. disapprove – gives direction; four points – strongly or somewhat – gives intensity; and a middle point – neither approve nor disapprove – communicates uncertainty, unawareness, or indifference. Question wording is generally at the discretion of the pollster. It can also vary, depending on the in-country context. For instance, in Brazil, pollsters historically have asked a five-point "horrible to excellent" question, while in the United States a four- or five-point approve/disapprove question is typically employed.

Such questions have important analytic properties as well. First, they are strongly correlated with executive election outcomes and other political ones such as legislation, legislative elections, and referenda.[3] Approval

---

[2] In countries with parliamentary systems such as the United Kingdom, Spain, and Germany, party voting intention questions are the closest proxy for approval ratings. In Italy, it has been custom to ask both party voting intention and government approval ratings. For reference see Poll of Polls (www.politico.eu/europe-poll-of-poll) or the EAP (executiveapproval.org).

[3] Gelman et al. (2020) "Information, Incentives, and Goals in Election Forecasts," in *Judgement and Decision Making* Vol. 15, Issue 5, pp. 863–880; Lewis-Beck & Stegmaier

ratings are also important signals to the political market on how well the sitting government can be expected to push forward its agenda.[4] Strong approval ratings strengthen the ruling coalition, while weaker ones undermine the ability to build consensus. This is often why new governments are more successful at pushing legislation in the first year as they benefit from the early "honeymoon period" of higher approval ratings.[5]

Given all of the above, approval ratings are a critical input for the pollster. They can be used both as predictive and as diagnostic tools. The public can go hot or cold on a given government or politician as a function of a myriad short-term events. In other words, such trends result from within- not between-person change.

Approval Ratings = *Structural + Policy*

We conceptualize approval ratings (A) as being a function of both structural factors (S) and policy factors (P). By structural factors, we mean variables like the economy, uniqueness of a given presidency, time in office, wars, or corruption scandals (Table 10.1). Governments have little control over such exogenous impacts in the short term. But the pollster must have a keen understanding of them in order to determine future performance. By policy factors, we mean legislation and policies all driven directly or indirectly by the government. These are all initiatives over which the government has some control.

There is a large academic literature that assesses the factors that impact approval ratings over time; this literature employs multivariate statistical models parsing out independent effects.[6] But, how does the pollster operationalize all this?

Let's first detail the factors and then apply our learnings to a practical problem.

(2000) "Economic Determinants of Electoral Outcomes," in *Annual Review of Political Science* Vol. 3, pp. 183–219.

[4] Canes-Wrone & Marchi (2002) "Presidential Approval and Legislative Success," in *The Journal of Politics* Vol. 64, Issue 2, pp. 401–509; Lovett et al. (2014) "Popular Presidents Can Affect Congressional Attention, for a Little While," in *The Policy Studies Journal* Vol. 43, Issue 1, pp. 22–43.

[5] Carlin et al. (2018) "Public Support for Latin American Presidents: The Cycle Model in Comparative Perspective," in *Research and Politics* July–September, pp. 1–8.

[6] See Mueller (1970) "Popularity from Truman to Johnson," in *The American Political Science Review* Vol. 64, Issue 1, pp. 18–34; Ostrom & Simon (1984) "Promise and Performance: A Dynamic Model of Presidential Popularity," in *The American Political Science Review* Vol. 79, pp. 334–357; Lewis-Beck & Stegmaie (2000) "Economic Determinants of Electoral Outcomes," in *Annual Review of Political Science* Vol. 3, pp. 183–219.

Table 10.1 *Structural and policy factors shown to have a statistically significant effect on approval ratings in the United States*

Economic factors (structural)	Noneconomic factors (structural)	Policy factors
Inflation	Scandals	Legislative success
Unemployment	War casualties	Foreign policy
GDP	Time in office (Honeymoon effect)	Domestic policy
Gas prices	Wars/terrorist attacks (Rally around the flag effect)	Significant speeches
	Wars/terrorist attacks	Executive orders

STRUCTURAL FACTORS

In broad brushstrokes, we can divide structural factors between economic and noneconomic ones. Economic factors can refer to a range of possible metrics, such as the unemployment rate, inflation, household income, GDP, currency devaluations, and gas prices. The salience of the specific economic variable employed depends on country and context. But, as a general rule of thumb, bad economic scenarios damage the sitting government's approval ratings while good ones help it.

Context indeed matters. In our experience, economic downturns have a more immediate impact in emerging markets than industrialized ones. This stands to reason. More disposable income and more savings in richer countries serve as a buffer against bad economic times. For these same reasons, the impact of the economy on approval ratings is greater in developing countries compared to industrialized ones.

In the United States, unemployment can have effect on approval but only at higher levels. Research shows that the tipping point is at about 7% unemployment.[7] Graph 10.1 depicts average approval ratings from 1948 to 2022. As you can see, lower levels of unemployment improve the average approval rating by 5 points. Inflation, in turn, has a stronger impact. Here, we find a 13-point difference in approval ratings between high and

---

[7] Choi et al. (2016) "Presidential Approval and Macroeconomic Conditions: Evidence from a Nonlinear Model," in *Applied Economics* Vol. 48, Issue 47, pp. 4558–4572.

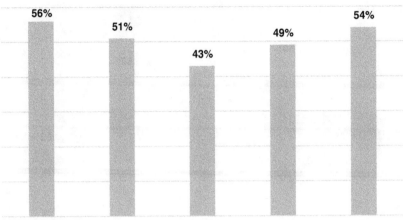

Graph 10.1 Approval rating by different levels of inflation and unemployment, 1948–2022 average
Source: Yearly Average Approval Ratings 1948–2022 from Gallup and Ipsos; Inflation and Unemployment from BLS[8]

low inflation regimes. There is an intuitive logic to this. Inflation has a far wider reach and direct impact on pocket books across all income levels. Think about the impact of a spike in gas prices or increase in the cost of basic foodstuffs. Everyone feels the pinch, albeit to greater or lesser extents.

Most important in our minds is that the academic literature can be operationalized into simple averages as shown earlier. Of course, we should be careful and remember that simple averages do not take into consideration multivariate complexities. But pollsters often employ such rules of thumb.

Turning now to noneconomic structural factors, these might include variables such as the incumbent's time in office, scandals, wars, terrorist attacks or natural disasters. The impact of how long a sitting government has held power shows a common trend across contexts and countries. Here, the general rule is that a new government can maintain strong approval ratings through the second quarter and sometimes into the third.[9] Many refer to this positive moment as the "honeymoon" effect.

---

[8] Definition of inflation categories: low inflation (–1% to 2.4%); medium inflation (2.4% to 5.9%); and high inflation (5.9% to 13.5%).
[9] Choi et al. (2016) "Presidential Approval and Macroeconomic Conditions: Evidence from a Nonlinear Model," in *Applied Economics* Vol. 48, Issue 47, pp. 4558–4572.

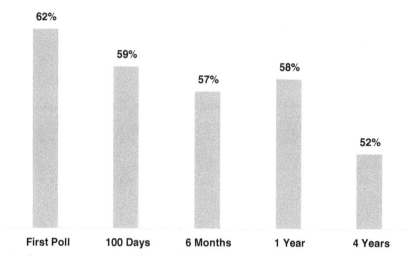

Graph 10.2 Average approval ratings by time in office, the United States, 1948–2022
Source: Approval Ratings from 1948 to 2022, Gallup and Ipsos

Observers find that this period generally lasts between 100 days and the first six months of an incumbent's time in office.

However, approval ratings tend to decline as governments inevitably have to make tough choices that will alienate at least some of their base (see Graph 10.2). Cumulative events take their toll. While the general trend is downward, there are some cases where approval ratings do improve later on in an administration's life cycle, particularly as election season approaches. Take, for instance, Clinton in 2000 or Lula in 2010. Both finished out their presidencies with numbers on the rise.

Scandals, wars, and natural disasters can also be thought of as non-economic, exogenous shocks. These typically have short-lived, but nevertheless profound, impacts on the opinion of the incumbent and his or her ability to enact policies. Wars and terrorist attacks have what is called a "rally around the flag" effect as detailed in Chapter 3. As this name would suggest, it is a moment when approval ratings climb in the aftermath of an attack. Existential threats typically bring people together, inspiring them to set aside their partisan differences. But that initial rally can fade if the conflict drags on too long or becomes a drain on resources.

Think of the jump in approval ratings for George H. W. Bush immediately before Desert Storm or George W. Bush's approval rating in the immediate aftermath of 9/11 (about 33 points). In contrast,

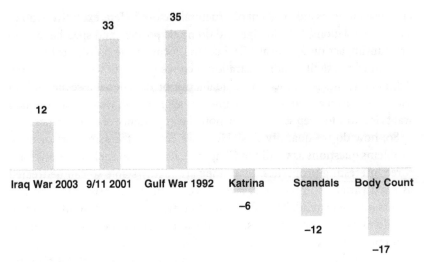

Graph 10.3 Effect of events on yearly approval ratings
Source: Approval Averages 1948 to 2022, Gallup and Ipsos

military commitments, such as Vietnam, scandals, and natural disasters, can be negative dampers on approvals ratings. These negative impacts range from 6 to 17 points (Graph 10.3).

While it is helpful to provide a rough number to quantify the effect of these events, pollsters should focus much more on the directionality of them. We know that "the rally around the flag" effect can have a strong positive impact, while scandals like Watergate or the Brazilian vote buying scandal have a significant negative drag. Such events can move the approval numbers by more than 10 points. This is substantively significant by any measure.

All of our analysis here is context-specific. The exact approval impact will vary by country and by context. But the logic remains pretty much the same. With context-specific data, the pollster can easily estimate the structural effects and directionality as we did earlier. Luckily for the pollster of today as compared to the pollster's lot of yesteryear, such data is readily available on aggregation websites, official statistics portals, and Wikipedia entries.

POLICY FACTORS

Do governments have control over any variables? At first blush the answer seems to be "no." But, by our estimates, about 10–20% of the variance in approval ratings is independent of structural factors.[10] Here, executive actions, such as legislations, bills, foreign and domestic policies, and speeches all can have an impact on approval.[11] The central focus of the pollster is to determine to what extent an administration is convergent with what people want. Admittedly, this is a much more qualitative or directional assessment. But asking if a given action by a government is aligned with what public opinion wants is a way to keep score. Again, note the importance of convergence.

So, how do we quantify this? Here, we employ the same sort of main problems questions as we did in Chapter 9. Remember such questions have three interesting properties. First, they are highly stable so can be treated as fixed variables in the short term. Second, they are correlated with real events on the ground. This allows for longer-term prediction of the main problems as the context shifts. And third, the candidate strongest on the main problem has a higher likelihood of winning an election.

Pollsters then assess each initiative by a given government. Our assessment normally seeks to address two questions. First, is the initiative aligned with the main problems? And second, is the initiative well regarded by public opinion? One classic example of policy misalignment is George W. Bush pushing forward social security reform in 2005 when Americans were most concerned about the war in Iraq. He truly doubled down on an issue that was unimportant to the public at the time. This resulted in a misfit between the policy offer and the public's priorities. Was this a foreboding sign of things to come? Well, at least in part.

Again, a check list of initiatives is more qualitative in nature. But it is the bulwark of a pollster's activity outside election season. Here, the pollster assesses individual initiatives and then determines if they are aligned with what people want. We will show an example of this next.

BRINGING IT ALL TOGETHER

So, how does this play out in practice? Let's turn now to a specific example – Biden's approval ratings circa August 2022. At the time, Biden was president with an anemic 39% approval rating, the midterms were around

---

[10] This is a back of the envelope calculation that considers that the average R-squared of published models is around 80%.

[11] Ostrom & Simon (1984) "Promise and Performance: A Dynamic Model of Presidential Popularity," in *The American Political Science Review* Vol. 79, pp. 334–357. Ostome and Simon employ an extensive coding scheme that shows the effect of nonstructural factors on approval ratings.

the corner, the world had just emerged more fully from the coronavirus pandemic and public concern had now shifted to inflation.

Many were wondering whether Biden – and by extension, the Democratic party overall – were dead in the water. Would Biden's approval ratings be able to recover sufficiently to support the Democrats on the ballot in the 2022 midterms? Or would it wind up being a red wave favoring the GOP?

Remember approval trends have similar patterns from country to country and context to context. But context-specific data is critical. In the case of the United States, we take the approval time-series from 1948 to 2022.[12] And we take inflation and unemployment data from the BLS (Bureau of Labor Statistics). We link the economic data with the approval ratings. Finally, time effects can be easily calculated: such as the honeymoon effect (100 days and 6 months), first-year approval rating, and the final approval rating. For other countries, the sources may be different but the logic is the same.

To illustrate how this analysis would work, let's consider where Biden began, and where he was by mid-year 2022. Biden started out his tenure with a 54% approval rating in January 2021.[13] But by August 2022 his approval ratings had dropped to 39% – a 15-point decline (Graph 10.4). Why? Was it just timing? The sudden and unexpected inflationary surge? Or both?

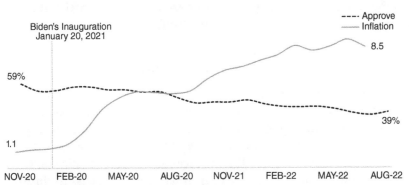

Graph 10.4 Biden's approval rating falls with rising inflation
Source: Ipsos Core Political, Bureau of Labor Statistics CPI and unemployment rate retrieved from the St. Louis Federal Reserve

---

[12] Taken from the academic aggregator the "ExecutiveApprovalProject.org" as well as from Ipsos.
[13] Note this puts Biden's starting approval numbers at the historic average (56%); see www .ipsos.com/en-us/cliffs-take-bidens-house-built-solid-ground.

Let's first focus on structural factors and more specifically timing effects – at six months, the average approval decline is 5 points, and at one year it is 4 points. At one year and eight months the average timing effect is about 9 points. In sum, in a world where everything is running smoothly, we would expect Biden to be in the low 50s or high 40s. Biden was lower than this. Why?

Things weren't going so well on the economic front. First, let's discard unemployment as a driving factor. In August 2022, the unemployment rate in the United States was around 3.5%; well below the 7% tipping point noted earlier in the chapter. But there was a substantial increase in inflation during Biden's administration, climbing from 1.1% to a four decade high of 9.1% in June 2022. By August, it had modestly cooled off, hovering at 8.3% despite the Federal Reserve's efforts to battle inflation down to more manageable levels. As noted, inflation does have an impact on approval ratings. Indeed, the average approval decline from a low inflation regime to a high one is 13 points.

So, what can the analyst deduce? In this case, we can say that Biden's numbers in August 2022 were indeed well within the range of what would be expected given the average time effect and the spike in inflation. Roughly, a 9-point timing effect plus a 13-point inflation effect. From this perspective, it looks like most of the decline is a function of structural factors.

Here, it is worth noting that we did not run a sophisticated multivariate regression model to parse out the independent effects. We could have done this of course, but in practice we seldom have the time. Instead, we drew on the academic literature together with empirical data to arrive at rough estimates. This is the grist of the pollster's mill.

MAIN PROBLEMS AND RATINGS

The pollster always triangulates. Here, we do so by assessing how the public perceives the government's performance on the key issues of the day. Remember how main problems are critical in assessing the odds of an election victory. Pollsters also use them to evaluate how a sitting government or presidency is faring. Critically, the success of an administration or leader rests on how the public views their performance on the top issues. In 2022, public concern shifted from COVID to inflation as noted in Graph 10.5. Such shifts generally signal problems for a government.

Americans went from assessing Biden on the pandemic to evaluating him on the economy and inflation. This was a remarkable shift that is only possible due to the unprecedented global impact of the pandemic and its reverberations. Unfortunately for Biden, COVID was his signature strength. He won the 2020 election on this issue and surfed the COVID

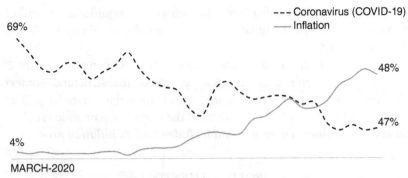

Graph 10.5 Inflation surpassing COVID as the main issue of the day
Source: Ipsos Global Advisor, What Worries the World

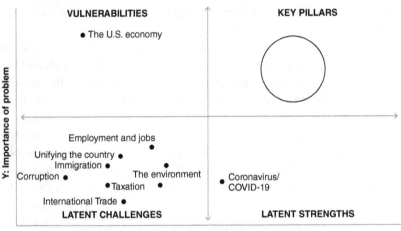

Quadrant 10.1 How Biden fares on the public's top priorities
Source: Ipsos Poll August 2022

wave for the first year. However, the perception of Biden's performance on inflation was far inferior to that of COVID. It is only natural that such a change in agenda would hurt Biden numerically.

As discussed in Chapter 2, building a four-box quadrant analysis (Quadrant 10.1) can help us determine where a leader's strengths and weaknesses lie. Such an analysis helps pollsters determine the key drivers, from both a positive and negative perspective. In August 2022, the US economy was the primary factor driving down Biden's numbers – see the vulnerabilities box. COVID was no longer a priority though remained Biden's strength – see latent strengths box. In contrast, no single factor was keeping

Biden afloat – see key pillar box. This reflects the significant downward pressure caused by high inflation and explains the seemingly rudderless Biden administration.

Just a year prior, the story was quite different. Remember Chapter 2. COVID was Biden's bailiwick. But, as noted, the structural context changed as did the public's priorities. This is important granular polling data to reinforce our previous analysis of the impact of economic variables on approval ratings. ***Taken as a whole, Biden had an inflation problem.***

POLICY AGENDA

But is it fair to say that presidents are at the whim of external forces out of their control? Structural factors are critically important in determining government popularity. But they don't explain everything. Every administration has some control over its own agenda.

The question here is whether Biden was effective (or not) in his tenure as of August 2022? To assess this, we simply list the big achievements and initiatives. And then we ask if they are aligned or not with the public's agenda. Normally a pollster would be polling on this in real-time. Here, we find that Biden's legislative agenda was primarily economic in focus (Table 10.2).

Consider the legislative slate and its generally lukewarm to positive reception by the public, Biden's policy agenda could be expected to be net-neutral to positive for him. As already mentioned, our policy analysis is typically more qualitative in nature. But such a score card was a good sign for Biden. The Biden administration's core agenda ***was convergent*** with what the public wanted. At the very least, they could be expected to exist as positive proof points when communicating the government's accomplishments during the 2024 presidential contest.

SUMMING IT UP

Would Biden be able to recover from his 2022 doldrums? Would he get above that magical 40% threshold? To answer these questions, we must examine the impact of different structural and policy factors on Biden's future approval ratings. Most importantly, let's triangulate, combining estimates with different assumptions.

Here, pollsters typically take inputs from other experts, such as economists. As of August 2022, the expert consensus was that inflation would be around 3–4% on an annualized basis by the end of the 2023. Based on this projection, approval ratings could hypothetically improve by about 8 points if the United

Table 10.2 *Policies, initiatives, and speeches during the Biden administration, 2021–2022*

Policy	Percent support	Date	Description
Democracy speech 2022	41%	Sep 22	In early September 2022, President Biden gave a speech in Philadelphia on the threats to democracy. When asked in a Reuters/Ipsos poll directly following the speech whether Americans thought Biden's speech would divide the country further or if the remarks would increase unity, 41% chose increase unity.
Inflation Reduction Act	48%	Aug 22	As the Inflation Reduction Act was working its way through Congress, Reuters/Ipsos poll found that half of Americans (48%) support passing the Inflation Reduction Act.
Build Back Better	56%	Nov 21	Ahead of the House passing the Build Back Better plan in November 2021, Reuters/Ipsos polling finds that many Americans support the Build Back Better Framework. Though, weeks later, in December 2021, Senator Joe Manchin (D-WV) announced his opposition to the bill, effectively killing it.
Student Debt Forgiveness	55%	Jun 22	NPR/Ipsos polling from June 2022 found that 55% of Americans supported forgiving up to $10K in student debt. Later, in August 2022, President Biden announced his plan to forgive $10K in student loans.
American Jobs Plan	45%	Mar 21	An early March 2021 Reuters/Ipsos poll found that when asked if Americans support or oppose the American Job Plan, a piece of infrastructure legislation released by the Biden administration, 45% of Americans supported this bill.
American Rescue Plan	70%	Mar 21	In late March 2021, Reuters/Ipsos polling found that most Americans support the American Rescue, a bill that allotted $1.9 trillion in taxpayer dollars for vaccines and medical supplies, sending a new plan round of emergency financial aid to households, small businesses, and state and local governments.
Joint speech to Congress	78%	Apr 21	President Biden delivered his first public address to a joint session of Congress on April 28, 2021.
Sending weapons to Ukraine	53%	Aug 22	President Biden has signed weapons packages sending aid to Ukraine. Based on polling from mid-August 2022, half of Americans support sending weapons to Ukraine.
State of the Union Address	41%	Mar 22	President Biden delivered his first State of the Union address to Congress in March 2022.

Source: Ipsos Polls 2021–2022

Table 10.3 *Biden's projected approval ratings in 2023 under five possible scenarios*

Scenario 1	Scenario 2	Scenario 3	Scenario 4	Scenario 5
Approval rating as of August 2022	Approval rating in 2023, assuming a shift from high to medium Inflation	More conservative inflationary impact	Unemployment surpasses 7%	Average
39	47	43	34	41

Source: Numbers derived from Ipsos Approval Ratings 2022

States were to shift from a high to medium inflation regime. This would equate to a 47% approval rating, although this probably overstates the uptick (Table 10.3). Remember that improving economies help less than shrinking ones hurt.

Alternatively, let's say that the effect is halved when the economy is improving. Why half? Pollster prerogative. That would still give us an approval rating of 43%.

What about an economic slowdown? Many analysts fretted about an overly aggressive Fed. However, most economists foresaw a soft landing for the economy with an unemployment rate of 3.7–4.6%. A negative signal but nothing earth-shattering. But let's assume a disaster situation for Biden – inflation does not improve and unemployment goes above 7%. This would have a 5-point impact and would equate into an approval rating of 34%.

So, which forecasted approval rating would be right? On the balance, the signals were more positive than negative. The best course of action is to take a simple average of the four approval scenarios. We have a mix of positive, negative, and status quo scenarios. Even here, Biden does pass the 40% tipping point. This, of course, is contingent on weak timing effects over the next few years and a soft economic landing after inflation.

What chance would we give to Biden to rise above the 40% threshold? Remember pollsters need to think probabilistically. Such a likelihood is much more a judgment call than an empirically derived number. We believe that he has a better chance than not to get there. Let's give him a 60/40 likelihood. But the proof ultimately will be in the pudding.

CONTEXT-BASED ANALYSIS

The Brazilian Quality-of-Life Agenda

Pollsters utilize main problem questions for more than just election forecasting. They are an important gauge on what public policies and which

Table 10.4 *Distribution of Brazilian social classes from 2005 to 2011*

	2005 (%)	2006 (%)	2007 (%)	2008 (%)	2009 (%)	2010 (%)	2011 (%)
A/B	15	18	15	15	16	21	22
C	34	36	46	45	49	53	54
D/E	51	46	39	40	35	25	24

Source: Ipsos/Cetelem Consumer Tracking Poll

governments will be successful. Here, success means both pushing through a policy agenda as well as winning elections.

Take the case of Brazil between 2005 and 2013. During this time, the Workers Party and Lula reigned supreme, social and economic mobility were the zeitgeist, and Brazilians were optimistic about their future. The driver here was the growth of the Brazilian middle class. Approximately, 40 million went from the lower classes to the Brazilian middle and upper-middle classes (Table 10.4). In all, the lower class declined by 27 points as a share of the population (from 51% to 24%). This was a significant transformation, and the primary reason why the Lula government ended with higher approval ratings than it started with in 2003. It is also why his handpicked successor Dilma Rousseff encountered few problems in her electoral bid in 2010, despite initially being a relative unknown.

As a result of this unprecedented social mobility, expectations of the average Brazilian significantly changed. They were no longer worried about basic economic necessities, such as food, shelter, and a paying job. Instead, they yearned for the trappings of a middle-class life – better public transportation, education, healthcare, and public safety. This aspiration was clearly reflected in the priorities of the Brazilian public as they shifted from basic economic needs to middle class worries (Graph 10.6).

At the time, we called this "the rise of the quality-of-life agenda."[14] Such shifts in priorities affect both policy and electoral outcomes. This was a period of time that produced more socially and policy-orientated governments. No longer was the focus only on macroeconomic stability. Take, for instance, the Paes government in the city of Rio, considered the example of empirically based policy at the time – or Dilma Rousseff who won the presidency on the mantra of maintaining the gains of the Lula years. Or, predating the aforementioned examples, take Lula's second government and its socially

---

[14] Garman & Young (2013) "Brazil's Protests Are Not Just about the Economy," in *Reuters OpEd* June 2013.

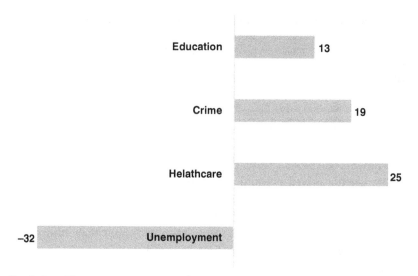

Graph 10.6 Change in priorities, Brazil 2005–2013
Source: Ipsos Pulso Brasil

oriented, but expensive, policies such as the FIES college loan program[15] and
the Farmácia Popular Program,[16] designed to broaden access to medicines.
All of these show the importance of context for understanding outcomes.

However, with rising expectations also came greater risk. As Langston
Hughes once asked, "What happens to a dream deferred?" The consequences
of frustrated hopes were seen in 2013 when millions of Brazilians took to the
streets to protest the anemic speed of change. Sparked by demands for cheaper
public transportation, the protests morphed into a push for better services in
general. Dilma's approval ratings took a hit. She ultimately won reelection in
2014, *but* the aura of unchecked improvement had been shattered. Ultimately,
she was impeached and removed from office in 2016. Her demise was at least
in part a function of these frustrated expectations. Context matters.

The contours of the political fallout in Brazil are clarified in light of shifts
in the main problems. Worldwide, as in Brazil, they are a powerful analytical tool, providing the observer with insight into both electoral and policy

[15] Niskler, Homridas-Caldas, & Batourina (2018) "Student Loans in Brazil: Investment or
Expenditure." *Inside Higher Ed*, May 13, 2018. Retrieved from: www.insidehighered.com/
blogs/world-view/student-loans-brazil-investment-or-expenditure.
[16] Emmerick et al. (2015) "Farmácia Popular Program: Changes in Geographic Accessibility
of Medicines during Ten Years of a Medicine Subsidy Policy in Brazil," in *Journal of
Pharmaceutical Policy and Practice* Vol. 8, p. 10. Retrieved from: www.ncbi.nlm.nih.gov/
pmc/articles/PMC4403833/.

outcomes. Most importantly, they give meaning and context. In our opinion, no analysis should go without an assessment of public opinion's priorities at the time. Such analysis is made easier for pollsters as main problems are a common question tracked by most polling firms.

THE RISE OF GLOBAL ANTIESTABLISHMENT SENTIMENT

Pollsters also look at values and beliefs to understand context. Take Brexit in 2015 or Trump's victory in 2016. They signaled the rise of a new strain of politics throughout the world – one that was more populist and antiestablishment in nature. This trend further continued as more nonaligned, counter-establishment candidates came into power in countries such as Mexico, Brazil, France, Poland, and Hungary. Such candidates came from both the right and left, underscoring the omni-political nature of this set of antiestablishment beliefs. So, what was going on?

Many analysts argued that the world was witnessing a rise in populist politics – one characterized by a desire for strong leaders with heterodox bents.[17] But what was the public's role in fomenting this shift?

Our story starts in the United States in 2015. At the time, we were trying to understand Trump's ascendency and resilience in the polls. To do this, we employed a five-item index developed in the early 2000s to gauge the rise of populist candidates in Latin America, including Luiz Inácio Lula da Silva, Hugo Chavez, Evo Morales, and Cristina Kirchner.[18] We refer to this as the "broken system" or "system is broken" index. We believed that much of Trump's signature rhetoric resonated with such sentiments. For instance, his rallying cry "make America great again." So, what did we find?

We found a broken America – one where a supermajority believed that the system was broken, that parties and politicians no longer cared about the average person, and one in need of a strong leader to take the country back. Here, such an index serves as a contextual variable helping us understand politics at a given point in time. As an analyst, think of it as stage setting or a starting point. From an electoral perspective it helps define the consideration

---

[17] See Young (2016) "Its Nativism," in Ipsos POV 2016; Pippa (2020) "Measuring Populism Worldwide," in *Sage Perspectives* Vol. 26, Issue 6, pp. 697–717; Mounk (2018) *The People vs. Democracy: Why Our Freedom Is in Danger& How to Save It*. Knoff.

[18] Gonzalez & Young (2017) "The Resurgence and Spread of Populism?" in *SAIS Review of International Affairs* Vol. 37, Issue 1, Winter–Spring, pp. 3–18.

Table 10.5 *Instances where antiestablishment sentiment has been a factor in political events*

Country and Year	Person(s)	Description
UK 2015	Brexit	"Yes" to exiting the EU wins; strong antiestablishment and nativist bent.
US 2016	Trump	Trump an outsider candidate beats Clinton an establishment candidate. Strong nativist and antiestablishment undertones.
Brazil 2018	Bolsonaro v. Haddad	Bolsonaro a strong outsider candidate wins against the establishment candidate Haddad. Known as the "Tropical Trump," Bolsonaro has a strong antiestablishment and right-wing orientation.
Mexico 2018	AMLO	Obredaor wins on an anti-corruption, antiestablishment plank. But left-leaning.
France 2017	Marcon v. Le Pen	Marcon and LePen go to the two second round. Both are nonaligned with traditional parties.
US 2020	Trump v. Biden	Biden, the establishment candidate, beats Trump. Again, strong nativist, anti-system rhetoric in the campaign. Trump supporters storm the Capitol to protest the election results.
Chile 2021	Boric v. Kast	Boric, the establishment candidate, wins. But Kast runs a strong nativist, anti-system, right wing campaign.
Colombia 2022	Petro v. Hernandez	Petro – an establishment candidate – edges out Hernandez, a self-stylized Trump acolyte.
Brazil 2022	Bolsonaro v. Lula	Lula beats out Bolsonaro. Two antiestablishment candidates. One on the right; the other on the left.

set of politicians, and it also forebodes heighted uncertainty as it is correlated with measures of disorganization and disruption (Table 10.5).[19]

Critically, we have used the index primarily as a gauge of a given country's predisposition to antiestablishment politics. Take, for instance, the 2018 Brazilian presidential election. Early in that electoral year, many discounted Jair Bolsonaro's chances to make it to the second round. That said,

[19] Young & Jackson (2023) "Defining and Validating the System Is Broken Index," in *Social Science Quarterly* Vol. 104, Issue 1, pp. 5–10.

Table 10.6 *The enduring nature of antiestablishment sentiment, 2016, 2019, and 2021*

Questions that form the "system is broken" index	Global			The United States		
Percent agree...	2021 (%)	2019 (%)	2016 (%)	2021 (%)	2019 (%)	2016 (%)
[Country's] economy is rigged to advantage the rich and powerful	71	70	68	71	66	69
Traditional parties and politicians don't care about people like me	68	67	64	72	67	66
To fix [Country], we need a strong leader willing to break the rules	44	46	46	43	35	40
[Country] needs a strong leader to take the country back from the rich and powerful	64	63	63	70	66	69
Experts in this country don't understand the lives of people like me	65	63	61	70	65	64

Source: Ipsos Global Advisor

a super majority of Brazilians held strong antiestablishment views, which indicated a strong possibility for an antiestablishment outcome.[20] The context suggested that Bolsonaro would be a strong candidate, if not the outright favorite (Table 10.6).

We see this antiestablishment trend in many other countries as well. This is a stable phenomenon with little change in the short term as shown earlier. But antiestablishment candidates don't always win at the ballot box. Take Trump's loss in 2020. Or, José Antonio Kast in 2021 Chile whose antiestablishment bent failed to translate into a win.[21] Even if antiestablishment

---

[20] Cascione (2018). "Social Tensions Flare in Brazil Ahead of Election," in *Eurasia Live*, June 1, 2018, www.eurasiagroup.net/live-post/social-tensions-flare-in-brazil-ahead-of-election.

[21] Funk (2021) "The Rise of José Antonio Kast in Chile," in *America's Quarterly*, October 26, 2021. Retrieved from: www.americasquarterly.org/article/the-rise-of-jose-antonio-kast-in-chile/.

credentials do not always ensure victory, such values-based analysis provides critical context and meaning.

So, how should the pollster conduct such analysis? Here, we understand that most analysts would not have the same resources at their disposal as we had in developing our index. But there still is a lot of data out there. A quick read of the academic literature on a given topic can shed light on any issue. And there are a considerable number of values trackers out there, including the International Social Survey Programme, General Social Survey, World Values Survey, and the Pew Research Center's work.

Pay close attention to the milieu surrounding an issue. This means read, analyze, and incorporate new information as it comes your way. We developed an index to understand the early naughts in Latin America and then employed it to better understand present-day America. Data and important contextual information are all around us. As pollsters, we just need some situational awareness to use it.

PART IV

THE POLLSTER AS SPIN DOCTOR

"Talk to someone about themselves and they will listen for hours."
—Dale Carnegie

INTRODUCTION

The pollster is also a spin doctor who works with decision-makers to engage public opinion and change it. This can be done for corporations, governments, and political campaigns and organizations. Think COVID vaccinations; corporate social responsibility initiatives; political campaigns (elections and otherwise), or public diplomacy engagements at the country and subnational levels. These are all examples that use empirically based communication approaches to move public opinion.

The objective of the three-hatted pollster here is to ensure that a given initiative is embraced by the public. In the case of COVID vaccinations, this might mean convincing people to vaccinate themselves, while on the corporate-side it might entail convincing key stakeholders of the economic, social, or environmental virtues of a given company. Similarly, a political campaign looks to get people to vote for their candidate, while a public diplomacy campaign aims to improve a country's image. In all cases, public opinion is a critical decision input. Here, the pollster may focus on all people – the general population – or some subset of it. Remember our discussion of **effective public opinion** in Chapter 2.

The pollster's role is to provide inputs to the marketer or PR professional, so that they might devise impactful communications pieces. In our experience, there is clearly a difference in the role between the pollster and the communication professional. Pollsters bring to the table public opinion inputs, while marketers take those inputs and turn them into impactful messages. When it comes to messaging to the public, there are two seemingly opposing perspectives on how the pollster's job can best be done.

Table IV.1 *Three-hatted pollster as spin doctor*

	Part II	Part III	Part IV
	The data scientist (to assess)	The fortune teller (to predict)	The spin doctor (to convince)
Primary client type	Media and all other clients	Private sector and financial sector	Politicians, governments, and private sector
Analytical focus	Maximizing accuracy	Forecasting outcomes	Developing the most convincing message
Typical questions	Is my public opinion data bias?	Who will win the next presidential election?	What is the winning message?

On the one hand, *the structural perspective* sees public opinion as stable and predictable and uses its very structure to engage it.[1] Here, the pollster focuses on the basics of opinion measurement: specifically, the decomposition of attitudes into rankings and ratings. Think of our **static model** in Chapter 3. This perspective also sees communicating to public opinion as part of a larger message ecosystem that includes the target, the message, and the messenger. In such cases, the pollster asks a simple question: how do we meet public opinion where it is?

On the other hand, *the packaging perspective* believes that if only the right message were said at the right time in the right way, the needle would be moved. Emotions and visceral reactions are key here. This perspective sees public opinion as malleable.[2] Think of words, hot buttons phrases, cues, and slogans. "Make American Great Again"; "Yes, we can"; "Clean Coal"; "Build Back Better" and so on. This perspective incorporates fundamental elements from our already discussed **dynamic model**. Here, the pollster asks the question: what message – packaged in the right way – has the greatest emotional impact?

---

[1] See Manheim (2011) *Strategy in Information and Influence Campaigns: How Policy Advocates, Social Movements, Insurgent Groups, Corporations, and Governments, and Others Get What They Want*. Routledge.

[2] Luntz (2007) *Words That Work: It's Not What You Say, It's What People Hear*. Hatchet Books; Health & Health (2006) *Made to Stick*. Random House; Carnegie (1936) *How to Win Friends and Influence People: The Only Book You Need to Lead You to Success*. Gallery Books.

Table IV.2 *Structural versus packaging perspectives*

Structural perspective (static model)	Packaging perspective (dynamic model)
Messenger credibility	Slogans
Target and targeting	Hot button words
Message themes, messenger/message fit	Emotions
Familiarity versus unfamiliarity	Priming/cuing
Rankings/priorities and ratings	Cues and clues
Priority linkage	Sticky message

Which is right? Well, both. Each perspective provides important tools for pollsters. We detail this in the next two chapters. In Chapter 11, we talk about our spin doctor perspectives – both conceptually and practically. We will use a sprinkling of examples together with conceptual frameworks. In Chapter 12, we take the 2022 Brazilian election that pitted Lula against Bolsonaro as our case study. Here, we break it into three parts. First, we determine what people want. What are the demands of public opinion? Who is more credible on the main issues? Who are the persuadables or those who should be targeted? Second, we focus on the emotional cues and clues that might positively or negatively trigger a reaction. Pollsters often use a combination of qualitative and quantitative methods to get at the crux of an issue. And finally, any empirically based communications program includes some sort of assessment. This typically includes the tracking of primary metrics like familiarity, favorability, ballot questions, and key message themes. Ultimately, the pollster as a spin doctor understands that public opinion is stable, but can be mutable under certain conditions.

A POLLSTER'S TALE: YOU CAN'T BE WHAT YOU AREN'T

Now, much of my experience as a pollster finds its start in the early 2000s. Again, we are in 2001–2002 Brazil – the presidential campaigns are beginning to ramp up. In 2001, it looked like the three-time presidential hopeful Lula da Silva of the Workers Party would be running against FHC's hand-picked successor Jose Serra – the minister of health. The third-party candidates were less expressive.

At the time, I was working with some private sector clients to understand the election as well as the Serra campaign as one of several polling vendors. The polling community was small; mostly located in the City of Sao Paulo; and was porous enough to know what was going on.

Lula was up in the polls early. He looked stronger than he ever had. Why? Brazilians were frustrated with the promise of the 1994 Real Plan. Stability after years of hyper-inflation yes! But stability without social mobility was no longer acceptable. Brazilians wanted a larger slice of the pie. Not good news for the government. GDP growth in 2001 was a paltry 1.4% and 2002 was not looking much rosier. It appeared to be a change election by any metric.

The Serra campaign was in a dilemma. Their candidate was "government" – Serra had been both chief of staff as well as minister of health to FHC. But a government finding itself in a change context was in a bad place. Ultimately, the decision by the political strategists was to try to split the baby – to be government **but not** government. The slogan roughly translated into "Continuity without Continuism." Or more crassly "the good without the bad." Hmmmmm?!

The inexperienced in me had a lot of questions. Is this even possible? I mean Serra was a creature of FHC. Will people really believe this? What is our experience with similar situations? Ultimately, can you really separate yourself from the government if you are the government? Not sure.

I never got concrete answers. Just scoffs and the moniker "the kid from Ohio." BTW I am from Illinois. Y'know – one of the other flyover states.

What happened?

Well, Serra lost; Lula won. The second-round election wasn't even close with a 22-point advantage to Lula.

So what did I learn? Context matters. And not just for prediction **but also** for communications. You must be aligned with what public opinion wants; otherwise, you lose credibility. As they say, "you need to walk the walk **not just** talk the talk."

You can't just spin yourself out of a problem. Yes, Serra's situation was difficult. Brazilians wanted change. But how much did this PR subterfuge hurt Serra in the long term? Not sure; but it did dim his shine. In the end, this experience sent me on a journey to understand how everything fit together. I came to understand that public opinion sets the limits of effective communication, not the other way around.

11

Engaging Public Opinion

Theory and Practice

In this chapter, we discuss both the structural and the packaging perspectives in conceptual terms. It is worth noting that the communications literature is diffuse and poorly integrated. Some of it reads more like self-help books. To be fair, it does draw on many different disciplines – some more rigorous; others less so. As such, our purpose here is to provide a clear framework for the pollster and practitioner. There is considerable art and creativity to effective communications. Look at Cannes Lion every year- the Oscars of the PR and Marketing world. There is incredible creativity in the crafting of impactful messages. But public opinion is public opinion – with a few basic compositional truths. By nailing them down, the pollster is able to provide structure to the communications process.

THE STRUCTURAL PERSPECTIVE

Let's start with the big picture first and then work from there. Here, we start off with a three-variable messaging framework taken from the political communications literature.[1] All successful messaging initiatives follow such a model either implicitly or explicitly (Figure 11.1).

We think of the framework as a message ecosystem – which includes: the target, the messenger, and the message. We believe that this 30,000-foot view helps the pollster see the big picture. Ultimately, it is a conceptual framework that provides a measurement model – what inputs should (and should not) be included in the analysis. Let's define our terms.

---

[1] See Manheim (2011) *Strategy in Information and Influence Campaigns: How Policy Advocates, Social Movements, Insurgent Groups, Corporations, and Governments, and Others Get What They Want.* Routledge.

Figure 11.1 Message ecosystem

THE TARGET

By target, we mean a group or population of individuals who is the intended recipient of a message or engagement. Targets can vary considerably. At its broadest, a target could include public opinion or the population in general. This typically is not done. Why? It is costly and ineffective to focus so broadly. Indeed, priorities and values vary greatly within a given population. Identifying more specific targets allows the pollster to be more focused. How does the saying go? "One size does not fit all." This is a classic example of **effective public opinion** as discussed in Chapter 2.

The pollster normally segments the population into multiple potential targets through a process called **segmentation**.[2] This can be done in a number of different ways. We detail two such approaches next.

The first is what we call **three-variable political segmentation** where the segments or targets are defined as supporters, persuadables, and detractors. This is a common scheme in politics. Supporters are those constituents that make up your base. It is critical to meet their basic demands – both in concrete actions and messages. Detractors make up your adversary's base and are most likely intractable when it comes to your message and engagement efforts. Focus less on them. Finally, persuadables are those that can be convinced to come to your side. These are often called swing voters in elections or fence sitters more generically. Much of the focus is here. Keep in mind that your adversary will target them as well. Simple and logical.

---

[2] Meyer (1996) *Segmentation & Positioning for Strategic Marketing Decisions.* Southwestern Educational Publishing, 1st Edition.

Table 11.1 *Main problem by a three-variable political segmentation*

	Detractors	Persuadables	Supporters
	Republicans (%)	Independents (%)	Democrats (%)
Economy	40	26	27
Immigration	13	6	6
Environment	2	6	13
Crime	11	10	7

Source: Ipsos Core Political Tracker August 2022

See Table 11.1 as an example. Let's describe it from the perspective of the Biden administration. His supporters are those Americans that identify as Democrats. The detractors are Republicans. And finally, persuadables are Independents. We also learn from the segmentation that the economy is the most important issue for all segments. For Biden's base, the second most important issue is the environment, while for Republicans it is immigration. Independents also worry about crime. The focus, of course, should be on the economy. This is the most important issue. For his base, other social issues like the environment should also get attention. For Independents, immigration and crime are important secondary issues. At a high level, the messaging scheme is clear.

Alternatively, segmentation can involve the definition of multiple groups by demographics, professional groupings, or psychological traits. Typically, this sort of segmentation is done in conjunction with decision-makers to align with organizational or institutional objectives. When it comes to companies, often such targeting includes key stakeholders such as NGOs, regulators, consumers, employees, the press, or key demographics if looking at consumers or citizens. In Table 11.2, we have a five-variable segmentation scheme. We took the same main problems question and broke the American population down into relevant demographic and political segments. Some of these segments are important to the Democratic coalition like Black and young Americans, while others are key for Republicans including less educated White men and Republican women. All the aforementioned segments are worried about the economy; however, other issues vary in their importance. We see how crime is the number two issue among Black Americans, while immigration is the same for white men and female Republicans. Again, segmentation is key to identify such variability.

In modern political marketing, microtargeting has become a standard tool. This involves the compilation of data from multiple sources often

Table 11.2 *Main problems by a five-variable segmentation scheme*

	Female Republicans (%)	Black Americans (%)	18- to 34-Year-olds (%)	White men with high school degree or less (%)	55+ Years of age (%)
Economy	41	27	32	32	27
Immigration	12	3	1	13	10
Environment	1	4	9	8	9
Crime	10	13	11	9	12

Source: Ipsos Core Political Tracker August 2022

coded at the geographic level.[3] Here, the aspiration is that individuals can be targeted to receive specially tailored messages at scale. More sophisticated methods are required, but we thought it important to note this trend.

THE MESSAGE

By message, we mean a communication or statement conveyed from one person or group to another. It can be an idea, a word, a slogan, or a concept. The structural perspective thinks of messages in terms of "message themes" or issue priorities. Yes, messaging uses the basic building blocks of public opinion as well. Similar to when pollsters forecast, the basic question is – what do people want? There are always a multitude of ways to get at this. But we always start with the main problem question. Let's take a few examples to illustrate this.

The Democratic primary for the NYC mayor was on June 22, 2021 (Graph 11.1). Let's assume we are working for the Adams campaign – he was a mayoral candidate and the Brooklyn borough president at the time. So, what was the winning message theme for the election? What did New Yorkers want? A simple look at the main problems helps tell the story.

Here, we see that it is all about crime. This makes sense. Crime is a very common local issue. This was especially so coming out of COVID – a disorganizing event that undermined the sound functioning of large cities. So, the message theme here is **crime and security** and any successful communication plan should be built around it. Remember you need to meet

[3] Issenberg (2012) *Victory Lab: The Secret Science of Winning Campaigns*. Random House Press.

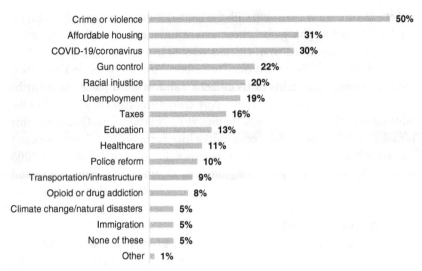

Graph 11.1 Top issues in the 2021 New York mayoral race
Source: Spectrum/Ipsos Poll June 10–17, 2021

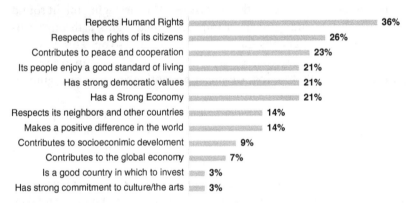

Graph 11.2 Rank order of ideal characteristics of a superpower
Source: Ipsos Global Advisor 2008; 23-country average

public opinion where it is. Adams, ultimately, did that and won both the Democratic nomination and general election for mayor.

Let's take another example – one of public diplomacy and country image (Graph 11.2). An important objective of any country's foreign service is to improve its image abroad. A strong image makes "winning hearts and minds" that much easier; this is often called "soft power."[4] Countries want to improve and extend their image around the world.

---

[4] Nye (2004) *Soft Power: The Means to Success in World Politics*. Public Affairs.

Let's assume we are working with the United States in this case. So, what do we do? We look at what global citizens want and meet them where they are.

We specifically asked what citizens wanted in a global superpower. And what did we find? They want one "to respect human rights" in first place; then "to respect the rights of its citizens"; and in third place "to contribute to peace and the cooperation." Any communication plan should take advantage of these key message themes as its central focus. Of course, this is easier said than done. Remember, like Jose Serra in 2002 Brazil, we can't run away from who we are. Let's remember that the United States in 2008 was still in Iraq and Afghanistan and had detainees at Guantanamo and Abu Grab. This is bad news for the United States given that the key message theme is "respecting human rights."

So, what can be done?

Remember you can't run away from your problems. Instead, you must focus on your strengths. Here, this might include using the economy and reframing other issues through this lens. The United States has been historically strong on the economy given its economic dynamism. And the economy is tied for fourth place with other issues. The messaging might sound like: "through economic growth we improve human rights"; "through economic growth we foster cooperations and peace," and so on. This is exactly what the United States tried to do around this time.[5] This is an example of **framing** an issue. By framing, we mean presenting an issue or argument from a certain perspective.

We want to detail two additional concepts: **proof points** and **priority linkages**. By proof points, we mean, concrete facts, actions and events. This could mean specific policies, like Biden's "build back better." Or events like "the Muller Report" in the United States or the "Car Wash" scandal in Brazil. This includes actions like keeping detainees at Guantanamo or occupying Iraq. They can have positive or negative connotations. And they become important facilitators of good communications. As such, the pollster must identify, measure, and understand them.

By priority linkages, we mean linking a lower-order priority with a higher order one. In the case of the NYC mayoral race, this might mean associating crime – a higher priority issue – with housing a lower priority one. For instance, let's say you are the housing director of NYC and

---

[5] Durra (2006) "US Public Diplomacy in the Arab World: The News Credibility of Radio Sawa and Television Alhurra in Five Countries," in *Global Media and Communication* Vol. 2, Issue 2, pp. 183–203 and Durra (2020) "US Diplomacy in the Middle East & the Digital Outreach Team," in *Place Branding and Public Diplomacy* Vol. 16, Issue 1, pp. 1–15.

running for mayor. How do you build credibility if the main issue is crime? This could be done by showing how housing policy contributes to greater public safety. As you can see, linking and framing are often done in tandem. We frame an issue to link it to a higher order one. We see this especially in speeches all the time – start with an issue with a broad consensus and then pivot to a more controversial or less important one.

THE MESSENGER

By messenger, we mean the person, institution, or organization that delivers a given message. Here, we think more specifically of messenger credibility and ask the simple question: is the messenger credible? The pollster measures credibility with favorability scores. Other measures can include confidence, approval ratings, or trust.

Messenger credibility can also be measured on specific issue domains. One candidate might be very credible on a specific issue like crime or housing or the economy but not on other issues like the environment or immigration. The pollster wants very specific measures of credibility to gauge messenger and message effectiveness. We will examine specific messenger credibility later in this chapter.

Graph 11.3 is an example of the credibility scores of companies. See how Home Depot, Amazon, and Visa all have high scores, while Twitter, ExxonMobil, and Philip Morris have low ones. Here, all other things being

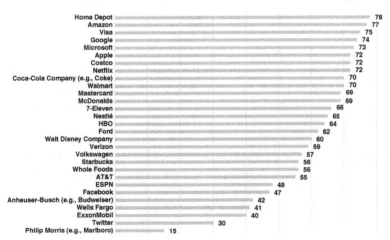

Graph 11.3 Credibility of companies as measured by favorability
Source: Ipsos 2023; Facebook maintained to ensure comparison year-over-year

equal, the best messenger would be Home Depot, while Philip Morris would be the worst. Of course, context always matters.

In today's word, messenger credibility is often more important than the message itself.[6] As we saw in Chapter 3, information credibility is critical to ensure further cognitive elaboration. Remember how messenger cuing affected the relative support for the infrastructure bill. Republican messengers were credible with Republicans; Democrat messengers with Democrats. Put differently, if the messenger is not credible, the message has little chance of having an impact. It is thus understandable why *ad homiem* attacks are so common; they go to the underlying credibility of the messenger.

FAMILIARITY AND FAVORABILITY: YOU GOT TO BE KNOWN TO BE LIKED

Messenger credibility, or favorability, is also strongly linked to familiarity. As the old adage goes, "you got to be known to be liked." Ultimately, it is critical for pollsters to include familiarity levels in their analysis. Many times, the difference in favorability scores is due to differential familiarity levels. Remember the discussion of name recognition in Chapter 2. Serra found himself ahead of Dilma in the polls as a result of his greater prior national exposure and correspondingly higher name recognition. Such advantages are often zeroed out during a campaign.

See the strong relation between familiarity and favorability in Graph 11.4. Here, we examine the image profile of some large companies in the United States. But such a relationship exists across all domains. As such, improved familiarity (or name recognition) is typically an element of any communication plan. We will discuss this in more detail in the next chapter.

So, what do we learn from such an analysis?

Here, the pollster always asks – is the company well known? And, if so, are they above or below the regression line? Quickly, companies like Philip Morris or Twitter or ExxonMobil have lower familiarity levels. They are not well known and hence not well liked. Only a strong communications effort or media exposure can improve their name recognition. In contrast, Home Depot and Amazon are well liked and well known; therefore, there is not much room for growth. Notably, they perform better than one would expect given their familiarly scores. See how they are above the regression line. This suggests that there is something about their

---

[6] Martin & Marks (2019) *Messengers: Who We Listen to, Who We Don't, and Why*. Public Affairs.

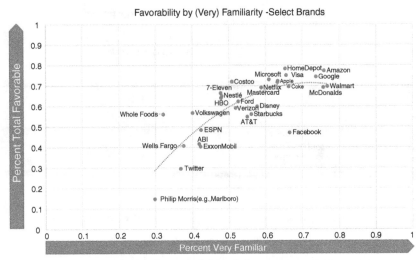

Graph 11.4 Companies by familiarity and favorability
Source: Ipsos 2023; Facebook maintained to ensure comparison year over year

image that distinguishes them positively. In contrast, Disney and AT&T, though higher on favorability, fall below the regression line. This suggests that there are negative aspects of their image that are weighing them down.

Lastly, both Facebook and Whole Foods distinguish themselves for being well off the line *but* in different directions. In the case of Facebook, they have a credibility problem as they underperform relative to their familiarity. In contrast, Whole Food has a significant credibility advantage being above the line by outperforming their familiarity. Note Big Tech – most perform at or below the average. In Chapter 13, we discuss the impact of hyper-polarization and misinformation on company image, which especially affect Facebook and Twitter. As we can see, such a simple analysis can provide the pollster with significant insight.

BRINGING TOGETHER RANKINGS AND RATINGS

The pollster can bring together priorities (rankings) and specific issue favorability scores (ratings) to better understand the most resonant messages and the messengers that are best able to carry forward such messages. Remember our multi-attribute model. This is just another application of it. We call this **message-messenger fit**. We often detail this graphically using our four-box quadrant analysis (see Quadrant 11.1).

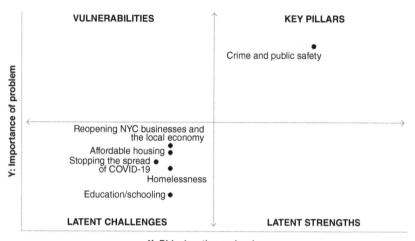

Quadrant 11.1 Issue priorities by ratings for Adams on issues
Source: Ipsos/Spectrum Poll April 2021

Let's go back to the NYC mayoral race. See how Adams is very credible on the most important issue. Crime is his key pillar. Remember he was a NYC cop before he was the Brooklyn borough president. This view makes it clear that Adams should push a crime agenda in his campaign, and he would be effective in doing it. In fact, his campaign did just this by emphasizing *the need for leadership in a time of crisis, disorganization, and rampant crime*.

Decision-makers often ask if they have any control of rankings and ratings. In our experience, ratings are much easier to move than rankings. Ratings can change as people learn more about your accomplishments. The central objective of any communication is simply to shine light on your good deeds and bring into relief the foibles and flaws of your adversary.

In contrast, rankings are more difficult to move in the short term. It is hard for political or economic actors to convince public opinion to change what is important. Think about it. If the color of a car is the most important factor in your purchase decision, it will be hard to convince you otherwise.

Along these lines, remember our discussion in Chapter 3. There is a very strong rank order correlation of priories from wave to wave. This is why pollsters typically treat main problem questions as fixed in the short term. Now, this is not to say the public's priorities can't be changed by political actors. Take Donald Trump 2017–2020. He was able to push the issue of immigration to the number one concern.[7] But this is the exception not the

---

[7] Young (2019) "Is Trump Distracted?" *Cliff's Take* Ipsos November 6, 2019.

rule. A clear example of framing, Trump painted immigration as an existential threat to the nation. The simple story here is that pollsters should always keep their eyes on the main problem question as it is a critical decision input.

THE PACKAGING PERSPECTIVE

The pollster as spin doctor first identifies the structural aspects of public opinion on a given issue. As a reminder, this includes issue priorities, credible messengers, credibility on the issues, segments, and the familiarity profile of the subject in question. But all this says very little about how to best impact people emotionally.

Part of this falls to the talents of communication professionals to divine the cognitive triggers. However, the pollster can help in the process. Here, the focus is on "words" and how to frame, or package, them in an optimal way. We often call this **message stickiness**. Remember what we learned in Chapter 4 – that our memories are organized into networks of concepts. Words Matter.

As discussed, information processing happens in three stages: attention, elaboration, and evaluation. Let's take our infrastructure bill example and use it to walk through each of the three stages.

ATTENTION

The first stage of cognitive processing is to grab people's attention. People process most information unconsciously, but if we can get people to pay conscious attention to our message, it has a chance of making a bigger impact. This is easier said than done. We are bombarded by information every second and advertisers and communicators alike have to keep finding novel ways to make their message stand out from the rest.

To do this, there are a number of different strategies as detailed in Table 11.3. In the case of the infrastructure bill – **belief confirmation** and **personal relevance** are two possible strategies to break through the clutter. Here, you want to align your messaging with preexisting beliefs and expectations. Let's be serious. There is nothing particularly sexy or scary about infrastructure as a subject matter.

Such alignment might involve showing how infrastructure policy helps the economy or how this impacts people in real terms – such as more jobs and a better local economy. Later in the chapter we will test the impact of economic messages. It is no wonder that the Biden administration named their infrastructure bill "build back better."

Table 11.3 *Strategies to grab attention*

Distraction-free	When possible, present the message in a context that is free from distraction. This allows the recipient to focus on the argument without disruption.
Repetition	Repeating the message gives the recipient greater opportunity to consider the content. However, this only works up to a point and then repetition results in a negative reaction of boredom and annoyance.
Personal relevance	Increase the personal relevance of the message by describing how the information will affect the individual personally, using second person pronouns (e.g., "you"), and framing the message to align with their values (e.g., generosity, beauty, wealth).
Personal responsibility	Increase the sense of personal responsibility about evaluating an issue by emphasizing the impact that the recipient's decision will have on the outcome.
Rhetorical questions	Use rhetorical questions ("Wouldn't you want to vote for this candidate?") rather than assertions in your argument. This encourages people to think about how they would respond, even when the questions are rhetorical.
Novelty	When possible, present information that is unexpected (e.g., a surprising headline).
Belief confirmation	Align the message with the beliefs and attitudes that people already hold. New information that confirms currently held beliefs is easily assimilated and accepted, whereas information that challenges currently held beliefs is discounted, ignored, or countered.

Anti-smoking campaigns provide another good example of grabbing attention. They often use visually shocking images of deformed or dying people. The message is clear – "if you do this you will end up like this." Fear is a great motivator.

ELABORATION

The second stage of information processing is interpreting the information we take in and storing it in our memory. This is why it's important to create a message that's not only attention-grabbing, but "sticky" as well. A "sticky" message is one that people see as credible – they have considered it more fully and mapped it into their existing memories. There are several strategies to help facilitate this process, as listed in Table 11.4.

Key is the credibility of the messenger. Remember messages that are not credible will be discarded. Here, it is important to remember that

Table 11.4 *Strategies to increase stickiness*

Hot Cognition	Pair the message with a cue that automatically elicits positive or negative emotions skipping deeper elaboration. In general, positive feelings lead to more positive evaluations and negative ones to more negative feelings.
Source Credibility	Make the source of the information appear as credible as possible. People are more influenced by messages that they perceive as coming from a credible source (e.g., an expert, a prestigious university).
Source Attractiveness and Likeability	Have the message come from someone that people find attractive and/or likeable (e.g., a well-liked celebrity or sports star). People are more likely to agree with messages by attractive or likeable sources.
Number of Arguments	Increase the number of arguments in the message. A greater number of arguments gives the impression that a message has more merits.
Priming	Create a favorable first impression by presenting positive information first. Information presented earlier in the process biases how the subsequent information is processed.

the messenger can be a person, organization, brand, group, and so on. Credibility ensures deeper elaboration.

Credibility can also be established using "cues and clues" that emotionally trigger people positively or negatively. By cues and clues, we mean bits and pieces of information that signal different emotional connotations or partisan leanings.[8] Words like "pickup truck," "diversity," or "Hollywood" are such examples. On the negative side, you might use such triggers against your adversary, or your adversary might against you. Political psychologists call this *hot cognition* – the process by which a cue produces a positive or negative emotion which short circuits deeper elaboration. Think of jumping straight to the answer. This is where knowing that our memory is made up of networks really plays an important role – words matter. Here, the question for the pollster is: what words trigger positive or negative emotions?

Finally, **priming** can increase the stickiness of a message. This includes creating a favorable (or unfavorable) first impression. This too might include cues and clues to set the stage. Just think of any difficult conversation you might have had with someone. You often start off talking

---

[8] Young (2018) *Our Age of Uncertainty: A Less Trusting, Browner, Tribalized America.* Ipsos POV. March 2018.

Table 11.5 *Select cues and clues (favorable-unfavorable)*

	Total (%)	Democrat (%)	Republican (%)	Independent (%)	NET D-R (%)
Donald Trump	−17	−78	68	−27	−146
Wall Street executives	−31	−44	−3	−49	−41
Country music	34	21	60	25	−39
Mitch McConnell	−23	−36	−1	−37	−35
Halo Top Ice Cream	24	18	34	20	−16
Small business owners	87	86	93	91	−7
Socializing	71	73	75	77	−2
Good personal hygiene	88	88	87	93	1
Paramedics	86	90	86	81	4
Jet.com	20	25	18	21	7
Trader Joe's	56	67	49	58	18
Tom Hanks	75	84	60	81	24
The National Football League (NFL)	22	36	8	11	28
NPR	24	53	7	17	46
LGBTQ people	44	74	10	33	64
Nancy Pelosi	−18	19	−55	−37	74
NBC News	38	80	−1	32	81
Barack Obama	30	92	−42	24	134

Source: Ipsos Age of Uncertainty Polling 2018

about positive things then pivot to the more difficult ones. This is priming. Politicians do this is in speeches all the time.

Let's take our infrastructure bill again. So, who or what might be our credible messenger? And what words or concepts are most positive and negative?

Table 11.5 shows cues, clues, and personalities. Pollsters often produce such lists and then test them using both quantitative polling and qualitative methods. Here, we simply ask the favorability of the objects in question. Then, we take the difference in net favorability between Republicans and Democrats to assess the degree of polarization. Note how Obama and Trump are the most divisive. They also have large partisan splits. These messengers would not bridge the partisan gap.

Tom Hanks, on the other hand, is well regarded – high favorability scores – and is not very partisan. He is a neutral figure. Perhaps such a figure might be an option when presenting the bill. In politics such pristine figures do not exist. They already have been tainted by the political wars. Alternatively, a jointly sponsored bill – think McConnell–Pelosi – might work. Or a bill supported by past presidents – Republican and Democrat – might garner sufficient credibility. These are imperfect strategies but all attempt to build credibility and elicit positive emotions. The logic is simple.

From a cues and clues perspective, an infrastructure agenda should use words that unite and avoid those that divide. We often stress to decision-makers that words matter so chose them carefully. Take "small business." It positively reinforces the infrastructure agenda. Something like: "new roads and bridges will only pave the way for small business." In contrast, words like "big government" or "the Biden Bill" paint infrastructure negatively. Ultimately, in today's communications environment, tread carefully.

MISINFORMATION

Misinformation plays a role in attitude formation. By misinformation, we mean false or inaccurate information used to deceive or confuse. And it goes directly to the credibility of the information. Again, information that is credible, even if false, is more likely to make an impact than less credible but factual information.[9] Think of COVID in the US. Democrats thought the death rate was higher than Republicans. Why? Republican leaders like Trump were signaling to their base that COVID was being exaggerated by the experts. In contrast, Democratic leaders were emphasizing the gravity of the situation.[10] Ultimately, myths, exaggerations, and outright lies can be sticky if coming from the right messenger.

How to counter? There is a large and growing literature on this.[11] The short answer is *to inoculate*. This might mean debunking myths, fact checking, and countering untrue claims. This is done either proactively or reactively. In the reactive case, this is countering already existing misinformation. In the proactive case, this means pushing forward measures before the problem rears its ugly head. Ultimately, misinformation comes down to the credibility of the message. Even false messages, if credible, are likely to be sticky.

CREDIBILITY BUILDING THROUGH PRIORITY LINKAGE

Building credibility is also about meeting people where they are. Again, think about a conversation with someone. If you start it off talking about

---

[9] Linden (2022) "Misinformation: Susceptibility, Spread, and Interventions to Immunize the Public," in *Nature Medicine* Vol. 28, Issue 3, pp. 460–467.

[10] Young et al. (2022) "What Tech Executives Should Know in Today's Polarized Society," in Ipsos POV February 16, 2022.

[11] O'Connor & Weatherall (2019) *The Misinformation Age: How False Beliefs Spread.* Yale University Press.

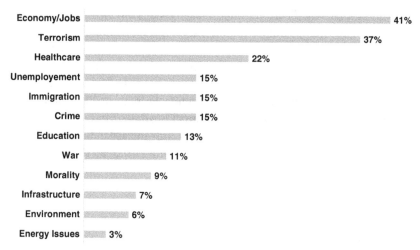

Graph 11.5 Main problems in the United States
Source: Ipsos/CGLA 2016

something interesting to them, you will gain credibility in the process. We all do it. Remember what Carnegie said in his seminal book *How to Win Friends and Influence People* – "You can make more friends in two months by becoming interested in other people than you can in two years by trying to get other people interested in you." One way to do this is by linking lower priorities with higher ones. Our infrastructure example is a great one.

Infrastructure alone is a lower priority (see Graph 11.5). The economy is typically a number one or two issue. Starting our conversation with infrastructure will probably be boring and one that will lose interest fast. However, linking it to the economy has a better chance of succeeding. People are interested in the economy as it has direct relevance to them. By starting with it, one can build credibility and then segue into other less interesting issues.

MESSAGE TESTING

As pollsters, we know that priorities, words, and credibility matters. And we can directly test this. So, let's take the example of infrastructure. We know the importance of the economy as a priority; it also tests very well as a stand-alone concept together with economic growth, employment, and jobs. Ideally, we would link economic growth with the concept of infrastructure.

How does it work? Well, it definitely polls well (see Graph 11.6). There is supermajority belief among Americans that infrastructure does indeed

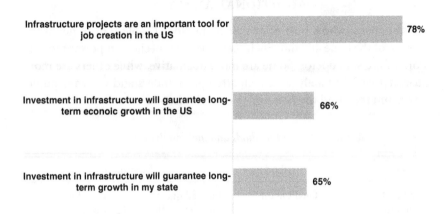

Graph 11.6 Testing linkage of economy and job creation with infrastructure
Source: Ipsos/CGLA Poll 2017

help the economy. We have asked similar questions that have produced analogous results. Public opinion believes that infrastructure is a motor for a better life. It makes total sense why Biden framed his infrastructure bill as "Build Back Better."

So, credibility is the name of the game at this stage of information processing – credible messages, credible messengers, and credible words. *In practical terms, credibility makes the message sticky as it ensures it will be more deeply considered.*

EVALUATION

Evaluation is the last stage of information processing. Here, people come to a positive or negative attitudinal predisposition toward an object. Often, we think of such a step in a very static way. This is our **multi-attribute model** at work: combining rankings and ratings into a weighted average in order to arrive at a summary judgment. Of course, as discussed in this chapter, much of this assessment happens in a subconscious, automatic way. We also learned that a key part of the process is the relative credibility of the information ingested. Here, we think of the structural perspective as providing the meat and bones, while the packaging perspective the skin. Ultimately, this stage results in a positive or negative assessment of the bill itself.

ADDITIONAL ANALYSES

Pollsters use a whole host of analytical methods (Table 11.6) to get at the essence of the issue at hand. Such methods are especially important for the work of the spin doctor. Some are more qualitative, while others are more quantitative. Ultimately, all are an attempt to understand what the public wants and then find the best way to communicate it.

Table 11.6 *Different methods and their analytic implications*

Method	Method type	Description
Open-ended questions	Qual/Quant	Unaided questions in a poll. They are good to collect and assess words associated with concepts. Usually in word clouds.
Focus groups	Qual	8 to 12 people lead by a moderator. Good to assess the reaction and structure of arguments. And gets at context and meaning
In-depth interviews	Qual	Individual interviews that get at meaning and context. Especially rich content
Key driver analysis	Quant	Rankings and Ratings analyses and derivative methods. Quadrant analyses in this book are examples
Experiments	Quant	Controlling or isolating the exposure of different content. Can more easily make causal inferences. Varying support for infrastructure is an example in this book.
Multivariate models	Quant	Linear regression (or some derivation) with dependent and independent variables. Fundamentals models are an example
Indexes and agree/ disagree items	Quant	Batteries of items to capture underlying beliefs. Antiestablishment index is an example.
Force-choice questions	Quant	Attempt to see what "pops" from a messaging standpoint. Example of corruption (versus economy) in next chapter
Ballot questions	Quant (can be asked in qual)	Choice among options. Can be electoral or nonelectoral.

Table 11.7 *Example of table with strategic inputs*

	Main problem	Ballot question	Matchup on main issue	Favorability of messengers	Familiarity of messengers	Key words	Context variables
Total							
Target 1							
Target 2							
Target 3							
Target N							

PUTTING IT ALL TOGETHER

After pollsters analyze all the data, they then put it into a nice simple summary table (Table 11.7). We will detail this further in the next chapter using the Brazilian 2022 presidential election.

Once a strategic plan is put into concrete terms and operationalized by the communications professionals, the pollster will then put together an evaluative tracking program to assess the relative effectiveness of the communications. Such a program typically includes the key metrics as defined earlier. This, of course, can vary from situation to situation. We detail this in the next chapter.

12

Communicating in the Brazilian
Presidential Election

INTRODUCTION

In this chapter, we define a communication strategy for the 2022 Brazilian presidential election using public opinion inputs. We ask a simple question – what is the winning message?

To do this, we deploy polling results from three 2,000 interview face-to-face polls and a battery of focus groups. These are what we call **a benchmark,** designed to identify key message themes and other public opinion inputs. To assess the campaign in course, we will analyze about 40,900 interviews conducted during 152 days of tracking. Note that we did not work for any campaign in Brazil. But we polled for private sector clients who wanted to understand and predict the election. In that capacity, we used our polling to mimic campaign dynamics in order to assess their relative effectiveness.

We start out with the structural perspective. We will focus on the context, key message themes, and messenger credibility. Remember our triangle. These metrics also will be lined up against our three-variable segmentation scheme. After which, we shift to the packaging perspective. What are those words, cues, and clues that really matter? How can the emotional impact be maximized? And then, finally, we track key metrics to assess campaign effectiveness.

For the sake of this exercise, let's play the role of the Lula campaign. But we could just as easily have taken the side of Bolsonaro. In many ways, one strategy should mirror the other. We will see this in the data and comment on both as we go.

PRACTICAL CASE STUDY: BACKDROP

In early 2022, Brazil was not in a good place. The boom years of the late 2000s were but a memory. Many argued that Bolsonaro's 2018 electoral victory resulted from just this – a frustrated middle class, disillusioned by corruption and pummeled by a relentless economy. Bolsonaro was an antiestablishment politician promising to fix a broken system. He beat Fernando Haddad – the Worker's party candidate – in a second-round runoff by more than 10 million votes. However, Bolsonaro soon faced challenges: the pandemic and inflation. He was no longer the unassailable figure of 2018.

As an incumbent, Bolsonaro entered the 2022 presidential election year with a stagnant economy, high inflation, and real income sitting about 10% lower than it had been a few years before. He also was accused of mismanaging the pandemic. Bolsonaro's main adversary was Lula – a two-time former president who was convicted and then exonerated for corruption. Other third-party candidates like Simone Tebet and Ciro Gomes also ran but were less expressive.

As the 2022 election progressed, the poor economic conditions that depressed Bolsonaro's numbers were easing quickly.[1] Would the situation improve in time to help Bolsonaro? This is the context within which the campaigns organized themselves. Officially, the electoral season started on August 16th; this is when the campaigns could air their ads on TV, radio, print, and social media. Brazil has two rounds of voting. The second round only occurs if a 50% threshold is not met in the first. In 2022, the first-round election was on October 2nd and the second-round on October 30th. Lula won the first against Bolsonaro (48% to 43%). This necessitated a second round where Lula won by the slightest of margins (51% v 49%).

Let's now walk through our public opinion-based communications assessment.

SEGMENTING THE 2022 BRAZILIAN ELECTORATE

The first thing we will do is to segment the Brazilian electorate. In Table 12.1, we detail our three-variable segmentation scheme. Remember the segments include **supporters, detractors, and persuadables**. Here, we define supporters (of Lula) as those Brazilians who are likely to vote for him; they represent 36% of the population. Detractors (of Lula) are those who are likely to vote for Bolsonaro making up 27% of Brazilian adults. Persuadables – 37% of the population – are those Brazilians who have no clear preference.

---

[1] Young & Feldman (2022) "The Brazilian Election Heats Up?" in *Ipsos Week in Review*, August 12, 2022.

Table 12.1 *Three-variable segmentation scheme*

	All	Detractors (Bolsonaro)	Supporters (Lula)	Persuadables
Segment Size	*(100%)*	*(27%)*	*(36%)*	*(37%)*
Female	52	42	54	57
College plus	16	27	12	13
High school or less	30	31	27	33
Northeast	26	14	36	25
Southeast	43	49	40	42
Evangelical	27	39	18	27
Auxilio Brasil (Cash Transfer)	24	22	31	19
White	35	43	30	34
16–24	18	12	17	13
55+	28	33	28	25

Source: Ipsos Poll May 2022

We cross this segmentation by key demographics. Look at how the results vary. Bolsonaro's base is more educated, from Southeastern Brazil, male, white, and evangelical. Lula finds most support among the less educated, Brazilians from the Northeast, and those who receive cash transfers. Finally, persuadables are similar to the average Brazilian *but* more female.

Communication professionals use such demographic segmentation schemes to target their advertising. Practically speaking, this means identifying the most appropriate media, such as TV, radio, print, and social media. We will not go into further detail on this subject as it is not the purview of the pollster.

THE CONTEXT

Context matters. It is important for both prediction and messaging. Here, think of context as the broadest kind of frame. Take a simple conversation about a difficult topic – a reprimand at work. If the supervisor enters the room all giddy and joyous, their message loses credibility. In contrast, a more serious demeanor will be more credible as it signals the gravity of the conversation. Context for the pollster ensures that message tone is adequate.[2]

---

[2] Klein & Mason (2016) "How to Win an Election: An Interview with Mark Mckinnon" in *The New York Times*, 2016.

We typically look at two contextual variables. The first is very simple – how is the country feeling at any given time – more positive or more negative? We often call this **relative optimism** which can be measured in a number of ways, including by approval ratings, right track/wrong track questions, and consumer confidence indexes. At its core, the pollster wants to gauge whether it is a change or continuity election. Remember our discussion about this heuristic in Chapter 9. This will determine how to position the candidate relative to the context. Practically we ask is this a change or continuity election? And how does the candidate stack up against this context or frame?

Second, values and beliefs are also important contextual variables. In Chapter 9, we looked at the rise of antiestablishment sentiment and how it conditions sociopolitical outcomes. We will do the same here. But our focus in this chapter will be on how it affects communication.

So, what do we find?

CHANGE ELECTION (WITH CAVEATS)

First, we find a Brazil that is more negative than positive. In our opinion, this makes Brazil at best a middling election and at worse a change election in early 2022 (see Table 12.2).

To assess the change context, we use a number of different measures. See how Bolsonaro's approval ratings are below 40%; only a plurality (34%) of Brazilians believe that the country is on the right track; and how consumer confidence is below the average. Brazilians, indeed, were frustrated. Taken as a whole, 2022 appeared to be a change election year.

Table 12.2 *Key context metrics to gauge relative optimism*

Metric	(%)	Description
Approval ratings	38	Below the 40% tipping point
Consumer confidence	47	Scale of 0 to 100; a score below 50 is a more pessimistic perspective
Right track	34	Right Track / Wrong Track Question. A majority (50% +1) on right track is considered good
Excellent + good	27	Five-point scale where a top two box score of over 35% is considered strong

Source: Ipsos Poll; Pollingdata.com.br; Ipsos Global Advisor

Table 12.3 *Who is to blame for the present conditions of Brazil*

	All respondents (%)	Persuadables (%)
The global economic crisis	42	47
President Jair Bolsonaro	37	24
The governors	16	22
Other	2	4
Not sure	3	5

Source: Ipsos Poll May 2022

From a communications perspective, the ideal would be to position one-self as a change candidate. This is exactly what Lula did. Take Lula's campaign message "Brazil deserves better." In contrast, Bolsonaro finds himself in a tougher place. He can't run away from who he is; he is the sitting president after all.

Understanding this, what are Bolsonaro's options? There are a number of things he can do strategically. First, blame something or someone else. The blame game works. Bolsonaro does this over and over again during his campaign. And public opinion gives him license to do this. Indeed, a strong plurality of Brazilians see the "global economic crisis" as responsible for their present woes, not Bolsonaro. This is especially so among persuadables (see Table 12.3).

Second, Bolsonaro needs concrete proof points that show how he is helping the population. Take, for instance, "Auxilio Brasil" –an income transfer program that granted 800 additional reais per month to poor families.[3] This is just one example among many. To be successful, Bolsonaro must hammer on these achievements. Finally, Bolsonaro could only hope that the scenario would improve enough so that his messaging would be made easier by a more positive frame. Hope springs eternal.

BROKEN BRAZIL AS CONTEXT

As already discussed, values and beliefs can also be important contextual variables. These are typically fixed in the short term as they are driven by generational replacement. We discussed this in Chapter 9. Here, we want to assess the Brazilian appetite for antiestablishment rhetoric and behavior. So, what do we find?

[3] **Auxílio Brasil** is a social welfare program of Brazilian government, created during the Jair Bolsonaro administration. It replaced Bolsa Familia and offered up to R$ 800 to at-risk families.

Table 12.4 *Antiestablishment attitudes in Brazil (% agree)*

Brazil needs a strong leader to take back the country from the corrupt and powerful	94%
The mainstream media is more interested in the making of money than telling the truth	91%
Systemic corruption in Brazil helps the rich and the powerful	89%
The Brazilian economy is rigged to the advantage of the rich and powerful	85%
To fix Brazil, we need a strong leader willing to break the rules	78%
Traditional political parties and politicians don't care about people like me	74%

Source: Eurasia/Ipsos Poll May 2022

Table 12.4 clearly shows that there was a widespread belief that the system is broken in Brazil. So, how does knowing this help the pollster from a communication perspective?

In our experience, antiestablishment attitudes are predictors, even if weak ones, of electoral outcomes.[4] And they do condition the environment making certain messages and behaviors stickier. As such, it is no wonder that Brazil had two strong antiestablishment candidates in 2022 – Bolsonaro and Lula. We should expect that their behavior and messaging would reflect this context. Take Lula saying, "the Brazilian people need someone to take care of them" or Bolsonaro harping on a "corrupt system." These manifestations only build credibility with the Brazilian populace. Again, context matters.

So, in sum, this is a change election. It is a negative frame that Lula can take advantage of as the opposition candidate. Bolsonaro, in contrast, must confront it by showing concrete solutions and playing to some of the beliefs about the origins of the present realities.

MAIN ISSUES THEMES

Now, let's turn to our main problems question. This is the cornerstone of any communications strategy. Here, we ask – what do people want? And how can we meet public opinion where it is? Pollsters often treat main

---

[4] Young (2016) "Its Nativism" in *Ipsos POV*, September, 2016; Young & Clark (2016) "Even Odds for Trump & Clinton: Is Trump a Spooler or a Game Changer," in RealClearPolitics, June 2016.

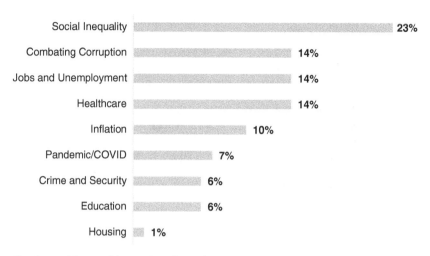

Graph 12.1 Main problem in Brazil March 2022
Source: Eurasia/Ipsos Poll March 2022

problem questions as contextual variables as well. So, what were Brazilians most worried about in early 2022 (Graph 12.1)?

We find two broad themes. First, Brazilians were most worried about social inequality. And second, they were concerned about the economy. To flush this out, we conducted focus groups. They too validated the importance of a "social and economic agenda." For instance, "I just can't get ahead," "I don't think my family will ever have nice things" and "we are stagnated right now." The average Brazilian saw the system as a barrier that wouldn't allow them to get ahead. This in turn was exacerbated by the poor economic conditions.

This suggested a broader agenda – one that fused in the public's mind both social inequality and economic issues. In our opinion, this "aggrieved economic agenda" would be the message theme for the 2022 Brazilian election. **Who owned this agenda would win the election.**

We also employed our three-variable segmentation scheme and find that the main problems vary across groups (see Table 12.5). Among Lula's detractors (Bolsonaro base), we see that corruption is the main priority. For Lula's base, social inequality is key; this goes for the persuadables as well. This segmented perspective truly gives insights into potential messaging strategies. Lula's path is clear – focus on social inequality and the economy. Bolsonaro, however, has to emphasize an anti-corruption message together with that of social inequality and the economy. ***He will need to link and pivot.***

Table 12.5 *Main problems themes by key segments*

	All respondents (%)	Certain to vote Lula (supporters) (%)	Certain to vote Bolsonaro (detractors) (%)	Soft Supporters of candidates (persuadables) (%)
Social and Economic issues	47	56	27	48
Security and corruption	20	14	33	21
Healthcare issues	21	20	24	20
Assorted issues	12	10	17	11

Source: Eurasia/Ipsos Poll March 2022

MESSENGER CREDIBILITY

We know that social inequality and the economy are close number one and two worries among Brazilians. Now, we need to determine who is the credible messenger? So, who is the stronger messenger? There are two ways to answer this.

First, we look at the familiarity-favorability profile of potential candidates in 2022. Here, we find three clusters of candidates (Graph 12.2).

The first cluster are those candidates like Simone Tebet and Eduardo Leite who are both unknown and not well liked. They have upside to improve on their favorability scores by increasing exposure and getting their name out there. Some, like Tebet, were able to improve their familiarity over the course of the campaign (from 24% to 57%). The second cluster includes candidates, such as Ciro Gomes, who are reasonably well known and hence liked. These candidates have had national exposure in the past. They are in a good place to start the election, but still need to work on their familiarity. Finally, the third cluster includes the two heavy weights – Bolsonaro and Lula – both nationally recognized figures who are well-known and well liked. As such, they both are relatively credible given their high favorability scores; though Lula has the advantage (80% versus 65%). There is little room to grow from a familiarity perspective. But they can differentiate themselves on the key issues.

Note how Lula is above the line, and Bolsonaro is below it. From this view, Bolsonaro appears to have an image problem relative to Lula. Why?

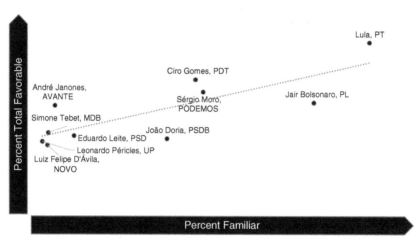

Graph 12.2 Familiarity/favorability of potential candidates in March 2022
Source: Ipsos Poll March 2022

In our assessment, there are two reasons. First, the Bolsonaro government was widely seen as mismanaging the pandemic; this had been a significant drag on his image. Second, as we will see, Bolsonaro is weaker on the main problems of the day – social inequality and the economy – a residual of the pandemic. So, our overall conclusion is that both Bolsonaro and Lula are generally good messengers. But Lula is in a stronger position. Ultimately, this ***will not*** be a campaign about improving name recognition ***but*** about being differentiated on the key issues.

Second, messenger credibility can also be issue specific. Any given candidate might be more credible on one issue versus another. Here, we are particularly interested in **the message-messenger fit**. So, what do we find?

We like to use our four-box quadrant analysis to assess issue specific credibility. Here, we look at Bolsonaro and Lula (Quadrants 12.1 and 12.2). Let's put the two side by side and compare quadrants. Their stories are almost mirror opposites of each other.

Lula's central pillar is social inequality – it is the most important issue, and he is more credible on it relative to other issues. Lula's strategy is clear: to wrap his messaging around social inequality and the economy by telling his story and detailing a credible plan for the future. His campaign will follow this course. This is an example of good message-messenger fit.

Bolsonaro, on the other hand, has a more difficult road forward as already mentioned. His strongest pillars are corruption and crime. Indeed, he won on them in 2018. But these are ***not*** the most important issues today.

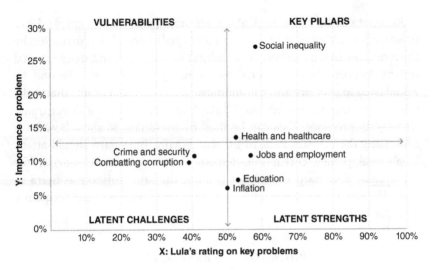

Quadrant 12.1 Lula's priorities and ratings on key issues
Source: Eurasia/Ipsos Poll March 2022

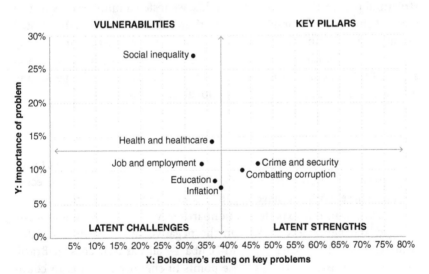

Quadrant 12.2 Bolsonaro's priorities and ratings on key issues
Source: Eurasia/Ipsos Poll March 2022

Essentially Bolsonaro does not have a key message pillar in early 2022. Look at the upper right-hand quadrant. Nothing! This gives insight into why he was below the line on our fav-fam chart. Bolsonaro definitely has an image problem.

So, what can he do? It is all about reframing and reinforcement. First, Bolsonaro would need to link the social inequality agenda to corruption by showing how Brazil has been kept behind by a corrupt and dysfunctional system. As noted, he is most credible on corruption and crime. Second, he would need to produce and communicate concrete proof points that make this positioning more credibility. Take "Auxilio Brasil" – a direct transfer poverty program. This can be used by Bolsonaro to show how he is addressing the primary issue of the day. Finally, Bolsonaro should attack Lula's weak point – corruption. Remember Lula spent time in prison for corruption. Bolsonaro should not commit the same mistake as Serra in 2002. He needs to embrace who he is, while pushing the social inequality and economic agenda.

PACKAGING PERSPECTIVE

Now, what about the packaging of the messaging? Let's examine those emotional triggers that make the message stickier. Let's add meat to the structural perspective's bones. To do this, we tested a number of words to assess their relative favorability and partisan leaning. We then stress tested key messages. Again, let's remember one of the key requisites for grabbing attention and building credibility is to talk about what people want and expect. Our structural perspective helps us with this. But the packaging perspective gives us that layer of emotional stickiness.

CUES AND CLUES

In Table 12.6 we rank a series of phases by their favorability and partisanship. Bolsonaro often uses words like "thief," "mess," and "fraud" directed at Lula. These words all have negative connotations **but** are not particularly partisan. In our experience, nonpartisan words are less emotionally charged and hence less sticky. On the negative side, Lula is associated with "Communist," "Chaves," and "Cuba" – all partisan cues in Brazil. Bolsonaro consistently makes these points to energize his base. In counterpoint, words such as "poverty" and "fome zero (zero hunger)" are more squarely associated with Lula. They also have positive connotations in Brazil and historically some of Lula's most differentiating characteristics.

In contrast, Bolsonaro is most associated with "the rich" and "privatization," which are more negative in feeling in Brazil. The overall takeaway is that the cognitive landscape favors Lula over Bolsonaro. Class division still cuts strongly in Brazil, while corruption less so.

Table 12.6 *Favorability toward each word by those who support Lula or Bolsonaro*

	Lula (supporters) (%)	Bolsonaro (supporters) (%)	Difference (Lula–Bolsonaro) (%)
Supreme Court	78	14	64
Northeast Region	88	58	30
Abortion	26	5	21
Cuba	26	9	17
Communist	25	8	17
Bolsa Família	84	70	13
Fome Zero	64	51	13
Venezuela	15	3	12
Hugo Chávez	16	4	12
Hunger	28	21	7
Poor	39	33	7
Mess	22	16	6
Poverty	26	22	4
Fraud	21	19	2
Disorder	18	17	2
Leader	74	73	1
Bum	11	10	1
Unprepared	18	18	0
Thief	16	16	0
Petrobras	56	57	−1
Stagnation	15	17	−2
Family	92	95	−3
Auxílio Brasil	76	83	−7
Southeast Region	73	84	−10
Minimum Wage	30	40	−11
Country	79	91	−12
Employee	71	83	−13
Middle Class	63	80	−16
Patriot	43	65	−21
Rich	41	68	−27
Privatization	36	67	−31

Source: Eurasia/Ipsos Poll October 2022

MESSAGING TESTING

We also test key messages. Specifically, we were interested in the malleability of the concept of corruption. It was Bolsonaro's strong suite and would be his jumping off point for other issues. So, what do we find?

Table 12.7 *Stress testing corruption against jobs (which would you rather have?)*

	All respondents (%)	Detractors (%)	Supporters (%)	Persuadables (%)
Government that creates growth and jobs, even if it results in corruption	48	32	63	42
Government with no corruption charges, even if this means fewer jobs	41	59	27	41

Source: Eurasia/Ipsos Poll March 2022

In Table 12.7, we see that the economy beats corruption. Here, we see clear evidence for Bolsonaro's linkage strategy. See how both his base and the persuadables are less receptive to the "corruption is tolerable" argument. This is evidence that Bolsonaro can make inroads. In contrast, the data also shows that Lula can counter accusations of corruption with a strong economic argument. This is exactly what both do in the second round.

This is only one example of message testing. Such an exercise can include dozens of different statements. Often, the vetting is done both qualitatively in focus groups and quantitatively with surveys. We focused on just one example here.

PUTTING ALL TOGETHER

After having conducted a benchmark like the previous one, the pollster then puts the inputs into a strategic presentation to share with communication professionals. They ultimately will be the ones to convert the findings into action. In our case, we like to organize the inputs into a table like Table 12.8.

See how the table lays out our public opinion inputs. It details the key message themes, credible messengers, and the targets. The table is built for Lula, but could have easily been created for Bolsonaro.

The table is clear. Lula performs well on the key message themes – social inequality and the economy. These will be his primary message pillars. In contrast, as already detailed in this chapter, we know that Bolsonaro has a more difficult task. He will need to reframe his strengths – corruption and crime – as the primary impediments to social mobility and economic growth.

Table 12.8 *Key message themes for Lula*

	Main issues	Secondary issue	Strongest issue (Lula)	Weakest issues (Lula)	Positive words (Lula)	Negative words (Lula)
All Brazilians	Social inequality	Economy	Social inequality	Crime corruption	Bolsa Familia, Fome Zero	Thief, Communist, Cuba
Persudables	Social inequality	Economy	Social inequality	Crime corruption	Bolsa Familia, Fome Zero	Thief, Communist, Cuba
Supporters	Social inequality	Economy	Social inequality	Crime corruption	Bolsa Familia, Fome Zero	**
Detractors	Corruption	Economy	Social inequality	Crime corruption	***	Thief, Communist, Cuba

Source: Eurasia/Ipsos Poll March 2022

Lula should use words, such as "poverty" and "the poor" reinforce his image as the man of the people. In contrast, he should push back against negative aspersions like "thief" and "bandit" by talking about the good things he has done in the past, such as "Fome Zero" (Lula era Hunger Program) or "Bola Familia" (Lula era income transfer program).

The persuadables will ultimately decide the election. They want solutions to social inequality and the economy. And Lula is strongest on this issue.

TRACKING AND PERFORMANCE

After the communication's strategy is defined and then operationalized, the pollster's job is not done. Our next task is to assess the performance of the campaign using daily tracking polls. This provides important feedback that allows the communication professional to adjust tactics and messaging. Here, we assess movement on the electoral ballot questions and on the key issue matchups. But to do this, let's first evaluate campaign dynamics and assess to what extent each campaign was on message.

THE SECOND ROUND AND CAMPAIGN ACTIVITY

The first round ended with a bang. Bolsonaro performed better than many had expected (48% v. 43%). Many criticized the polls for missing the mark. However, a closer look showed that the average of the polls came close to the actual results. The problem was their wide dispersion that caused confusion and uncertainty.[5] Most importantly, the Bolsonaro campaign came to the second round emboldened and energized, while the Lula campaign had to initially contend with a weaker than expected performance.

Second-round races are different from their first-round cousins. In our experience, campaign communications in the first round tends to be more diffuse and less effective. This is because clear contrasts are more difficult given the number of candidates. The focus, instead, is typically on increasing familiarity. In contrast, second-round races take on the personality of American-style general elections – where two candidates battle it out *mano-a-mano.*

Here, we want to provide some concrete campaign metrics in order to put our public opinion tracking data into proper perspective. In Brazil, campaign media time is closely regulated. In the first round, it is allocated

---

[5] Young & Garman (2022) "Pesquisas-Mitos E Ajustes Adequados" *OpEd Estadao*, October 29, 2022.

Table 12.9 *Second-round five-minute ads for Bolsonaro and Lula*

	Main issues (social inequality and economy)	Bolsonaro strengths (crime and corruption)	Context (blame and change)	Total
Bolsonaro	20	14	18	20
Lula	22	19	****	22

Source: Poder360.com.br

by the relative size of the candidate's party or coalition in congress. In the second-round, the candidates get equal time.

We conduct a simple assessment of second-round communications for both the Bolsonaro and Lula campaigns. Our central focus is to determine if each campaign was on message. Simply put, are the campaigns focused on the main problems? To capture such activity, we analyze 42 five-minute TV spots – 22 for Lula and 20 for Bolsonaro (Table 12.9). The five-minute spot is the workhorse for campaigns in Brazil and are aired during peak viewing hours. There are hundreds of other shorter TV, radio, and print spots. But here we focus on the workhorse. So, what do we find?

First, both Bolsonaro and Lula are consistently on message – hammering on social inequality and the economy. By our counts, all of their spots address these issues.

However, for Bolsonaro, only fourteen of thirty of his ads actually attempted to reframe or link the main issues with his strong points. Remember Bolsonaro was strongest on crime and corruption and weakest on social inequality and the economy. To be effective, he would need to pivot from his place of strength to gain credibility on the main problems. "Corruption keeps us back" and "Lula likes the corrupt" are good examples. But Bolsonaro does not make such linkage as consistently as he should in our opinion. Indeed, in the first ten days of the second round, only 50% of Bolsonaro's ads make this connection. What is the old adage in advertising? Repetition, Repetition, Repetition.

By the time of the first debate on the 16th of October however, Bolsonaro finds his footing. The debate is a great example of Bolsonaro attacking Lula on his weakest point – corruption – and making the linkage with the social inequality and economic agenda. Finally, Bolsonaro hammered home consistently (18/20) that the sad state of the economy was not his fault. Here, he toggles between two arguments: (1) Macro global forces were the cause of the problem and (2) that conditions in Brazil were improving.

Lula focuses on the main message theme in all of his commercials. Lula also spends considerable time (19 of 22 spots) attacking Bolsonaro's strengths with messages such as "fake news," "lies," "Bolsonaro is corrupt," "runaway crime wave," and "Bolsonaro only governs for the rich." By our assessment, Lula was much more consistent in his attacks on Bolsonaro, than Bolsonaro was on Lula. Remember Bolsonaro depended on his strong points to reframe his weak ones; Lula didn't. Did Lula win because of this? Maybe.

As the second-round unfolded, Bolsonaro became increasingly effective at attacking Lula. "Corruption holds Brazil back," "the PT is the party of lies," "Friend of Cuba," and so on. Hence, Lula began to counter-attack. Here, Lula did a good job of defending himself by debunking critiques – much in the vein of **misinformation inoculation** as discussed in Chapter 10 – and then pivoting to a positive agenda.

How do these campaign activities impact public opinion? Let's take a look.

PERFORMANCE METRICS

The ballot question is typically our key evaluative metric in an election. All interested parties watch its ebbs and flows closely. In Graph 12.3, we track the second-round matchup between Lula and Bolsonaro. This is a very typical example of what communications professionals would receive daily.

The story is clear. Bolsonaro makes up ground slowly throughout the first and second rounds. Lula goes from an 18-point lead in late May to a 3-point one by October 29th. The second round saw an especially acute narrowing. Tracking ballot questions like this allows the pollster to gauge campaign performance. But it is not a good diagnostic tool. There is no direct answer to why the changes are occurring. To get at this, we also track key matchups. Here, the pollster can zero in on the main message theme and see how each candidate performs on them over the course of electoral campaigning.

Graph 12.4 shows the trend on key matchups. Note the two issue sets. Lula is strongest on the most important issue up top. Bolsonaro, in turn, is strongest on the issue below.

Lula went into the electoral season with a public opinion advantage. But Lula loses ground across all issues relative to Bolsonaro especially on **social inequality** (29 versus 12). The decline is especially acute in the second round. Here, Bolsonaro's increased issue linkage had its effect. Our feedback to Lula would have been to defend his weak points by attacking Bolsonaro on his strong ones – crime and corruption. And our counsel to Bolsonaro would have been the mirror opposite – keep attacking Lula on his weak points and make those linkages between your strong points and the main problems.

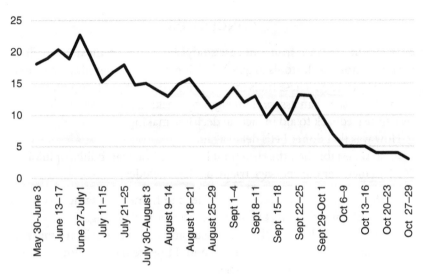

Graph 12.3 Trends in election ballot question (Lula–Bolsonaro), May–October 2023
Source: Eurasia/Ipsos Tracking Poll 2022

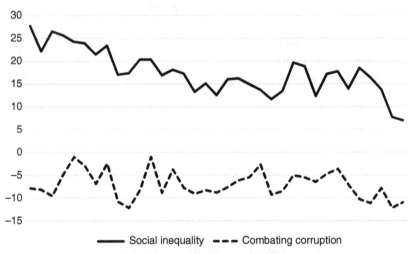

Graph 12.4 Trends in key matchups (Lula–Bolsonaro), May–October 2023
Source: Eurasia/Ipsos Tracking Poll 2022

Ultimately, all this was a too little too late for Bolsonaro. In our assessment, his campaign was better in the second round, especially in the second half of it. But time was not Bolsonaro's friend. Lula would be president.

CONCLUSION

So, what did we learn from our case study? First and foremost, the pollster as spin doctor has the tools to guide decision-makers in defining a communications strategy. These tools are the primordials of public opinion itself. Second, pollsters can assess campaigns by tracking them, which allows for real-time feedback to aid in tactical decision-making.

How was that done? Let's detail again.

First, we established the structural inputs of Brazilian public opinion in 2022. Remember our message triangle. They include:

- This was a change election year. Need to frame messaging relative to it, with the only caveat being the context was changing.
- Social inequality was the main issue and hence the primary message pillar; the economy is a close second. Message themes should always address the concerns of people.
- Lula was more credible on social inequality and the economy; Bolsonaro on corruption. Lula needed to focus on who he is and what he has done. Bolsonaro needed to pivot showing how his fight against corruption also improves the lives of people.
- Persuadable Brazilians represented 37% of the voting population and were worried about social inequality and the economy much like the general population.
- A supermajority of Brazilians believed that the system is broken. Both Lula and Bolsonaro polled well on many antiestablishment attributes. Such a positioning will help to reinforce their credibility when combined with concrete policy issues.

Second, we identified the packaging inputs as well. Here, we are looking for those high impact cues and clues that will trigger emotional reactions. They include:

- Lula positive words: poor, poverty, northeast
- Lula negative words: Cuba, Venezuela, communist
- Bolsonaro positive words: Savior of the Country, Strong Leader
- Bolsonaro negative words: the Rich, Upper Middle Class, Privatization
- Negative Words: Thief, Bandit, Mess, Fraud, Corruption
- Message testing: "Economic growth beats corruption"

Third, we tracked key metrics, including the election ballot question and matchups on the key issues. Such a tool allows for real-time feedback. Specifically, Bolsonaro made significant headway once he linked his strong points with the main issue themes. Lula's counter-attack at the end of the second round just might have given him the presidency. We see how daily public opinion tracking can provide essential tactical inputs to the communication professional.

Finally, this was an election-focused case study. But the same approach can be applied to all other domains, including private sector companies, governments, and other politically oriented endeavors such as referenda, impeachments, and significant legislation.

We have worked with innumerous clients and decision-makers, and the logic of public opinion always is the same: Meet public opinion where it is and you are more likely to be successful.

13

The Pollster in Society

We have covered a lot of ground in this book. Our objective was to produce a toolbox for the practitioner. We told most of this story through the eyes of the pollster. *But* the pollster was not the sole focus. Indeed, the audience for the book is much broader. Ultimately, it is for anyone who wants to analyze public opinion and use it in decision-making. We never delve into the role of the pollster and what the future holds for the profession. This seldom is done in a methods-oriented book. But we will in this last chapter.

To wit, we have three specific goals here. First, we want to review the activities of the three-hatted pollster. We do this to provide greater context for each type of pollster. Some of us are all three; others are some combination of these. Any pollster worth their salt must at least be a data scientist, or they risk losing credibility.

Second, we explore the role of the pollster in society. Ultimately, what is the purpose of the pollster? In our view, pollsters are critically important in any democracy. We believe this is often overlooked due to the ranking frenzy after every electoral cycle. Here, we put the profession into proper perspective.

And third, we discuss the use of non-survey, or alternative data, inputs as proxy measures for public opinion. We provide a framework for pollsters to think through them in a critical manner. Validation is a key concept that we reintroduce here – one more tool for the data scientist.

Many expound the end of the poll. We, though, see the poll and non-survey inputs as complementary. Ultimately, whether pollsters use a poll, non-survey inputs, or some combination of the two, they bring voice to people and provide that continual feedback loop between those in power and the public.

RECAPPING THE THREE-HATTED POLLSTER

The activity of the pollster is multidisciplinary in nature. We developed a framework –the three-hatted pollster – which we believe captures the vast array of what pollsters do and simultaneously shows how the pollster deploys public opinion as a decision input. To reiterate, our framework breaks the pollster's role into three buckets: (1) the data scientist, (2) the fortune teller, and (3) the spin doctor. So, what did we learn?

The pollster as data scientist is concerned with the quality of public opinion data. The pollster asks – is our data biased or not? A pollster's credibility is only as good as the quality of the data. We singled out the media as a typical client for this type of pollster. Media publication of election polling is a high stake, high reward game. But all clients demand high quality data. To this end, pollsters can use our *simplified total survey error framework* to guide them. We detailed this in Chapters 5–7.

The pollster as fortune teller is a rarer bird. The polling profession nibbles around the edges of the forecasting industry. Yes, pollsters might use their polls to say something about who will win the next election. We see this often. However, as we have learned, the use of just the poll, or a single input, is fraught with problems. In contrast, aggregators (statisticians) and forecasters (political scientists) have filled the election prediction vacuum.

Table 13.1 *Summary of the three-hatted pollster*

	Data scientist	Fortune teller	Spin doctor
Activity	To assess	To predict	To convince
Key questions	Is my data biased?	Who will win the election? What will happen?	What is the winning message?
Framework	Total survey error	Triangulation	Structural-packaging perspective

Framework detail	(1) Sampling error
	(2) Non-sampling error
	  (a) Coverage bias,
	  (b) Nonresponse bias,
	  (c) Measurement error
	  (d) Estimation error
		(1) Heuristic Model,
		(2) Poll-based model,
		(3) Fundamentals model
			(1) Message,
			(2) Messenger,
			(3) Target,
			(4) Emotions,
			(5) Words

Mantra	There is more to error than the margin of error	Beware of single input forecasts	Meet public opinion where it is

Many even use multiple inputs, such as poll aggregation, modeling, and past elections. Remember triangulate, triangulate, triangulate.

The pollster in recent years has been left behind as forecasters. But, the pollster puts public opinion into context. Think about our discussion of the rise of antiestablishment sentiment or the growth of the quality-of-life agenda in Brazil. Only the pollster can tell such a story with data and credibility. The role of the pollster as fortune teller is critically important. We just need to upgrade our tools. And our **triangulated forecasting framework** – as detailed in Chapters 8–10 – helps along these lines.

The pollster as spin doctor is a harder story to tell. Much of this world goes on behind closed doors, never seeing the light of day. The pollster here does proprietary research for their clients, including parties/politicians, corporations, public sector agencies, and NGOs. That said, we think the 2022 Brazilian election case study helps to chronicle the life of the spin doctor. Keep in mind that rarely are such engagements so data rich. It is more common to conduct a single benchmark poll and maybe some focus groups. However, on the extremes, fully funded national campaigns might include even more polling than we presented, including state-level tracking and full batteries of focus groups conducted intermittently over time. The modern campaign also employs all the sophisticated sorts of forecasting and aggregation approaches detailed in this book. Whether data intensive or not, the objective is the same – to identify where the public stands and then meet them where they are. The pollster does this by understanding the basic building blocks of public opinion and then applying them through a single **structural** – **packaging framework** that we detailed in Chapters 11 and 12. Simple, right?

At the most general of levels, the pollster provides data to illuminate the world. This might mean polls about "extreme weather" or "support for military aid to Ukraine" or "the state of society's mental health." We did not go into much detail in this book on this more descriptive aspect of the pollster. But it fills a need for any democratic society: to understand the stance of the public on those issues that affect the greater good.

We can think of such "descriptive elucidation" as a form of context-based analysis detailed in Chapter 10. However, the aforementioned usage is more for description than prediction.

PURPOSE AND THE POLLSTER

Our three-hatted pollster brought us a long way in understanding the activity of the pollster. It goes to providing considerable granularity to our definition in Chapter 1. That a pollster is "an individual or organization that measures, analyzes and interprets public opinion." This, however, leads to other questions. What is the pollster's purpose? What does it mean to be a pollster?

At their core, pollsters are the critical link between those who govern and those who are governed. Their activity gives an ongoing tally of how those in power are doing relative to their constituents. Yes, elections fill such a role. But they are a slower feedback mechanism. Polls and pollsters allow for timely response to those in power. Modern democracy would be deficient otherwise. We expand on these ideas next.

POLLSTERS BIG AND SMALL

Public opinion can be big business. Take Ipsos, Gallup, Yougov, Morning Consult, Kantar, Westat, RTI, and NORC. Some of the largest research firms must understand public opinion in order to answer client questions. Here, the citizen is the unit of analysis. Governments and the private sector are the clients in need of inputs. And the broader goal is to understand citizens and in turn meet their needs.

But the polling landscape is also made up of smaller private sector polling firms and university research centers. They fill a critical role in bringing voice to people where others won't. Take state-level politics in the United States or any small to mid-sized democracy. The organic production of new pollsters is critically important. One example of this "spontaneous generation" is Brazil. It has gone through a generation shift where venerable firms have taken a back seat to new ones. Those in power need to know what the public thinks and wants. Such demands will always spring "evergreen" in free societies.

Professional associations undergird the polling community. Take AAPOR (the American Association of Public Opinion research) in the United States or WAPOR (the World Association of Public Opinion research) globally. Many regional and country-specific organizations also exist. All such associations convene professional conferences where knowledge is shared; take positions on controversial subjects, such as polling restrictions, and set up professional standards for transparency and disclosure. These all give musculature to the polling profession.

Critically, the profession of polling is central to the very concept of modern democracy. And both polling organizations and associations play an important role in it.

PUBLIC OPINION AS A DECISION INPUT

So, what about public opinion as a decision input? We talk a lot about this in the book. But, thus far, we have not defined it.

Public opinion as a decision input is contingent on three key factors: (1) public attitudes, (2) the decision-maker, and (3) the expression of it. Let's define our terms.

- **Public attitudes** are a positive or negative evaluation of an object, such as a president or government. They are linked to the public good, such as public policies or other issues of public or collective import. This is in opposition to private attitudes or opinions – our inner thoughts such as our favorite color or secret valentine.
- **Political and economic actors** – decision-makers – must be able to act on **the public will**. Again, the link between the two is key.
- There must be **the ability to express** public opinion because, if not, how is it acted upon? We typically think of elections or polls as the means to gauge public opinion. But, others exist including rebellions, revolutions, riots, demonstrations, organized interest groups, social media, and strikes.

The pollster is the modern lynchpin that holds together the decision maker, the public, and the expression. In our view, without these three factors at play, public opinion is irrelevant as a decision input. The poll and the pollster are catalysts in this delicate ecosystem.

TRUST IN POLLSTERS

Are pollsters seen as credible actors? Given their importance to society, we would hope that they would be. Let's turn to polling to answer our question on the pollster. Ironic, no?

Here, we look at the pollster against other professions at a global level and ranked ordered across thirty countries (Graph 13.1). Pollsters fall about in the middle of other professions. Better than politicians; worse than doctors and scientists. Lawyers edge us out. Pollsters and News professionals are about even.

The data shows that pollsters have a trust deficit. This is especially so in some of the oldest and more venerable democracies. Look at the United States and the United Kingdom in Graph 13.2

Pollsters, of course, are never noticed unless an election prediction goes south. Think Trump in 2016 or Bolsonaro in 2022. One of the more disliked

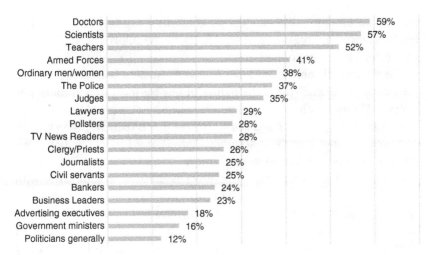

Graph 13.1 Trust in pollsters versus other professions: The average across countries
Source: Ipsos Global Advisor 2022

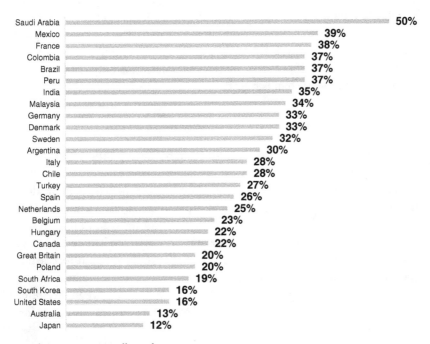

Graph 13.2 Trust in pollsters by country
Source: Ipsos Global Advisor 2022

institutions among pollsters is the ranking of polling firms by their electoral accuracy.[1] Aggregators and academics are the culprits here. The scorn
of pollsters; the catnip of journalists.

We are agnostic on rankings. In our career, we have been at the top and
the bottom of them. This is the nature of our business. It will inevitably
happen. Ultimately, how will the pollster use it? At a very high level, they
show how well a given method works. However, it is reductionist in nature.
The pollster is not just about accuracy. Indeed, this is only one hat of the
three-hatted pollster. We do so much more.

Part of the lukewarm trust in pollsters is the lack of familiarity with
them. Indeed, it is not a top-of-mind profession. I remember back in the
early years of my carrier having a nice conversation with a woman at the
dentist's office. She thought I said that I was an "upholster." A bit surprised
after a long conversation on philosophy and current events, she wanted my
card because she had some sofas that needed attention! I clarified. We have
a name recognition problem.

So, does this middling position hurt pollsters in the performance of their
activity? Yes, we think it does. Trust is essential for any profession. Our
credibility gap manifests itself in multiple ways. First, it can affect response
rates. If polls and surveys are not credible, why participate in them? Logical
question. And second, it is just another element among many that erodes
belief in the system. If pollsters are seen as unfair, this only reinforces the
perception that the system is rigged.

PUBLIC AND PRIVATE POLLSTERS

As a profession, we often make a distinction between **public pollsters** and
political pollsters. We think it worthwhile exploring this. Public pollsters
are those that work for media outlets. Their primary activity is to produce
robust public opinion data for elections and non-electoral topics. They draw
the lines at political clients. Political pollsters, in contrast, do work with parties and politicians. But most of their work is proprietary. The central focus
is on messaging and engagement (pollster as spin doctor) but forecasting
(pollster as fortune teller) can be an important tool in their toolbox.

In some countries, pollsters may do both. But media credibility often
requires the avoidance of a conflict of interest. The political pollster unfortunately is conflicted.

---

[1]   See as an example https://projects.fivethirtyeight.com/pollster-ratings/.

Table 13.2 *Net favorability score of select companies (favorable-unfavorable)*

	Total (%)	Republicans (%)	Democrats (%)
Google	56	30	81
Amazon	48	51	54
Microsoft	39	25	56
Apple	24	8	45
Facebook	−1	−13	14
Twitter	−18	−40	4

Source: Ipsos Poll 2021

We made only a few references to the private sector. This is because the nature of our work is confidential. Here, the pollster helps companies navigate regulatory and societal issues. And central to this is a company's reputation or credibility. Sound familiar? Think sectors such as "Oil and Gas," "Big tech," "Mining," and "Consumer Goods." They all must operate in highly regulated environments. The same sort of logic applies here as in elections. The pollster must determine priorities, ranking, ratings, favorability scores of companies, and other contextual issues. The primordial elements of public opinion are the same independent of the outcome variable.

For example, in the "tech sector," societal context helps explain its challenges today. Misinformation, political violence, and hyper-partisanship are all negative factors that affect the reputation of "big tech" companies (Table 13.2). We find that the more exposed a company is to this polarized world, the more severe their reputational problems.[2] Again, context matters.

SUMMING UP THE POLLSTER

Considering all of this, we believe that the pollster should be thought of as a steward or guardian of public opinion.[3] Pollsters bring "voice to people." And, more fundamentally, they serve as a link between those in power and the public. They also must do this with robust, credible data. What did Lord Levin say? "When you **cannot** measure, your knowledge is meager and unsatisfactory"? Pollsters must live by this credo.

---

[2] Young et al. (2022) "What Tech Executives Should Know in Today's Polarized Society," in *Ipsos Quick Facts.*

[3] See https://hdsr.podbean.com/e/pollsters-the-discoverers-and-guardians-of-public-opinion/.

Ultimately, all free societies require the skills of the pollster. If pollsters didn't exist, an alchemist would have to conjure them up.

THE POLLSTER AND NON-SURVEY DATA

We spend most of this book using the poll to measure public opinion. But we also recognize increasingly that the poll is not the only way that public opinion can be captured. Alternative data sources are being employed and include everything from social media to behavioral sensor data to aggregate cell phone data, and more. Pollsters must learn how to navigate this data eclecticism, while at the same time being true to their calling. We explain our logic as follows.

Even today, many analysts use such information as a proxy for public opinion. Take Elon Musk's use of Twitter to gauge his standing in the world. Or using Twitter data to forecast the migration of Syrians in Europe after a mass exodus due to the ongoing civil war. Or, using cell phone data to assess trust in government in conflict zones by measuring foot traffic in government buildings. Our data world is changing and so is the way we track public opinion.

We understand that non-survey data usually comes from a wide range of large data sets. Can you use social media to say something about public opinion? Or, can aggregate cell phone data accurately depict behavior? Or, can drone data say something about the health of a given social group?

A priori, we can't really say. Indeed, unlike the sample survey, or poll, which has known inferential properties, each non-survey data source is a mystery unto itself.

So, the natural question is – can alternatively sourced data represent public opinion? Here, the same methodological tools used to assess the quality of a poll, such as bias, error, validity, and reliability, are also employed when analyzing alternative data sources.[4] Such scientific concepts are transportable.

These are the tools that the pollster must employ prospectively in the treatment of non-survey data. So, let's take a few examples of validating non-survey data against external benchmarks. When it comes to public opinion, social media data are the most commonly used proxy.

---

[4] Salganik (2018) *Bit by Bit: Social Research in the Digital Age*. Princeton Press.

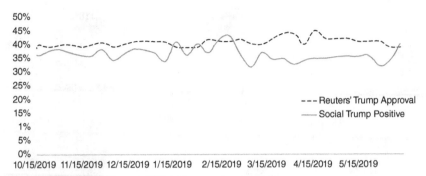

Graph 13.3 Trump approval ratings and positive sentiment
Source: Ipsos Core Political and Social Media Sentiment Analysis

Convergent Validity: Presidential Approval

Social media data can include a vast array of data sources including Twitter, YouTube, Facebook, TikTok, and Instagram. Unstructured text-based data – raw social media posts – are then organized into attitude-like forms using NLP algorithms. In Graph 13.3, we organize social media mentions into groupings of positive responses.

So does this work? Let's validate.

First, we need an external benchmark. Here, we take a Trump approval question from our Reuter/Ipsos poll and compare it to algorithmically generated positive sentiment from social media. We find that Trump's social media sentiment is more negative (about 5 points) on average and more variable (or less reliable) over time.

So, what does this say? The social media sentiment data corresponds fairly well to poll-based approval ratings. Substantial research reinforces this point – that social media sentiment can be a good proxy for presidential approval and main problems.[5] This said, such estimates are highly subject to analyst specification as well as the quality of the underlying data. Our takeaway is "trust but verify" – or rather validate.

PREDICTIVE VALIDITY

Similarly, how predictive is social media sentiment? Let's look at the 2018 US midterm elections. Here we are looking at 435 congressional races, 35

---

[5] O'Connor et al. (2010) "From Tweets to Polls: Linking Text Sentiment to Public Opinion Time Series," in *Association for the Advancement of Artificial Intelligence*.

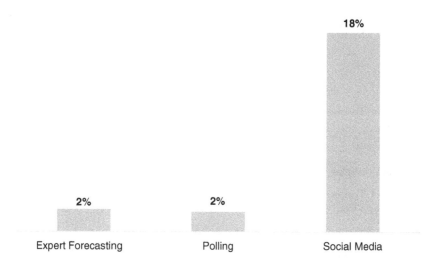

Graph 13.4 Percent of races picked incorrectly
Source: Ipsos Political Atlas 2018

Senatorial, and 36 gubernatorial. We then use positive sentiment to determine electoral victory. If a given candidate has more than 50% positive sentiment, we designate them as a winner. If not, then they are a loser. We also
have two external benchmarks – polls and expert forecasts (Graph 13.4).

See how both the polling and expert forecasts do much better than social
media at predicting winners. Social media got 82% of the races right – better
than a flip of the coin. But still far from the prediction accuracy of polling
(~98%) or expert forecasting (~98%). Social media ultimately is directionally correct **but** just an above-average forecast performer.

Races in rural areas were especially off. Here, the data was sparse and
more Democrat than Republican contrary to expectation. This looks like
traditional coverage bias. So, our takeaway here is that social media–as a
single input – is only a weak predictor of elections. That said, the research
shows that, in conjunction with other inputs, social media data can improve
electoral accuracy.[6] Again, multiple inputs outperform single inputs.

Use of Non-Survey Data with Polls

There has been much talk about the poll and how it has seen its best days
and that the future will be all about alternative forms of data capture. But

---

[6] Brito et al. "A Systematic Review of Predicting Elections Based on Social Media Data:
Research Challenges and Future Elections," in *IEEE*.

Table 13.3 *Non-survey uses as proxy measures for the poll*

	Enhancement	Substitution	Extension
Description	Complements the polling data.	Replaces polling as the capture mechanism.	Captures public opinion in situations where polling can't.
Examples	Social media sentiment as an additional input into a fundamentals model.	Using social media sentiment to track presidential approval in place of polling.	Using aggregate cell phone data in conflict zones to assess confidence in local government by estimating foot traffic at government buildings.

our short exercise earlier and the extant literature suggest there still is a lot of fuzziness around non-survey estimates. Much more research is still needed and validation is key to the way forward.

But this begs the question – how should pollsters use non-survey data? In practice, we have employed it in three distinct ways: (1) enhancement, (2) substitution, and (3) extension. We do believe non-survey data will increasingly be used by analysts and pollsters. This is inevitable. And our framework is a useful roadmap for the future. Let's define our terms.

Enhancement is when non-survey inputs complement the polling data. This might mean contextual data to understand the campaign dynamics. Take our example of the 2022 Brazilian presidential election in Chapter 11. We employed social media data to understand Lula and Bolsonaro's punch/counterpunch. Or, as mentioned earlier, the use of social media together with other inputs to forecast elections. **Substitution** is the outright replacement of polling by non-survey data. Evidence suggests that social media data does a good job of tracking job approval and main problems. Perhaps in the future we no longer will need presidential tracking polls. But the stumbling block here is that we still need a benchmark to validate our non-survey inputs. And **extension** is the use of non-survey data on issues that the poll can't solve. Take for instance the example of the use of aggregate cell phone data to gauge citizen fatigue in war-torn Ukraine.[7] This ***could not*** have been done by surveys given

---

[7] Lapowsky (2023) "New Data Paints a Picture of a Year of War in Ukraine," in *Fast Company*.

the need for speed, large sample sizes, and the inaccessibility of certain regions of the country due to open conflict.

SUMMING IT UP

We are quite bullish on the future of the pollster. The profession fills a critical role in society as detailed in this chapter. Pollsters are the caretakers of public opinion. This is very clear. But the poll need not be the sole method by which we capture public opinion. Alternative data sources are increasingly being employed to measure public opinion and are showing promise. The pollster should not be shy.

There has been much talk about the end of the poll as non-survey AI-enabled methods take over. Terminator meets polling! We think that this is "much ado about nothing." First, we aren't close to wholesale substitution. There is too much variability due to human specifications and data quality issues. Instead, we are in a time of validation. Some things will work; others will not. Validity should be the pollster's guiding principle.

Second, the pollster will still be a pollster independent of the tools employed. We bring context and meaning to decision-makers. We are the guardians of data robustness and serve as the bridge between those in power and the people. How will computer scientists do that? Not sure. Ultimately, pollsters should welcome the next decades as they catalogue and validate non-survey inputs against – the profession's workhorse – the poll. There is a lot of work to be done.

Now, there should be concern given the level of trust people have in the pollster. Are we seen as part of the solution? Part of the problem? Or just irrelevant? Probably a mix of the three. But ultimately, we can only control what we can control. This includes being ever vigilant about the quality of public opinion data through the continued refinement of our craft. Remember our cause is noble – the stewards of public opinion.

Index

Printed in the USA
CPSIA information can be obtained
at www.ICGtesting.com
CBHW031941170924
14610CB00002B/157